THE BLACK
POPULATIONS
OF FRANCE

THE BLACK POPULATIONS OF FRANCE

Histories from Metropole to Colony

Edited by SYLVAIN PATTIEU,
EMMANUELLE SIBEUD, and TYLER STOVALL

University of Nebraska Press | *Lincoln*

Library of Congress Cataloging-in-Publication Data
Names: Pattieu, Sylvain, editor. | Sibeud, Emmanuelle, editor. | Stovall, Tyler Edward, editor.
Title: The Black populations of France: histories from metropole to colony / edited by Sylvain Pattieu, Emmanuelle Sibeud, and Tyler Stovall.
Other titles: Histories from metropole to colony
Description: Lincoln: University of Nebraska Press, [2022] | Includes bibliographic references and index.
Identifiers: LCCN 2021015364
ISBN 9781496228819 (hardback)
ISBN 9781496228994 (paperback)
ISBN 9781496229977 (epub)
ISBN 9781496229984 (pdf)
Subjects: LCSH: Blacks—France—History. | Blacks—France—Social conditions. | France—Race relations—History. | African diaspora. | BISAC: HISTORY / Europe / France | HISTORY / Africa / General
Classification: LCC DC34.5.B55 B54 2022 | DDC 944/.00496—dc23
LC record available at https://lccn.loc.gov/2021015364
Set in Fournier MT by Mikala R. Kolander.

Contents

Illustrations

THE BLACK POPULATIONS OF FRANCE

Introduction

A Historical Mosaic

SYLVAIN PATTIEU, EMMANUELLE SIBEUD,
AND TYLER STOVALL

In November 2014 a staging of the performance art program *Exhibit B* by the South African artist Brett Bailey at the Théâtre Gérard Philippe in Saint-Denis outside Paris provoked a series of lively debates. A petition and several demonstrations called for banning the performance, claiming it was degrading to Black people. Some groups like the Anti-Negrophobia Brigade mobilized energetically against the exhibition, whereas the CRAN (Representative Council of Black Institutions) showed itself more prudent, sensitive to the argument of freedom of expression advanced by the defenders of the exhibition.

This episode illustrates the sporadic way that the question of Blackness has erupted in public space in France. Further, the groups that have championed this concept that have not succeeded in making themselves durable spokesmen for it. For example, the creation of CRAN in 2005 was opposed by French Caribbean associations, and the organization was never able to establish a hegemonic position over questions of Blackness. Contrary to the United States, where the history of slavery, segregation, and the civil rights movement has created a strong common heritage, the Blacks of France have no unified linear history with which they can identify.

To say this is not to minimize the importance of Blackness as a social and political issue in France. The murder of George Floyd by Minneapolis police in May 2020 sparked a powerful protest movement across France; on June 2 tens of thousands marched in solidarity in Paris. The movement reflected participants' sympathy and empathy, as French Blacks protested their own abuse at the hands of the police. The movements of the summer and fall of 2020 thus underscored the transnational character of Blackness and antiracism in France, illustrating the fact that Black life in France embodies both difference and solidarity. To understand fully Blackness in France one must mobilize several diverse histories: those of colonialism, immigration, and the creation of the nation's overseas departments. Scholarly research will enable us to weave together these different pasts: that is the goal of our book.

Although Blacks have lived in France since before it was France, the African presence there dating back to the Gaul of the Roman Empire, France's Black history centers around the early modern and modern era. France played a leading role in the transatlantic slave trade that brought Europe, Africa, and the Americas together from the seventeenth to the nineteenth centuries; its colony of Saint-Domingue (now Haiti) was by the time of the French Revolution the wealthiest plantation economy in the world.[1] In the late-nineteenth century the French conquered a huge empire in sub-Saharan Africa that endured until 1960.[2] By the early years of the twentieth century Blacks from Africa and the Caribbean had begun to create small settlements in metropolitan France, a phenomenon that increased dramatically after World War II.[3] At the same time, small numbers of African Americans, in search for both opportunity and an escape from American racism, settled in Paris, bringing jazz and other aspects of Black American culture to France.

Today France probably has the largest Black population in Europe. No one really knows that exact number thanks to the refusal of the French government to acknowledge the existence of racial difference as a social reality by collecting demographic statistics on it, but some have estimated a Black population of three to five million.[4] Sizeable communities exist in major French cities, especially Paris, and since 2005 Blacks in France have had their own central organization, the CRAN.[5] The majority are people of African origin, but there is also a sizeable population from the French Caribbean living in the metropole. If one adds to this total the overwhelmingly Black populations of France's Caribbean overseas departments, over a million people, one finds that nearly one out of twelve French men and women today are Black.

In spite of these contemporary numbers, the history and historiography of Blacks in France has been fairly limited compared to that of Blacks in the United States. One school of research that brought these two histories together is the study of African American expatriates and exiles in Paris. The pioneering work of literary scholar and Anglicist Michel Fabre on Richard Wright followed by numerous studies of the great Black American *chanteuse* Josephine Baker inspired a school of writing on Black Americans in Paris.[6] Historians used this approach to consider diasporic and transnational perspectives on Blacks in both France and the United States and the relationship between them.[7] Other historians began writing about different aspects of Blackness in France, investigating the nation's colonial past and postcolonial present. Studies as diverse as William Cohen's *The French Encounter with Africans*, Marc Michel's *L'Appel 'à l'Afrique*, Alice Conklin's *Mission to Civilize*, and Tzvetan Todorov's *On Human Diversity* have all considered the history of race and Blackness in the context of French imperialism, national identity, and universalist ideology.[8] Beyond historiographical approaches, several social scientists from fields like sociology and anthropology have considered contemporary manifestations of Blackness in France, often focusing on questions of immigration and the rise of Black communities in the ghettoized *banlieue* surrounding Paris and other French cities.[9] Literary scholars have built on the work of Michel Fabre, exploring the interplay of literature, race, and identity in modern France.[10]

Taken as a whole, these works represent a substantial body of scholarly literature. It nonetheless remains true that the use of the concept of race, understood as a cultural and social fact rather than a biological one, remains in its infancy in French research.[11] However, the publication in 2008 of Pap Ndiaye's book *La condition noire* had a major impact on both scientific and public debates.[12] In this book, both an extended essay and a synthetic work, Ndiaye reviews the state of research on the history of Black populations in France and calls for the further development of this research field. Ndiaye also develops the idea that the Black populations represent a minority in French society, whose existence is shaped by the experience of being Black in a majority white society.

La condition noire is important because it helped launch the scholarly debate about Blackness in France. But whereas Ndiaye provides stimulating hypotheses and a useful synthesis of the relevant historiography, he does not engage in primary historical research, calling instead upon a new generation of scholars to rise to the task. It is therefore time to immerse ourselves in the archives, to explore concrete issues in order to write the history of the Black populations of France.

This is the perspective of our book. Over ten years after the publication of Pap Ndiaye's work, we must continue to explore the questions he raised with new primary research. We must further develop our research into this question on both a theoretical level and one grounded in archival research. Since 2011 the editors of this study have been running a regular seminar at the University of Paris 8 on the history of Black populations. Numerous young scholars have come to present their work, engaging in very stimulating discussions. As a result we have amassed a wealth of new research that we wish to highlight in this volume. We made the choice to work together, French and American historians, out of common interest but also as an example of the circulation of these questions across the Atlantic. These interchanges were not just a matter for historians and did not necessarily depend on academic discussions; on June 7, 2020, for example, the French soccer player Marcus Thuram celebrated a dramatic goal against the opposing team by kneeling in memory of George Floyd. The son of Guadeloupe-born Lilian Thuram, one of France's most successful players, he was named after the famous Black activist Marcus Garvey.

The recent debates over "woke culture" in France, responding to the influence of American universities, have underscored for us the importance of a transatlantic approach to these questions. Leaving aside the wild fantasies of certain politicians and journalists, this controversy has also been joined by French academics. While not sharing in the more odious aspects of this campaign, important scholars like Stéphane Beaud and Gérard Noiriel, the authors of pathbreaking research on the history of immigration in France, have also taken up this perspective. In their recent book *Races et sciences sociales* they argue that a focus on race has the effect of undercutting class analysis.[13] They consider research focused on questions of race a drift into identity politics and the misapplication of

American racial categories onto France. Their argument unfortunately devalues and misrepresents the work of some young scholars in both France and America today.

In contrast, in this book we rely upon empirical research to show how questions of race and class interact. The scholarship of the authors featured in this volume clearly shows how the dynamics of race have existed in French history, if not necessarily in the same ways as in the history of the United States. Our work represents not the importation of "woke culture" but rather archival work that shows how individual lives in both France and its colonies have been shaped by questions of race. As Marc Bloch wrote in his great book *The Historian's Craft*, "The good historian is like the giant of the fairy tale. He knows that wherever he catches the scent of human flesh, there his quarry lies."[14] Questions of race have unfortunately shaped the flesh and lives of humanity for many years, and the present day has been no exception.

The Black Populations of France is organized into three parts. Part 1 addresses circulations, the ways that different Black populations have moved through the French empire in Africa, focusing on the actions of these groups and the margins of maneuver available to them. It focuses particularly on African soldiers who were both integrated into and oppressed by the French colonial order. Emmanuelle Sibeud leads off this section with her study of the Sainte-Marie affair, involving colonial subject and later *tirailleur sénégalais* Joachim Firinga's demand for citizenship in 1910. Pitting the French national government against the colonial administration in Madagascar, the affair underscored the conflicts over race and citizenship in French colonial Africa; the residents of the island of Sainte-Marie did not win recognition of their status as French citizens until after World War II. In her chapter Sarah Zimmerman considers a very different aspect of the history of the *tirailleurs sénégalais*, discussing the experience of Black soldiers and their families in colonial Morocco on the eve of World War I. Zimmerman pays particular attention to the soldiers' wives, exploring how they negotiated the relationships between their families, their Moroccan neighbors, and their French rulers in considering the gendered nature of race and the legacies of colonial slavery. In contrast, Ruth Ginio explores the history of African soldiers who fought in France during the Second

World War and then returned home. She finds that the racial tolerance and interracial love they often encountered in France empowered them to demand more equal treatment back in colonial Africa. Their experience of the contradictions of French racial attitudes ultimately helped render the colonial order based in those contradictions untenable.

Part 2 considers the experiences of Blacks in metropolitan France, from the eighteenth to the mid–twentieth century. It addresses themes like the memory of slavery, the histories of Black women and gender, and the historical influence of African Americans on Blacks in France. In his study of three French families, Pierre Boulle directs our attention to the history of Blacks and race in eighteenth-century France. Starting with the 1778 royal decree that banned interracial marriages in the country, Boulle explores how people of African ancestry, both slave and free, existed as a part of French families. His chapter gives a valuable new perspective on French provincial life in the years before the Revolution. Minayo Nasiali's essay analyzes the interchange between Africa and France by telling the story of Somali sailors in Marseilles who deployed their connections to the French empire as a way of securing employment in the French maritime industry. She considers how they used their French identity as an advantage in their rivalries with Yemenite sailors during the interwar years, and in doing so portrays Marseilles as a city both French and African.

Whereas Nasiali's study considers men, Jennifer Boittin tells the story of Black women migrants in the interwar years. She focuses particularly on two groups: Black women from the Caribbean who came to Paris and those from French West Africa who went to Rufisque, Senegal. Studying an era full of descriptions of Black women as sexualized bodies, Boittin flips the script by considering these women's own ideas and writings about sexuality, in the process underscoring their complex, multifaceted humanity. This section's final essay shifts from personal to structural analysis, exploring the history of BUMIDOM (Bureau des migrations d'Outre-mer, or Overseas Migration Office), the French Agency that organized migration from the French Caribbean to France in the decades after World War II. In exploring the impact of the BUMIDOM, which he argues lies at the intersections of social, economic, and political history, Sylvain Pattieu shows how the interest of the French state in organizing immigration arose not only from the need for labor in France during the boom times of the Trentes Glorieuses but also from fears of labor militancy and unrest in both the metropole and the Caribbean. He explores how Caribbean migrants sought to avail themselves of the opportunities offered by the BUMIDOM while at the same time challenging its limits and restrictions.

Part 3 looks at contemporary France, considering racial policies and the rise of different kinds of discourse about race. It explores the interactions between state policies and ideas of race developed by individuals, organizations, and communities to illustrate the role of race in public debates. Audrey Celestine continues the story begun by Sylvain Pattieu in her article on the Interministerial Delegation for the Equality of Opportunity of Overseas French (DIECDOM). Founded in 2007, DIECDOM worked to ease the integration of the "overseas French," primarily from the Caribbean, to life in the metropole. Yet as Celestine points out, it did so in a contradictory manner by treating them as a special case, running counter to the French refusal to acknowledge racial difference. In her essay on images of Blackness, Sarah Fila-Bakabadio approaches the study of the representation of the Black body from the interesting and novel perspective of the Black feminine press that flowered in France during the early twenty-first century. She shows how popular magazines like *Amina*, *Miss Ebène*, and others propagated highly controlled and stylized images of Blackness as beautiful, and in doing so also gives us insights into the community of Black women in France today.

The last two chapters in this collection consider the role of African Americans and African American culture in the Black life of France. Franck F. Ekué's contribution studies the use of the English-language term Black in France, showing how it has been championed and adopted by French Blacks as an alternative to the French word *noir*. Ekué uses Stuart Hall's concept of the floating signifier to describe its multiple uses in contemporary French culture, drawing upon the history of Black American expatriates in France as well as the rise of African American liberationist politics back in the United States. He argues that the use of this term shows the ability of French Blacks to create their own identity while at the same time revealing the limitations on France's ability to accept Blacks as fully a part of the French nation. Tyler Stovall considers this issue from a different perspective, discussing the African American expatriates that live in contemporary France and their relations to the Black French communities around them. Exploring both the histories of Black American expatriates and the Blacks of France, he notes that today writers on Blackness in France tend to portray African Americans as peripheral to their communities and to France in general. He notes that ironically this tendency has increased precisely as the Black communities in France have become larger and more settled over the years, resembling less the African Americans of Paris and more Black Americans in the United States.

A few key themes emerge from these different studies of Blacks and Blackness in France. One is gender, in particular communities of Black men and women and the relationships between them. Some chapters, particularly those about soldiers and sailors, deal with African men, while others focus on the experiences of Black women in both colonial and metropolitan France. Together they illustrate the many complex and important intersections of race and gender in the life of Black France. Another theme is the relationship between different Black communities in France. Claude McKay's classic 1929 novel *Banjo* explored the often-contentious relations between African and Caribbean dockers in the port of Marseilles, and several of the articles in this collection consider what such relationships mean to the history and present-day reality of Blacks in France. Finally, in one way or another all of these chapters embrace the intellectual and political imperative to let the Black peoples of France speak for themselves. We do so in a humble recognition of the beauty and richness of these cultures, considering ourselves privileged to play a role in bringing their voices to different audiences in America and hopefully around the world.

The Black Populations of France constitutes a major intervention into the historiography of modern and contemporary France, underscoring the centrality of issues of race to that body of literature. In particular it emphasizes a pluralistic, hybrid approach to the study of the Black diaspora, one both nationally focused and transnational at the same time. These histories of Blacks in France will thus contribute to our understanding of the role of racial identities and practices in the modern world as a whole.

NOTES

1. Christopher Miller, *The French Atlantic Triangle: Literature and Culture of the Slave Trade* (Durham: Duke University Press, 2008); John D. Garrigus, *Before Haiti: Race and Citizenship in French Saint-Domingue* (New York: Palgrave Macmillan, 2006); Bernard Gainot, *La revolution des esclaves* (Paris: Vendémiaire, 2017); Laurent Dubois, *A Colony of Citizens: Revolution and Slave Emancipation in the French Caribbean* (Chapel Hill: University of North Carolina Press, 2004).

2. William Schneider, *An Empire for the Masses: the French Popular Image of Africa, 1870–1900* (Westport CT: Greenwood, 1982); Harry Gamble, *Contesting French West Africa: Battles over Schools and the Colonial Order, 1900–1950* (Lincoln: University of Nebraska Press, 2017); Ruth Ginio *The French Army and its African Soldiers: the Years of Decolonization* (Lincoln: University of Nebraska Press, 2017).

3. Gary Wilder, *The French Imperial Nation-State: Negritude and Colonial Humanism between the Two World Wars* (Chicago: University of Chicago Press, 2005); Philippe Dewitte, *Les mouvements nègres en France, 1919–1939* (Paris: l'Harmattan, 1985); Petrine Archer-Straw, *Negrophilia: Avant-Garde Paris and Black Culture in the 1920s* (New York: Thames & Hudson, 2000).

4. Michael Kimmelman, "For Blacks in France, Obama's Rise is Reason to Rejoice, and to Hope," *New York Times*, June 17, 2008.

5. Lozès, Patrick, *Nous les Noirs de France* (Paris: Danger Public, 2007).

6. Michel Fabre, *Richard Wright, la quête inachevée* (Paris: Lieu Commun, 1986); Michael Fabre, *La rive noire: de Harlem à la Seine* (Paris: Lieu Commun, 1986); Michale Fabre, *From Harlem to Paris: Black American Writers in France, 1840–1980* (Urbana: University of Illinois Press, 1991).

7. Tyler Stovall, *Paris Noir: African Americans in the City of Light* (Boston: Houghton-Mifflin, 1996); Andy Fry, *Paris Blues: African American Music and French Popular Culture, 1920–1960* (Chicago: University of Chicago Press, 2014); Rashida Braggs, *Jazz Diaspora: Race, Music, and Migration in Post–World War II Paris* (Berkeley: University of California Press, 2016).

8. William Cohen, *The French Encounter with Africans: White Response to Blacks, 1530–1880* (Bloomington: Indiana University Press, 1980); Marc Michel, *L'Appel à l'Afrique: contributions et réactions à l'effort de guerre en A.O.F., 1914–1919* (Paris: Presses universitaires de la Sorbonne, 1982); Alice Conklin, *Mission to Civilize: the Republican Idea of Empire in France and West Africa* (Stanford: Stanford University Press, 1997); Tzvetan Todorov, *On Human Diversity: Nationalism, Racism, and Exoticism in French Thought* (Cambridge MA: Harvard University Press, 1989).

9. Trica Keaton, *Muslim Girls and the Other France: Race, Identity, Politics, and Social Exclusion* (Bloomington: Indiana University Press, 2006); Crystal Marie Fleming, *Resurrecting Slavery: Racial Legacies and White Supremacy in France* (Philadelphia: Temple University Press, 2017); Paul Silverstein, *Postcolonial France: Race, Islam, and the Future of the Republic* (London: Pluto, 2018).

10. Miller, *French Atlantic Triangle*; Dominic Thomas, *Black France: Colonialism, Immigration, and Transnationalism* (Bloomington: Indiana University Press, 2007); Doris Y. Kadish, *Fathers, Daughters, and Slaves: Women Writers and French Colonial Slavery* (Liverpool: Liverpool University Press, 2012); Brent Hayes Edwards, *The Practice of Diaspora: Literature, Translation, and the Rise of Black Internationalism* (Cambridge MA: Harvard University Press, 2003).

11. This remains true in spite of the fact that a number of works have addressed the question of Blackness in France. Examples include Pascal Blanchard, Eric Deroo, and Gilles Manceron, *Le Paris Noir* (Paris: Éditions Hazan, 2001); "Black: Africains, Antillais . . . Cultures noires en France," *Autrement* 49 (April 1983); Claude Ribbe, *Les Nègres de la République* (Paris: Éditions Alphée, 2007); Rama Yade-Zimet, *Noirs de France* (Paris: Calmann-Lévy, 2007); François Durpaire, *France blanche, colère noire* (Paris: Odile Jacob, 2006).

12. Pap Ndiaye, *Les noirs de France: essai sur une minorité française* (Paris: Calmann-Lévy, 2008).

13. Stéphane Beaud et Gérard Noiriel, *Races et sciences sociales* (Paris: Éditions Agone, 2020).

14. Marc Bloch, *The Historian's Craft*, trans. Peter Putnam (New York: Vintage, 1964), 26.

PART 1

Colonial France in Africa

1

The Inopportune Citizenship of the Inhabitants of Sainte-Marie in Madagascar (1907–49)

An Imperial Contradiction?

EMMANUELLE SIBEUD

TRANSLATED BY TYLER STOVALL

"Therefore, born on French soil, of parents who were French in the legal sense of the term, I thought I was French and, being of adult age, entitled to all the qualities of citizenship. But, gentlemen, it seems I am not French. Oh, I know that between a Frenchman of France and the poor devil who has the honor to address to you the present request there is a physical difference that nothing can erase. My African profile, my kinky hair, my skin, even my style, all of these say that I am a Black man."—Comité de protection et de défense des indigènes, *6000 Français dépouillés* (1911)

In November 1910 Joachim Firinga submitted to the French parliament a petition denouncing the rejection of his citizenship and that of the six thousand residents of his small island, Sainte-Marie de Madagascar. The color of their skin seems to have been the real reason for this civic demotion, through which the French local authorities tried to impose a colonial administration on them. At the same time, Firinga had registered to vote in Paris. His rejection enabled him to apply for a judicial review, which a parliamentary deputy from La Réunion who supported his case immediately requested. The members of parliament and the appeals court agreed with him: the residents of Sainte-Marie had been French since the purchase of their island in 1750 and qualified citizens since 1848.[1] On July 22, 1912, the appeals court reaffirmed Firinga's citizenship with an order that would set a legal precedent.[2] But they did not reckon with the tenacity of the colonial administration, which refused to accept this position. The Saint-Marians were considered subjects until 1946 and it required the uprising of 1947, followed by a spectacular abstention in Sainte-Marie from the municipal elections of 1949, to force the administration finally to renounce its very long denial of their citizenship "on the basis of grossly erroneous affirmations."[3]

Citizen Firinga died in battle in Craonne, on the Western Front of World War I, in 1917. His incorporation into a unit of the African Rifles (*tirailleurs sénégalais*) maintained the equivocal nature of his case and the question of Sainte-Marie became an example that was systematically invoked to underscore the dangers of assimilation. The end of the First World War was a key moment in the revision of conditions for the access to citizenship of all French colonial subjects. The priority given in theory to those who had seen combat facilitated a redefinition of naturalization as a distinction in compensation for exceptional services and not as a right. Moreover, a culture-centric rhetoric overlapped with debates during the 1910s over attempts to downgrade citizens of color in Madagascar and Senegal.[4] It was not racial discrimination by colonial authorities or by European minorities that hindered the assimilation of colonial subjects. Rather, they disqualified themselves by refusing to renounce their personal status based in custom in order to embrace French civil law. The latent incompatibility between French citizenship and "Black" appearance denounced by Firinga in 1911 was not a scandal but instead arose from undeniable ethnological realities.[5] Thus the "color line" existed first and foremost in the conceptions and practices of colonial subjects themselves.[6]

Yerri Urban has stressed the fact that the Sainte-Marie affair played a key role in this evolution. While recognizing their citizenship, the appeals court affirmed in 1912 that it was conditioned by the acceptance and observation of French civil law.[7] The demand for the equality of all free men, no matter their skin color, as contained in the law of 1833 gave ground to an insistence on conformity with civil law. Unfortunately for them, the Saint-Marians were the first group used by the colonial administration to deny assimilation. The demotion inflicted on them became the symbol of the discretionary authority of the local colonial authorities, and in this sense Madagascar became an imperial laboratory. One must nonetheless go beyond local initiatives and the limits on the power of the colonial authorities both at a local and an imperial level to evaluate thoroughly the stakes of an insoluble question, one with many ramifications. Let's leave aside for the moment one of the most well-known, the important Malagasy assimilationist movement of the 1920s, in order to insist on the echo of more immediate effects and to analyze the different levels on which they took place.[8] I argue in effect that the issue of Sainte-Marie was an imperial contradiction that acted a priori as a foil for the jurists elaborating imperial law for both good and ill and one that nourished the reflections of other no less influential actors. Blaise Diagne in particular was a civil servant in Madagascar who was closely involved in local debates, drawing contradictory lessons from the Sainte-Marie affair. One must therefore return to what made Madagascar a strategic crucible for imperial racialization during the 1910s.

Neither Subjects nor Citizens

Starting in 1897 the inhabitants of the small island of Sainte-Marie were in a situation, not uncommon in colonial life, of dissonance between their status and that of their island. Sainte-Marie was purchased in 1750 to serve as a jumping off point for the Indian Ocean. Subsequently attached either to La Réunion or to Mayotte, depending on the year, it became a part of Madagascar in 1896 and received the relatively privileged status of *commune* the following year.[9] The status of the non-European residents of Sainte-Marie was less clear. They were a priori beneficiaries of the laws of 1833 and 1848 even though those measures hadn't been promulgated locally. They could not vote for a member of parliament but they did have a right to civil status, and a district court for local notables functioned regularly in Sainte-Marie from 1887 to 1894. Some Saint-Marians enlisted in the French army of conquest in 1895 and, until 1909, they were exempt from paying personal taxes, the head tax, and the tribute imposed upon defeated subjects, as well as from the special repressive measures that from 1904 on constituted the local colonial version of the poorly named native "code."[10] In sum, these were good subjects, but the question of granting full-fledged citizenship to some of them caused difficulties. Firinga, who came from a leading family in Sainte-Marie and was a member of the first regiment of the Malagasy Rifles in 1895 as well as a highly regarded interpreter with the headquarters of the army of occupation until 1900, requested his naturalization in 1897 so that he could apply to the school for junior officers in Saint-Maixent. He repeated this request in 1899.[11] No disposition having been taken to naturalize Madagascans, he was refused twice, but in 1899 he received a significant compensation: exemption from the requirement that natives engaged in mining pay special fees.

He learned, at his expense, that this exemption could be revoked unilaterally. In 1907 he was ordered to pay the duties required of natives and sentenced to three months in prison for rebellion, having greeted the local official who came to his house to collect this sum with a gun in his hand. After his sentence was confirmed he appealed to the appeals court. The court essentially ruled he was guilty but agreed to examine his appeal, thus recognizing that he was not a native subject since natives had no right to appeal. Firinga was not alone in his struggle. As of August 1907 twenty-five leading Saint-Marians addressed a petition to the president of the republic to demand a decree explicitly abrogating the native code in Sainte-Marie and reestablishing full citizen rights for all the inhabitants of the island.[12] In April 1908 the newly formed federal association of natives of the colonies also wrote to the colonial minister to protest against "the violations of the French status of the Saint-Marians" and to remind him that they were French citizens.[13]

The local colonial administration knew perfectly well that the status of the Saint-Marians was ambiguous and these protests, both locally and at the imperial level, prompted their disqualification in its eyes. The governor-general of Madagascar since 1905, Victor Augagneur, intended to champion a new imperial policy.[14] He ostensibly reformed the native decree of 1908 while at the same time affirming that the system was indispensable.[15] In particular, after having literally harassed the minister of the colonies, in March 1909 he obtained a decree allowing him to naturalize a few carefully selected Madagascans. Under the pretext of restarting the policy of assimilation, it in reality changed its meaning and practice. Naturalization became a rare distinction granted at the discretion of the local colonial administration, which was charged with evaluating the merits of the candidates. By collectively demanding the reestablishment of the rights that they claimed as their proper due, the Saint-Marians challenged this logic of the unilateral, drip-by-drip grant of citizenship. Their demotion henceforth became the counterpart of the policy initiated by Augagneur. In May 1909 the decree on native justice in Madagascar was the first to be applied without any accommodation for Sainte-Marie, although not without irony. Given the absence of any local custom other than French law, native justice was in effect made to conform to the Hova code—so named after a political category in the Merina Kingdom, the dominant Madagascan polity in the nineteenth century, that French authorities falsely used as an ethnic label—by a native tribunal presided over by the administrative mayor, flanked by native officials chosen by leading citizens. The Saint-Marians were thus required to pay the personal tax, becoming in effect subjects without any exemptions or their own customs.[16]

Their refusal was immediate and effective. On his return to Sainte-Marie in October 1909, Firinga obtained permission to open a shop and create a club, "L'Union."[17] He organized demonstrations at the residence of the administrative mayor (300 people in October 1909 and 1,200 in December, including 500 women) and meetings in all the island's villages. He convinced the leading citizens to resign their administrative positions so that, effectively, the administration was reduced to recruiting its own.[18] Finally he collected funds (five francs for men, one franc for women, fifty centimes for youths) that enabled him to run articles in the local press and to leave in August 1910 to place his case before parliament and the minister of the colonies. The colonial administration was forced to retreat on all fronts. In November 1911 the appeals court of Tananarive decreed that only the civil code applied to the Saint-Marians. The native tribunal therefore had no authority over them. In April 1913 four hundred Saint-Marians subpoenaed the governor-general of Madagascar to appear before the civil tribunal of Tananarive, accusing him of having wrongly inscribed them on the personal tax roll. The personal tax was then transformed into a municipal tax of the same amount.[19] This time it was the European inhabitants of Sainte-Marie who protested. Not only were they no longer exempt, but they also claimed their racial dignity had been violated because they were lumped in with natives and, like them, indiscriminately subject to colonial orders.[20]

Since the situation could not be resolved locally, in 1913 the colonial ministry took up the matter with the Conseil d'état to redefine by decree the status of the Saint-Marians, but it encountered the impossibility of amending the law of 1833 by a decree.[21] For want of anything better, the colonial administration chose to catch the Saint-Marians between two stools. They were not treated as subjects. This posed few problems in Sainte-Marie but was more difficult for the Saint-Marians living in Madagascar, who were prompt to demand rights that could not be entirely refused. The procedures that should have enabled Saint-Marians to take advantage of their citizenship became veritable obstacle courses that few were able to complete successfully. If their cause became permanently bogged down in this status quo, it underscored the effective limits of the ability of the colonial administration to intervene and the juridical limits of government by decree, which had prevailed in the colonies since 1854. The experience was so disturbing that imperial racialization, which Madagascar had been one of the crucibles of for a long time, appeared like a desirable backfire.

Madagascar, Crucible of Imperial Racialization

In the aftermath of the conquest, General Gallieni put in place in Madagascar a "policy of races" that he portrayed as both modern and republican.[22] Historians have shown that this policy was first of all an improvised response to the formation of Malagasy national sentiment around the Menalamba rebellion, and that it mobilized local categories in a rather confused fashion.[23] The debates around the Saint-Marian question underscored both the omnipresence of this racial rhetoric and its malleability. The administrative mayor of Sainte-Marie used ethnology to link the Saint-Marians to the Madagascan Betsimisaraka and to present them as the descendants of slaves jealous of their former Hova masters.[24] From his own perspective, Firinga challenged not only negrophobia but also the "Hovachization" that victimized the Saint-Marians. Beyond these contradictory usages, the policy of races linked up with imperial realities, with the governor-general of French West Africa intending to import it into this federation and Augagneur portraying himself as a republican herald of racialization.[25]

A doctor, Radical-Socialist, freemason, and member of the League for the Rights of Man, Augagneur was the ideal spokesman for the transformation of racial rhetoric. This rhetoric was a response to the establishment of a long-term style of imperial management, the anguish linked to Japan's defeat of the Russian empire in 1905, and the resurgence of the debate about the relations between the so-called inferior and superior races. Linked to the "advanced party," Augagneur contributed to the colonial party by developing a racist vision of the colonized populations in which the Madagascans occupied a strategic position. Unlike the "yellows" who had their own civilization and the "Blacks of the continent" who didn't have one at all, the Madagascans were at the same time sufficiently advanced and without "strong" traditions, which made them by default "the most likely to be penetrated by our civilization."[26] In 1907 during his first return to the metropole, Augagneur attacked more explicitly the "great doctors of the Declaration of the Rights of Man and of the Citizen" who preached racial equality in complete ignorance of colonial realities.[27] His arguments emphasized both pragmatic and cultural considerations: "Is it by chance that you will emancipate as a whole all the barbarian races in the middle of whom you find yourselves? Is it by a single stroke, by the sole power of a text or a decree, that you will proclaim that these men, attached to fetishistic practices, without the slightest intellectual activity will become French citizens, with all the powers one can give to all civilized men?"[28] Even if it was carefully omitted, the question of race was nonetheless the stumbling block of this new rhetoric. Augagneur and others thus overtly portrayed the assimilation of the "old colonies" as an error compromising the imperial future.[29]

It was not simply a matter of discourse. In December 1907 Augagneur submitted to the ministerial council a project to create an East Africa federation centered around Madagascar. La Réunion, Mayotte, and the Comoro islands would be its dependencies. The Saint-Marians would thus become the first of a series of Black French citizens reduced to the rank of colonial subjects, on the pretext of a change in the status of the territory where they lived and by reason of the color of their skin. Although this project provoked vehement protests in La Réunion and remained a dead letter, it nonetheless illustrated the contradiction between imperial logic and the increasing creolization of Madagascar, like many other colonial societies, at the beginning of the twentieth century. In search of a way out of the socioeconomic crisis that afflicted La Réunion until the First World War, the island's elected officials pleaded for the conquest of Madagascar and supported the establishment of Réunion colonial settlers in Diego Suarez after 1885.

The balance sheet was contradictory at the beginning of the twentieth century. If there were four thousand colonial settlers from Réunion in Madagascar in 1902, the majority were poor migrants, nonwhite or mixed race. Their reality had so little to do with the metropole's project that in 1908 Paul Leroy-Beaulieu recommended, in the fourth edition of his *De la colonisation chez les peoples modernes*, to import French Canadians in order finally to create a French population in Madagascar.[30] The white bourgeoisie from Réunion, also installed in Madagascar by colonial authorities, kept its distance from these proletarian citizens of color. In Diego Suarez, their point of entry, indigent Creoles were assigned to the native hospital in order to keep costs down, but also to avoid any mixing with Europeans. There were enough of them to exclude Madagascan natives from the hospital, even though it was funded by native taxes.[31] Tensions were just as bad in the countryside. The small creole colonial settlers, nicknamed *marécageux* (marshmen), lacked the necessary capital to exploit their concessions and thus instead tried to carve out a position as commercial intermediaries to their Madagascan neighbors. Following the same logic, they demanded a monopoly over mining concessions. Thus the "color line" constituted in Madagascar a frontier that intersected in a conflicting manner with the divide between subjects and citizens.

The white bourgeoisie of Réunion had a paternalistic relationship with the Saint-Marians. Thus in December 1907 the "old settlers" of Tamatave reminded Augagneur that the Saint-Marians had for a long time enjoyed the same rights as the Réunionnais, and it would be unjust to deprive them of those rights.[32] In 1910–11 Firinga published a "Saint-Marian Chronicle" in a weekly newspaper, the *Impartial de Diego-Suarez*, which regularly attacked working class Creoles. It was senator Félix Crépin of Réunion who in 1911 drafted the report favoring Firinga's petition, and it was moreover the Réunion network that contested his registration on the electoral lists of the fifth *arrondissement* in Paris, thus enabling him to turn to the appeals court. Still influential, these networks were nonetheless hard-pressed to keep up with political evolution in Réunion, where the question of race led to shifting boundaries. The first Black member of Parliament from Réunion, Lucien Gasparin, was elected in 1906. He broke with the conservative republicans of the white bourgeoisie who had supported him after arriving in Paris and joined the Radical-Socialists in order to represent the Black workers who were his voters.[33] He also had strong ties to Madagascar. Grandson of a Madagascan freed slave, he moved to Tamatave in 1897 and established himself as a lawyer, which enabled him to begin a political career in La Réunion. A privileged laboratory for the renewal of imperial racial rhetoric, Madagascar was thus the most unpredictable crucible for a debate about the place of Black citizens that erupted simultaneously on several fronts.

Citizenship and the Color Line

The press was a central site for this debate. Newspapers created and directed by French citizens benefitted from the law of 1881, and Augagneur used them as a sounding board for his new policy. In June 1907 a new title, the *Réveil de Madagascar*, was launched by Réunion and Mauritian journalists associated with Blaise Diagne, an *originaire* citizen of one of the four communes of Senegal and the principal agent for postal customs in Réunion since 1899 and Madagascar since 1902. Its editors ostensibly supported Augagneur. They invoked "the ideas of republican liberty, of democratic fraternity, of social solidarity, of human emancipation, of justice, in a word, which are the honor of our homeland and which justify its influence in the world," and also affirmed that to be French is an "honor," therefore justifying its ultra-Malthusian policy of naturalization.[34] They emphasized in October 1907 that the naturalization of the natives was "an exception to the laws of nature," calling for the greatest possible prudence.[35] Not only must the Madagascans guarantee their "intellect, morality, and devotion to our institutions" in order to become citizens, but they must also pay for this privilege through an extra tax because they were able to become citizens without leaving home, an advantage compared to citizens coming from the metropole or other French colonies.[36]

This barely-disguised rivalry between citizens turned into overt hostility to the demands of the Saint-Marians. Imitating the condescending attitude of Augaeur, the *Réveil de Madagascar* portrayed the "poor little Firinga" from time to time as a native "poor devil" badly advised by Augagneur's adversaries and as "his highness, Firinga," draped "with an excess of haughty belief in what he considered his right" at risk of "affecting the social order," or rather the imperial order.[37]

The problem in the decade preceding the First World War was that the imperial order remained uncertain, equally at the expense of the editors of the *Réveil de Madagascar*. In April 1908 the disappearance of one of the founders of the newspaper put its future in doubt. Diagne was then charged with selling printing material to the Tananarive Freemasons lodge, "La France Australe," of which he was a member, to create a new paper faithful to Augagneur. The sale did not happen, and during an altercation in August 1908 Diagne was publicly slapped and called "dirty n—" by one of the masons with whom he was negotiating. He sued and obtained recompense the following September after a trial, the deliberations of which were published in the *Réveil de Madagascar*, that showed how insoluble the question of race had become in Madagascar.[38] During the trial, the accused was defended by the president of the League of the Rights of Man in Tananarive, who did not hesitate to say to Diagne: "Don't forget you are a Negro, and that is not a point in your favor."[39] In response Diagne denounced the racism of the local masons who refused to initiate Madagascans. This public display of internal debates earned him a heavy condemnation from the Grand Orient of France, one that he had revoked when he returned to France in 1909.[40]

Augagneur's offensive policies exacerbated these tensions, giving them an unprecedented impact in France.[41] But they also grew out of broader changes, in particular those taking shape in neighboring southern Africa where the formation of a new British dominion after the Boer War institutionalized racism in a clear and eventually contagious fashion. Starting in 1908 a rumor circulated that twenty thousand Madagascans would be delivered for two years to South African mining companies in search of contract labor. The most influential settlers protested against this theft of their labor supply, but they also considered that this experience would make the Madagascans learn once again "the respect for Europeans that they have lost."[42] The demotion of Saint-Marians, whose only crime was to be Black, arose out of this paranoid logic, which also threatened better-integrated Black citizens like Diagne. Nonetheless, with its badly managed Creole composition, Madagascan colonial society was a site both of amplification of and challenge to this global evolution.

The *Réveil de Madagascar* immediately took up arms against racist discourses by refuting racial theories and pinning the ordinary prejudices of colonial society to them.[43] The editors of the *Réveil de Madagascar* were clearly divided between wanting to fit in and their conviction that they were "the stranger in the night that no one invites in, the troublemaker, the party-crasher, the bull in the china shop."[44] Like Diagne they tested the concrete possibilities that came to them. The 1908 altercation illustrated the very narrow limits of republican universalism. Diagne became a freemason in 1899, shortly after his arrival in Saint-Denis from Réunion. Reassigned to Tananarive in 1902, he joined the lodge there. The Grand Orient solicited his advice in 1902 when that lodge was dissolved for dysfunction and he was charged with forming a new lodge named "Madagascan Independence."[45] It attracted a large proportion of lower-level imperial administrators of colonial origin like himself who sought effective sponsorship.[46] In 1907 Diagne also organized the first Indian Ocean regional Masonic conference, with delegates from Madagascar, Mauritius, and Réunion. Two of the seven requests he presented concerned Madagascan native subjects exclusively. He called for primary schools and "the progressive naturalization of Madagascans with serious qualities of education and morality."[47] Though he could easily set himself up as the protector of native interests, his proposal concerning the education of children in European schools was set aside for fear of mixing up racial categories.[48] The voluntary assimilation practiced by Diagne thus ran up against the essential obstacle which lay at the base of the civic demotion inflicted on Saint-Marians: the question of race. It would certainly be naïve to suppose that the racist blows and insults of 1908 would be enough to make him revise his positions, but they were more than anecdotal incidents. In Madagascar between 1902 and 1908 Diagne literally saw the color line widen under his feet. But it was also in the island's first lodges that he observed Gasparin's strategy which transformed the increasingly heavy stigma of color into an electoral argument.[49] By 1909, therefore, he had witnessed very different imperial experiences with his long sojourns in Madagascar and Réunion.

In 1915–16 Diagne learned from the administrative elements of the rejection of the Saint-Marians when he demanded not respect for his constituents' established rights, but the possibility of fulfilling their duty as citizens. The colonial administration viciously recognized the efficacy of this strategy by deciding in 1916 not to enlist the Saint-Marians at the same time military recruitment was intensifying in Madagascar. That led the subjects to a bitter conclusion, that if the Sainte-Marie question had become an imperial contradiction, it had been to the advantage of other citizens. Diagne did not abandon them, however, and he completely revised his opinion of their case. In 1915 he, along with Gasparin and six other members of parliament, submitted a bill requesting that naturalization be a right for all colonial subjects with titles and demanding the immediate recognition of contested citizenship cases, notably that of the Saint-Marians.[50] The complex articulation between the fate of the Saint-Marians and that of the *originaires* of the four communes, the links between Diagne and Gasparin, shows that the common struggle of colonial parliamentarians of color arose not only from their encounters in the metropole nor from their going back and forth between the metropole and their constituents.[51] Their imperial and interimperial experiences also nourished them, giving them a critical expertise and the ability to make use of it. To return to the lessons that Diagne took from his ten years in the Indian Ocean suggests new perspectives on the complexity of his position at the end of the First World War, when he opposed colonial racism with a discourse of racial conciliation, while at the same time joining W. E. B. Du Bois and the pan-African networks in relaunching the campaign against negrophobia.

NOTES

1. *Journal official de la République française. Débats parlementaires, Sénat*, July 11, 1911, 1286–87.

2. *Recueil general de jurisprudence, de doctrine et de legislation colonials et maritimes* 1 (1913): 69–71.

3. Thus in 1939 the colonial administration estimated that there were 7,876 native subjects in Sainte-Marie out of 9,104 inhabitants. In 1946 these supposed subjects were registered in the second [electoral] college, provoking their refusal to vote in 1949 (only 2 percent participated). Archives de la République Malgache (ARM), F 74, Commune de Sainte-Marie, letter de Robert Delavignette au minister de la France d'Outre-mer, November 3, 1949.

4. George Wesley Johnson, *Naissance du Sénégal contemporain: Aux origins de la vie politique modern (1900–1920)* (Paris: Karthala, 1991).

5. *Rapport fait au nom de la commission des affaires extérieures, des protectorats et des colonies, chargée d'examiner les propositions de loi concernant l'accession des indigènes aux droits civils et politiques* par Marius Moutet, député (Paris, Imprimerie de la Chambre des deputes, 1918), 328; Document no. 4383, Chambre de deputes, 11ème legislature, session de 1918—Annexe au PV de la séance, March 1, 1918, 152.

6. This phrase was proposed by W. E. B. Du Bois during the first pan-African Conference organized in London in 1900. On the global logic of the color line, see Marilyn Lake and Henry Reynolds, *Drawing the Global Colour Line. White Men's Countries and the International Challenge of Racial Equality* (Cambridge, U.K.: Cambridge University Press, 2008); Tyler Stovall, "The Color Line behind the Lines: Racial Violence in France during the Great War," *American Historical Review* 103, no. 3 (June 1998): 737–69.

7. Yerri Urban, *L'indigène dans le droit colonial français, 1865–1955*, collection des theses, no. 36 (Paris: Fondation Varenne, 2010).

8. Solofo Randrianja, *Sociétés et luttes anticoloniales à Madagascar (1896 à 1946)* (Paris: Karthala, 2001).

9. In practice the island was run by an administrator named by the Governor General of Madagascar. This administrative mayor was assisted by a municipal council whose members were chosen among the leading citizens, then elected. See the attached chart.

10. On this arrangement see Sylvie Thénault, *Violence ordinaire dans l'Algérie colonial: camps, internements, assignations à residence* (Paris: Odile Jacob, 2011).

11. Archives Nationales d'Outre-Mer (ANOM), FM/SG/MAD, 326 dossier 844.

12. ANOM, Fonds Ministériels, SG Mad 326 d 844, petition, August 30, 1907, signed by twenty-seven Saint-Marians.

13. ANOM, Fonds Ministériels, SG Mad 326 d 844, letter, April 7, 1908.

14. Victor Augagneur (1855–1931) was the governor general of Madagascar from 1905 to 1910. See http://www.assemblee-nationale.fr/sycomore/fiche.asp?num _dept=261.

15. "Circulaire et arrêté du Gouverneur general réglementant le droit de repression, par voie disciplinaire, des infractions spéciales à l'indigénat," *Journal official de Madagascar* 8, no. 1161 (June 27, 1908): 430–35.

16. The personal tax was twenty francs, the equivalent of the monthly rent for a house. Gouvernement general de Madagascar, *Madagascar: Annuaire general* (Tananarive, 1912), 601–4.

17. The law of 1881 on freedom of assembly having been promulgated in Sainte-Marie, the administration decided it was more useful also to grant this authorization to the club so as to monitor its activities.

18. ANOM, Fonds Ministériels, SG Mad 369, letter du gouverneur general de Madagascar au Ministre des colonies, September 20, 1911, 10–11.

19. In November 1912 the director of the Colonial ministry's Indian Ocean service calculated the loss that would result from recognizing the citizenship of the Saint-Marians: more than 110,000 francs for Sainte-Marie and more than 450,000 for Nossi-Bé (whose residents were in the same legal situation). ANOM, Fonds Ministériels, SG Mas 326 d 844, Note du November 11, 1912. This calculation was nonetheless not based in reality. Firinga launched a very successful taxpayers' strike: 891 Saint-Marians out of 5,500 paid their tax in 1910 (915 in 1911), which brought down the tax revenues to 18,000 francs.

20. ANOM, Fonds Mnistériels, SG Mad d 844, lettres du colon Jean Biendiné au Gouverneur general le March 10, 1914 et au Ministre des colonies, June 19, 1914.

21. Archives Nationales (Pierrefitte), Conseil d'État, AL 3111–165973, projet de décret sur les Saints-Mariens.

22. Gallieni's report on his new policy was highly praised in Paris by prominent Republican figures such as Ernest Lavisse, who championed it in the influential *Revue de Paris* in 1899. Ernest Lavisse, "Une méthode coloniale," *Revue de Paris*, June 15, 1899, 681–98; Lavisse, "Une méthode coloniale," *Revue de Paris*, July 1, 1899, 54–71.

23. Stephen Ellis, *L'Insurrection des Menalamba: une révolte à Madagascar, 1895–1899* (Paris, Karthala, 1998); Françoise Raison-Jourde, "L'assignation d'un destin identitaire: L'enquête de 1908 sur race et caste des élèves malgaches," in Françoise Raison-Jourde and Solofo Randrianja, dir., *La nation malgache au défi de l'ethnicité* (Paris: Karthala, 2002), 45–60.

24. "What, in effect, is the population of the Dependency if not an aggregate of Betsimisaraka defectors from the *Grande Terre*, turned into pirates and contrabanders, and unhappy slaves transported in gangs from the Comoro archipelago; four fifths of the inhabitants were formerly indentured servants of the Governor or the wealthier planters. And Sainte-Marie which was, off the coast of Madagascar, at the avant-garde of civilization and a vital outpost of Greater France, is now in a state of backwardness. The Saint-Marians are practically where they were in 1750, they languish in their stagnant ponds; in fifteen years the Hovas, for whom they have a profound aversion, have advanced by several centuries, a level of progress they will maintain if the past is any guide to the future; it is a strange spectacle after 150 years of contacts with civilized peoples to see these people who owe France everything and demand racial equality now wish to vio-

late legality every day at the instigation of one of their own." ANOM, Mad. 369, rapport de l'administrateur maire au gouverneur general, August 30, 1910.

25. Alice Conklin, *A Mission to Civilize: The Republican Idea of Empire in France and West Africa, 1895–1930* (Palo Alto CA: Stanford University Press, 1997).

26. "Entretien avec M. Augagneur," *le Temps*, November 20, 1905, 1–2 "La question colonial et les partis avancés," *le Temps*, November 8, 1905, 1.

27. "M. Augagneur en France," *Revue de Madagascar* 12, December 1907, 578.

28. "M. Augagneur en France," *Revue de Madagascar* 12, December 1907, 578.

29. As the administrator Louis Spas, who in 1912 defended a law thesis on European and native justice in Madagascar, argued, "We can only deplore once more the capital error committed by the legislator of 1833 whose devotion to the idea of assimilation led to consequences that everyone regrets today. This error has already produced in the Caribbean and in Réunion results we do not believe it necessary to belabor further, and now almost 6,000 natives of Sainte-Marie will receive the same benefits of citizenship as the French! What have they done to earn that, and do they really deserve such a favor in general?" Louis Spas, *Étude sur l'organisation de Madagascar, justice indigene, indigénat, conseils d'arbitrage*, Thèse pour le doctorat, Université de Paris, Faculté de droit (Paris: Giard et Brière, 1912), 93.

30. This proposal is presented in G. L., "La colonization française à Madagascar," *Revue de Madagascar* 2 (1908): 20.

31. Claude Bavoux, "Les conditions d'insertion sociale des creoles à Diego Suarez, ville pluri-ethnique au début de la colonization," in Françoise Raison-Jourde and Solofo Randrianja, dir., *La nation malgache au défi de l'ethnicité* (Paris: Karthala, 2002), 229–45.

32. "M. Augagneur à Tamatave," *Le Réveil malgache* 52 (October 5, 1908): 2–3.

33. Danielle Maestri, "Lucien Gasparin, député de la Réunion, 1906–1942: éléments biographiques," *Revue historique des Mascareignes* 1, no. 1 (1998): 197–208;. David Gagneur, "Deux deputés réunionnais, incarnations républicaines au début du XXème siècle: François de Mahy (1830–1906) et Lucien Gasparin (1868–1948)" in Prosper Eve, dir., *Un transfert culturel à La Réunion: L'idéal républicain* (St. André de la Réunion: Océan Editions, 2009), 160–72. Firinga paid close attention to these evolutions. In December 1909 he reminded the administrative mayor of Sainte-Marie that the police charged with repressing a demonstration in Réunion the previous year had been greeted with a hail of rocks and suggested that the Saint-Marians could do the same. ANOM, Fonds Ministériels, SG Mad 369, letter de l'administrateur-maire de l'île de Sainte-Marie au Gouverneur general de Madagascar, December 15, 1910, 4.

34. Editorial board, "A nos lecteurs," *Le Réveil de Madagascar. Journal républicain. Politique, commercial, Industriel, agricole d'informations & d'annonces paraissant le mardi, le jeudi et le samedi*, no. 1, June 7, 1907, 1. At least half of these entries were not signed. The journal appeared three times a week for nineteen months.

35. "Echos-Naturalization," *Le Réveil de Madagascar*, October 19, 1907, 1.
36. "Editorial—Naturalisation," *Le Réveil de Madagascar*, March 7, 1908, 1.
37. "Lettre ouverte à M.J.F. colon indigene à Mahatsara," *Le Réveil de Madagascar*, July 30, 1907, 1–2; "Echos—Un pauvre diable," and "Arrestation de M. Firinga," *Le Réveil de Madagascar*, August 1, 1907, 1; "Echos—Sa grandeur, Firinga," *Le Réveil de Madagascar*, October 29 1907, 1.
38. GODF, carton 1884, loge "la France australe," Tananarive, 1909–21.
39. "Quelques explications," *Le Réveil de Madagascar*, September 23, 1908, 1.
40. He was condemned to be expelled for five years. This sentence was annulled in 1909 and in 1922 Diagne became the first Black member of the high council of the Grand Orient of France. The in-house brochure recently edited by Jean-Luc Le Bras, *Blaise Diagne à Madagascar (1902–1908), ou Le séjour mouvementé d'un franc-maçon, fonctionnaire colonial ambitieux* (GODF, brochure no. 3546) nonetheless suggests that the 1908 trial continued to be a Black mark on Diagne's Masonic career.
41. Rémi Fabre, *Francis de Pressensé et la defense des droits de l'homme: un intellectual au combat* (Rennes: Presses universitaires de Rennes, 2004).
42. "L'émigration de la main d'oeuvre de Madagascar," *Revue de Madagascar* 1 (1908): 219.
43. G. Mada, "La question des races," *Le Réveil de Madagascar* 2 (June 6, 1907). It was linked for example to the scandal provoked by the prospect of recruiting native monitors for the lycée in Tananarive. "Echos—Très naturels," *Le Réveil de Madagascar*, June 13, 1907.
44. "Editorial—Utiles explications," *Le Réveil de Madagascar*, July 1, 1908, 1.
45. GODF, carton 1887, loge "l'avenir malgache," 1903–5 et carton 1889, loge "l'indépendance malgache," 1904–9.
46. Owen White, "Networking: Freemasons and the Colonial State in French West Africa, 1895–1914," *French History* 19, no. 1 (March 2005): 91–111.
47. Archives GODF, carton 1889.
48. Emmanuelle Saada, *Les enfants de la colonie. Les métis de l'Empire français entre sujétion et citoyenneté* (Paris: La Découverte, 2007).
49. Gasparin and Diagne met in Dahomey at the beginning of the 1890s.
50. AN (Pierrefitte), C. 7645, projet de loi Lagrosillière, 11eme legislature, May 1915.
51. One must therefore qualify the analysis proposed by Dominique Chathuant in "L'émergence d'une élite politique noire dans la France du premer 20eme siècle," *Vingtième siècle, Revue d'histoire* 101 (2009): 133–47.

2

Colonial Misappropriations
of Trans-Saharan Legacies

Abid al-Bukhari and *Tirailleurs Sénégalais* in Imperial and Colonial Morocco

SARAH ZIMMERMAN

In 1911 in Zahiliga, a rural military post east of Casablanca, a Senegalese woman became impatient while queuing at a well and cut the line. This transgressive act elicited the contempt and criticism of a Moroccan woman waiting her turn to draw water. In the ensuing verbal exchange the two women traded verbal insults that asserted and questioned social hierarchies connected to legacies of trans-Saharan slavery. Skin color and sub-Saharan African origins took pride of place in this dispute; particularly how these physical attributes connoted cleanliness, propriety, and status. The quarrel devolved into physical assault and public shaming. Finally the Senegalese woman yelled, "Moroccans are savages! Moroccans have dirty faces, dirty clothes, and are all unclean! If we were dirty like you, our husbands would beat us."[1] This West African woman, known in French sources as *madame tirailleur* or *madame sénégalais*, had accompanied her husband, a *tirailleur sénégalais* (West African colonial soldier), to the French conquest of Morocco.

Pierre Khorat, a French observer, recorded this event in order to portray what he believed to be primordial and insurmountable animosities between Africans from north and south of the Sahara. It is unlikely that this altercation unfolded in a single language comprehensible to all participants and observers, which calls into question the accuracy or authenticity of Khorat's portrayal of this heated scene. Khorat likely embellished or invented wholesale aspects of the exchange between the Moroccan and Senegalese women at the well. The ways that Khorat portrayed this event, perhaps, better inform us of how French observers of Morocco's conquest sought to substantiate stereotypes of insurmountable differences between sub-Saharan and North Africans.

This chapter results from a concern with the ways that scholars have dealt with the historical legacies of the trans-Saharan slave trade in twentieth-century French colonial North Africa. Much of the scholarship concerned with race or social divisions focuses on the ethnic categories of Arabs and Berbers or the religious identities of Jews and Muslims.[2] Scholars concerned with racial divides resulting from the trans-Saharan slave trade often locate their work on the southern fringe of the Sahara.[3] Many also focus on precolonial North Africa.[4] Others are concerned with the misappropriation of the methodological and conceptual tools of Orientalism and abolitionism in the production of trans-Saharan history and its legacies. E Ann McDougall sought to discredit this intellectual imperialism by providing a critique of the hegemonic Western production of knowledge concerning racialized distinctions between sub-Saharan Africans and North Africans.[5] William Cohen's canonical text *The French Encounter with Africans* also argues that the history of slavery and abolition in the Atlantic World influenced French historical knowledge of sub-Saharan Africans prior to the nineteenth century. However, Cohen also posited that famous sixteenth-century North Africans like Leo Africanus influenced precolonial French representations of Black Africans.[6]

I follow Cohen's lead while interrogating a set of military debates concerning the *troupes noires* that illustrate how sixteenth- and seventeenth-century North African history influenced French perceptions of racial difference in early twentieth-century Morocco. During the conquest of Morocco, French military officials repurposed the Abid al-Bukhari—a seventeenth-century imperial Moroccan military institution made up of people with presumed sub-Saharan African origins—in order to incorporate civilian Moroccans and tirailleurs sénégalais into their vision of colonial modernity. Also known as the Black Guard, the Abid al-Bukhari provided a historical reference that paralleled French colonial military practice in Morocco and served to legitimate French colonial rule on both sides of the Sahara.[7] Colonial officials adopted and adapted Moroccan and trans-Saharan histories in a dialogic process that produced an exploitable colonial archive inextricably linking soldiering, slave ancestry, and sub-Saharan African origins.[8] The conjugal partners of the Abid al-Bukhari and tirailleur sénégalais in Morocco also played an important role in the production and reproduction of these military institutions. These women supplied essential auxiliary services, as well as provided conjugal support that increased soldiers' morale and upheld racial distinctions between people of African descent and Arabo-Berber Moroccans.

Lieutenant-Colonel Charles Mangin, one of the most strident voices in this debate, published *La Force Noire* in 1910. This text, and those who rallied behind its arguments, aimed to convince a broader military and civilian public of the utility of tirailleurs sénégalais in North Africa. Their success heavily influenced the introduction of military conscription in French West Africa and the deployment of those West African conscripts during World War I in France. French officials at all levels of military hierarchy and from the remotest corners of French Empire participated in the debates catalyzed by *La Force Noire*. Handwritten reports from outside of Figuig and elaborate debates featured in the military publication *Armée Coloniale* revealed a systemic shift in how military officials racialized their "Black troops" and validated fixed racial differences they perceived as social fact in North Africa. There was also a transformation in the ways that French officials perceived the presence of West African wives on colonial campaigns. The French believed that tirailleurs sénégalais were better soldiers when they lived "*en famille*" in Arab-dominated countries. West African wives, accompanying tirailleurs sénégalais to rural military outposts like Zahiliga, Colomb-Béchar, and Béni-Ounif, became embroiled in a military effort to maintain racial boundaries between sub-Saharan African soldiers and North African civilians.

Legacies of Slavery and *Tirailleurs Sénégalais*

In 1908, three years prior to the conflagration between women from opposite sides of the Sahara in Zahiliga, two battalions of tirailleurs sénégalais disembarked a French military steamer in Casablanca to participate in France's "pacification" of Morocco. Two years later, another 1,600 tirailleurs sénégalais descended naval gangways in Oran. They would eventually become part of French occupying forces in the arid commercial towns of Colomb-Béchar and Béni-Ounif. Even though tirailleurs sénégalais had participated in French imperial military conquest since the 1880s, their deployment to North Africa inspired new discussions about their utility in French empire. In order to justify and expand West Africans' military presence in Morocco and Algeria, military officials manipulated trans-Saharan history and the historical presence of sub-Saharan Africans in the Maghreb.

In *La Force Noire* Lieutenant-Colonel Charles Mangin provided a limited yet serviceable history of imperial Morocco's historical relationship with West African empires, sub-Saharan Africans, and their diaspora north of the Sahara. Mangin singled out the Abid al-Bukhari as an exemplary imperial Moroccan military institution made up of slaves and former slaves made up of sub-Saharan Africans and their descendants. Sultan Mawlay Ismail created the Abid al-Bukhari in the late seventeenth century. The Abid al-Bukhari was a military institution central to the expansion and consolidation of the Moroccan state under this third leader of the fledgling Alawi dynasty. Octave Houdas, a French Orientalist, translated several Arab-language histories of Moroccan dynasties that would have been available to Charles Mangin in the early twentieth century. According to Houdas's 1886 translation of Abdoulqasem ben Ahmed Ezzaini's history of the Alawi dynasty, Sultan Mawlay Ismail assembled the male and female Black slaves of Morocco in his imperial capital of Meknes in order to create the Black Guard shortly after his reign began in 1672.[9] Mawlay Ismail provided them with clothing and arms and then directed them to the Mashra ar-Ramla camp, located on the outskirts of Meknes.[10] The members of this racially segregated military encampment became the support system for and the members of the Abid al-Bukhari. In describing this process of induction, Houdas's translation of Ezziani's text collapsed the intricate and discrete distinctions between slave status, slave ancestry, and sub-Saharan African origins.

Mangin borrowed from Houdas and provided broader historical context in *La Force Noire* to explain how racially distinct slaves came to exist in Alawi-ruled Morocco. Eighty years before Mawlay Ismail's reign, Moroccan Sultan Al Mansur sent a large contingent of musketeers across the Sahara to conquer the Songhay Empire. Mangin claimed that Al Mansur invaded West Africa for the explicit and unique purpose of acquiring sub-Saharan African soldiers, who would ensure his rule in the Maghreb and defend his realm from Iberian and Ottoman threats.[11] Mangin's text disregarded the battle of Tondibi, where Al Mansur's musketeers routed Askia Ishaq's troops in 1591, as well as the subsequent conditions of surrender. Al Mansur's military commanders returned to Morocco with thousands of slaves. During the three or four generations separating Al Mansur and Mawlay Ismail's reigns, most of these sub-Saharan African prisoners and/or slaves assimilated into Moroccan communities. In the late seventeenth century Mawlay Ismail's agents identified their descendants by their physical appearance and registered over 150,000 of them for the Abid al-Bukhari.

In Arabic 'abid is the plural noun for slave, servant, and/or devoted follower of a person or deity. Historians John Hunwick and Eve Trout Powell note that by the mid–seventeenth century North African Berber and Arabic dialects employed a single term, 'abid, to denote skin color, sub-Saharan African origins, and slave status.[12] Their observation reflects the sociocultural consequences of Mawlay Ismail's military projects. The Abid al-Bukhari was not a slave army made up of conscripts from the furthest reaches of Moroccan empire. Instead, the Abid al-Bukhari resulted from the enslavement of many otherwise free men who were then required to provide military service for the Sultan. Illegally enslaved women found themselves among the ranks of the Abid al-Bukhari's support services—as wives, seamstresses, and cooks.[13] Historian Chouki El Hamel argued that Mawlay Ismail's illegal enslavement of tens of thousands of dark-skinned Moroccans made the Abid al-Bukhari a crucible where race, sub-Saharan origins, slavery, and military prowess cohered in new ways that led many Arabo-Berber Moroccans to view dark-skinned Moroccans, as well Africans from south of the Sahara, as biologically predetermined for servitude.[14]

Roughly two hundred years later, Mangin illustrated Moulay Ismail's success fusing Blackness to slavery and soldiering by repurposing abridged versions of Morocco's conquest of the Songhay and the inauguration the Abid al-Bukhari. Mangin claimed that the sub-Saharan African diaspora, with examples ranging from Mameluke soldiers in Egypt to African Americans serving in the American Civil War, provided incontrovertible evidence of the innate martial quality of Black peoples and of sub-Saharan Africans' ability to acclimate to a wide range of climates and geographies.[15] These martial characteristics were genetically inherited and cultivated by primitive lifestyles shot through with hardship.[16] Mangin believed that West Africans would provide France with versatile troops for all environments. He also promoted the tirailleurs sénégalais as the quintessential fighting force for Moroccan conquest due to the history and legacies of the Abid al-Bukhari. Louis-Hubert Lyautey, the highest French official in Morocco from 1912 to 1925, created his own Black Guard made up of tirailleurs sénégalais. His was the ultimate appropriation of imperial Moroccan history—adapting pre-colonial symbols of power to legitimate colonial rule.[17]

In 1910 Mangin's championing of the historical use of Black slave labor for military purposes conflicted with concurrent efforts in French West Africa (FWA) to eradicate the association of slavery with the tirailleurs sénégalais. During the first decade of the twentieth century former slaves and low-status men did not enlist precisely because many West Africans perceived the tirailleurs sénégalais as a military institution made up of slaves and former slaves.[18] High-level officials in FWA linked dwindling numbers of voluntary soldiers with the success of emancipation in West Africa, as well as increased wage labor opportunities in the expanding agricultural, industrial, and service sectors.[19] After 1909 Lieutenant-Colonel Charles Mangin and Governor-General William Ponty coordinated their efforts to encourage enlistment by altering the image of the tirailleurs sénégalais for potential recruits. They professionalized the ranks by standardizing and increasing pay, as well as systematizing recruitment practices across West Africa.[20] These efforts, in combination with the success of *La Force Noire*, resulted in the 1912 Recruitment Decree, which introduced quota-based conscription in FWA. With conscription, officials like Mangin and Ponty hoped that recruitment classes would better represent the demographic diversity of West Africa and ensure the longevity of the tirailleurs sénégalais as a colonial institution.

By 1912 French recruitment agents had identified the West African groups most predisposed toward military service. Their "racial" breakdown of West African people occurred along ethnolinguistic divisions, as well as by their professions, religious beliefs, and "civilizational" development—acquired through Islamic and/or French education. Commanding officers in North Africa requested recruits from specific ethnolinguistic groups from French West Africa. Idealized regiments were demographically balanced and consisted of recruits from each of the identified martial races in West Africa. Bamana-speakers, who the French labeled Bambara, were at the top of the martial race pyramid, followed by Malinké, Soninké Amoros, and Mossis. According to military documents, Dahomeyans were the most advanced French-language learners with Tukulors as a near second. Wolofs were intelligent but could not speak Bamana, which made them ineffective in most regiments serving in North Africa. Veterans of the Madagascan, Soudanese, Ivoirian, and Congolese campaigns were invaluable irrespective of their ethnic origins.[21] These divisions revealed French officials' impulse to categorize and establish static labels for West African communities, while simultaneously recognizing that instruction and experience could transform soldiers' utility.

French officials believed that military order would overcome sociocultural differences within the tirailleurs sénégalais; however, they also recognized and respected their perceived racial divisions and hierarchies among West Africans. These separations and rankings were based on communities' historical roles in the trans-Saharan slave trade. Mauritanians and Tuaregs could serve in camel-mounted units in the Sahara, but they were generally poor foot soldiers. These recruits refused to obey soldiers hailing from the agricultural/pastoral regions of the West African Sahel, savannahs, and forests. French military officials rationalized these issues via historical oversimplification. Mauritanians and Tuaregs had participated in the trans-Saharan trade as slave raiders and merchants. Thus, they viewed most West African communities as enslavable and inferior. The troupes noires debates reified racialized distinctions and hierarchies based on legacies of the Saharan trade, while simultaneously celebrating the martial potential of recruits with slave pasts or ancestry.[22] The French outlawed domestic slavery in FWA in 1905, yet slavery's legacies were apparent among the ranks of the tirailleurs sénégalais nearly a decade later. The military chain of command did little to countermand the power and authority of masters over their slaves. Once conscription began in 1912, slaves and masters served side by side in the ranks of the tirailleurs séné-galais. If the French promoted a slave to caporal or sergeant, he continued to defer to his master even if he was a second-class soldier.[23]

Over the next few decades, public perception of the tirailleurs sénégal-ais in West Africa improved, as did the institution's credibility in French military and colonial administrations. This was not the case in French colonial North Africa. The lived experiences of tirailleurs sénégalais and their families on campaign in Morocco reveal the epistemological errors made by French officials, who maladapted the Abid al-Bukhari to their twentieth-century military ambitions in the Maghreb. By employ-ing tirailleurs sénégalais—accompanied by their wives and families—in France's North African territories, the French hardened and reified racial differences in the Maghreb. In the seventeenth century Mawlay Ismail's Abid al-Bukhari may have been visibly distinct from other Moroccans, but they were members of Moroccan communities. The French military's tirailleurs sénégalais may have shared the Abid al-Bukhari's sub-Saharan African origins, but they were not Moroccans. They were West Africans dressed in French colonial military uniforms.[24] As a result North Africans tended to view tirailleurs sénégalais as interlopers in France's power play for North Africa. Known as "saligan" in Moroccan Arabic, the tirailleurs sénégalais caused ruptures in the traditional ways that North Africans interacted with and viewed people from sub-Saharan Africa.[25]

Arguments made in the wake of *La Force Noire's* publication rarely reflected the real experiences of tirailleurs sénégalais and their families in the Maghreb. Yet French officials throughout the empire increasingly used the racial language standardized by the 4,300 published articles and numerous public meetings associated with the troupes noires debates.[26] Documented accounts portraying interactions between tirailleurs séné-galais or mesdames tirailleurs with North African civilians sought to substantiate aspects of the preexisting debates. French officials framed anecdotes from the campaign to confirm insurmountable racial tensions between sub-Saharan Africans and North Africans. In Colomb-Béchar and Beni-Ounif in 1910 the presence of well-armed French West African soldiers disquieted residents. They attempted to limit off-duty tirailleurs sénégalais in their towns and rarely spoke to them.[27] The French absolved themselves from easing these racialized tensions by shifting accountability to legacies of trans-Saharan history endemic to Morocco.

In 1912 Morocco became a French Protectorate and France outlawed slave markets and other conspicuous aspects of slave trading and slavery in urban centers. Members of the French occupying forces, including tirailleurs sénégalais, participated in enforcing these prohibitions. One morning in 1912 Captain Cornet and a group of his French compatriots sought out the slave market in Marrakech. As they gawked at the indignity and inhumanity of the fettered, dark-skinned slaves for purchase, Captain Cornet asked his Bamana-speaking orderly, Nama Diara, to locate his fellow countrymen among the slaves.[28] Nama Diara was a tirailleur sénégalais from French Soudan. In this bizarrely orchestrated confrontation caught under the microscope of colonial observers, Captain Cornet confirmed that Nama Diara's physical features, cultural heritage, and geographic origins rendered him and other sub-Saharan African soldiers eligible for enslavement in twentieth-century Morocco. This anecdote sits uncomfortably with Mangin and Ponty's concurrent efforts to disaggregate slave status from the tirailleurs sénégalais in French West Africa.

Anecdotes of this nature equipped French officials with ethical justification for colonizing North Africa through the language of abolition. In another example that makes conspicuous the moralizing abolitionist rhetoric pervasive in French colonization north and south of the Sahara, a West African *spahis* serving in southern Morocco located his long-lost mother in a small hamlet named Talaïnt. Slave raiders had seized his mother in her natal village in West Africa prior to French colonization. In Talaïnt the mother assimilated into the community through marriage to a southern Moroccan (Soussi). The primary source does not comment on the degree to which the mother's slave status affected her marital status. The French commanding officer allowed the West African spahis to reacquaint himself with his mother and meet his half-siblings.[29] The spahis also passed on the moralizing rhetoric of French colonization in a conversation convincing his mother and extended relatives that the French had good intentions in North Africa.

Nama Diara and other West Africans serving in North Africa provided the French with anecdotes that they twisted into abolitionist rhetoric justifying France's colonization of Morocco. These examples illustrated how West Africans were ideal intermediaries who simultaneously challenged and reified Moroccan racial hierarchies linked to local histories of slavery and soldiering. Notably, French attention to slavery within the context of military conquest rarely highlighted the plight of enslaved women and the wives of tirailleurs sénégalais. The majority of slaves trafficked from West Africa into the Sahara and Maghreb were women. These women integrated into Saharan and North African societies as slaves and concubines who became wives and mothers.[30] Their importance in the social reproduction of their communities led to the generational assimilation of their descendants into Maghrebi communities.

Strikingly, mesdames tirailleurs' presence in North Africa did not facilitate the integration of tirailleurs sénégalais or their children into Maghrebi civil society. During French conquest, West African military families garrisoned and bivouacked in segregated, distinct camps called *villages nègres*, or Black Villages. West African military wives served to reinforce racialized ethnic and physical differences between sub-Saharan Africans and North Africans because their families lived exclusively within the ranks of the tirailleurs sénégalais. The next section analyzes mesdames tirailleurs' roles in France's colonial conquest of Morocco and how they echoed those of the wives of the Abid al-Bukhari. Mesdames tirailleurs were an integral component of debates concerning the modernization of the troupes noires, as well as their utility in North Africa. Yet the rhetoric that French military officials used to laud and denounce the presence of West African wives in Morocco demonstrated a disregard for the lived experiences of these women on Moroccan campaign.

Mesdames Tirailleurs and Villages Nègres

When battalions of West African troops disembarked at Casablanca and Oran in the early twentieth century, West African women were among them. Spousal accompaniment to active theaters of war was by no means a novel practice in the history of the tirailleurs sénégalais. During the nineteenth century mesdames tirailleurs accompanied their soldiering husbands to new frontiers of French conquest in West Africa, Equatorial Africa, and Madagascar. West African women's presence in the conquest of North Africa garnered new attention and heightened visibility because of the ongoing debates related to the troupes noires. French military observers repurposed mesdames tirailleurs' presence in the ranks of the tirailleurs sénégalais for their discussions about Black soldiers' epidemiological strength and the cultural legacies of the trans-Saharan slave trade. By deploying "en famille" in the racialized landscapes of France's conquest of Morocco, tirailleurs sénégalais served the French in gendered and racialized spaces comparable to those of the Abid al-Bukhari.

Sultan Mawlay Ismail racially engineered his Black Guard through arranged marriages that increased the racial distinctiveness of the sub-Saharan African diaspora in Morocco. When Mawlay Ismail inducted enslaved and free men into the Abid al-Bukhari, his representatives across Morocco also forced free and enslaved women to migrate to Meknes. The Sultan's agents brokered marriages between members of the Abid al-Bukhari and these women, whose eligibility for these conjugal relationships depended on the visible signs of their sub-Saharan African descent. Once incorporated into the expanding imperial state, these women received training in obedience and the domestic arts in Sultanic harems.[31] The children of these couples entered into domestic service in the Sultan's palace or other governmental spaces, and when they came of age, they became soldiers and wives like their parents.

This eugenic experiment effectively racialized military service in the Alawi Empire, racially segregated Moroccans, and simultaneously marginalized and increased the visibility of the sub-Saharan African diaspora in Morocco. The *maghzen*, or imperial government, isolated families of the Abid al-Bukhari from the general population and Moroccan civil society began to view them a racialized tool of the Alawi state.[32] Soldiers in the Abid al-Bukhari deployed to conflict zones with their families. Their family members provided domestic and auxiliary services that facilitated troops' performance and encouraged fidelity to their units. Families accompanied soldiers during the campaigning season in the southern Sous region and in the Atlas Mountains. The Abid al-Bukhari's temporary garrisons provided a "buffer zone to control tensions between Arabs and Berbers" in the outer reaches of the expanding Alawi state.[33]

More than two hundred years later the French colonial military followed suit. Military commanders created Black Villages, which physically and racially segregated tirailleurs sénégalais and their families from other colonial troops and Moroccan civilians. Similar to the Abid al-Bukhari, the French believed the Black Villages provided tirailleurs sénégalais with the appropriate space and components to reenact the social and cultural life affiliated with their ancestral villages, which would improve active soldiers' morale.[34] The French military introduced educational services and employment pathways for soldiers' offspring. Schools for the "Enfants de Troupes" offered literacy classes and drilling exercises for young children on campaign with tirailleurs sénégalais.[35] Postcards from the Moroccan conquest that bear captions reading "The Future Black Army" or "The Future Tirailleurs" portray groups of young West African children flanked by French soldiers with the conical tents of the Black Villages as the background.[36] Echoing a military strategy of the Abid al-Bukhari, a French general claimed that tirailleurs sénégalais provided a *cordon sanitaire* (a neutral buffer zone) between French *colons* and Algerian *indigènes*.[37]

French bureaucratic planning surrounding the transport of mesdames tirailleurs and the organization of Black Villages exposed tensions within the military regarding the professionalization of the tirailleurs sénégalais and their role in creating colonial modernities in the Maghreb. The Black Villages were simulacra of West African villages. They were adaptations of rural African livelihoods to the exigencies of colonial military life. These caricatural living arrangements failed to imitate West African villages in these confined militarized spaces due to the age and gender imbalances. West African conjugal partners had children while on campaign but could not rely on extended kin and older generations to assist in raising children in Black Villages. French commissariats at West African ports regulated freight and weight on military steamers bound for Casablanca and Oran, which led them to conclude that roughly 25 percent of tirailleurs sénégalais could deploy to North Africa with their wives. This percentage resulted from weighing women's contributions to soldiers' morale and military services against the added logistical burden of campaigning with women and minors. Officials further suggested that the number of West African children in Morocco should not exceed one child for every four women.[38]

If the French were attempting to emulate West African society in Black Villages, these regulated gender and age imbalances belied their efforts.

The presence of the families of tirailleurs sénégalais in France's conquest of Morocco was a twentieth-century tactical anomaly. By the mid–nineteenth century, most North American and European state-funded armies had removed civilian women that traditionally provided auxiliary services from regiments of soldiers. In mainland France, camp followers, sutlers, and soldiers' wives gradually disappeared from official military spaces.[39] Civilian women's relationship to the military evolved along two bureaucratic paths. First, the military financially transformed the relationship between the state and soldiers' marital partners with the introduction of family pay and widow's benefits. Second, the French military professionalized sexual services for soldiers through the creation of Bordelles Militaires de Campagne. These institutionalized and state-funded brothels employed local women for active French troops in mainland France and its empire.[40]

Black Villages on the Moroccan campaign were antithetical to contemporaneous French military efforts to professionalize the tirailleurs sénégalais. Members of the colonial military assumed that West African soldiers were incapable of participating in the modern practices of the French military. The postcard images of tirailleurs sénégalais "en famille" on Moroccan campaign were incompatible with French ideals of male republican citizens providing military labor for a nationally defined state. Instead, West African soldiers were family men whose particular brand of masculinity and patriarchal domestic roles continued on the battlefield. Similar to the Abid al-Bukhari, the presence of mesdames tirailleurs compelled the French military to segregate sub-Saharan African troops from civilian Moroccans and other French forces. By including yet isolating the domestic spaces of tirailleurs sénégalais, Moroccan civilians and other troops serving the French heuristically learned that the tirailleurs sénégalais were unable to serve in the military without their wives and families. Black Villages were living evidence that tirailleurs sénégalais were seemingly unable to surmount their inborn primordial propensity to live in villages. These closed communities also illustrated that the French military supported a prohibition on interracial sexual or conjugal relationships between West African troops and Maghrebi female civilians.

According to French doctors stationed in Morocco, mesdames tirailleurs and their children prevented the spread of so-called social diseases like homosexuality and alcoholism among West African troops. While there is little doubt that the French believed these troops were the pinnacle of masculinity and heterosexuality, military officials feared their susceptibility to North African sexual predilections. In their promotion of tirailleurs sénégalais as family men, the French military also assumed that they were faithful partners and committed fathers.[41] This belief was incongruous with practice, since many West African soldiers hailed from polygynous societies. In the Black Villages of Morocco and Algeria, the French reshaped West Africans' traditional social relationships and retooled the gendered divisions of space and labor common to tirailleurs sénégalais and their natal communities.[42]

Mesdames tirailleurs provided palliative care to injured soldiers or nursing assistance to those affected by communicable infections and diseases. Separated by the Sahara, West and North Africa are distinct epidemiologic and environmental zones. Tirailleurs sénégalais frequently contracted respiratory and pulmonary infections, as well as tapeworm and filariasis (which can cause elephantiasis).[43] Shortly after the first battalions of West African troops arrived in Morocco, soldiers outside of Casablanca succumbed to an outbreak of beriberi, a disease caused by deficiencies in thiamine, or vitamin B1, characterized by degenerative changes in the immune, digestive, and cardiovascular systems.[44] Thiamine is essential for the body's metabolic processes and is amply found in plants and animals, whereas many grains, like rice, are deficient in B-complex vitamins. West Africans were the only soldiers among the ranks of the colonial army affected by the outbreak of beriberi. In Morocco the most prevalent carbohydrate was couscous made from wheat semolina. The central carbohydrate in most West Africans' diets was rice or millet. The military imported rice and distributed it—and often little else—to tirailleurs sénégalais stationed in Morocco. The French military accommodated the dietary preferences of tirailleurs sénégalais, but inevitably failed to provide these troops with well-balanced nourishment. After the 1908 beriberi outbreak, the military diversified West Africans' food allocations. Turning the responsibilities of preparing meals over to mesdames tirailleurs may have also improved basic health among troops.

Wives provided their soldiering husbands with domestic services that improved the quality of their food and the cleanliness of their living spaces. French officials touted mesdames tirailleurs as panacea to medical ailments and low morale because they provided their husbands with sexual and domestic labor, which in turn reduced African soldiers' promiscuity and their likelihood of contracting sexually transmitted infections. The range of benefits provided by civilian West African women in the Black Villages of North Africa superseded the negative aspects of mesdames tirailleurs' so-called feminine nature. French officials like Pierre Khorat eagerly reproduced the so-called primordial acrimonies between Moroccan and sub-Saharan African women in order to illustrate their hysterical character. By passing the blame onto the character of women, the French military conveniently absolved itself from catalyzing or exacerbating these adversarial conflicts. Mangin's arguments that sub-Saharan African soldiers—read men—were loyal and hardwired soldiers stood unblemished.[45]

Significantly, these women were in a unique position because they belonged to regiments of the tirailleurs sénégalais but were not contractually bound to its discipline. Military expectations of obedience were not explained through formal training or enforced through chain of command. The French military provided mesdames tirailleurs' transportation, sustenance, and living quarters. As a consequence they expected wives to act in accordance with military order. These women had greater contact with local civilians because they required provisions for cooking, cleaning, and childrearing. They did not wear uniforms into Moroccan markets, which would have visibly communicated their official status as members of the tirailleurs sénégalais regiments. The dynamics of colonial conquest and the legacies of the slave trade weighed upon negotiations for basic foodstuffs. The smallest pretext could easily lead to an "explosion" that required the intervention of their husbands.[46]

The colonial army depended on tirailleurs sénégalais to supervise their wives' behavior and discipline them when appropriate. This system of disciplining and punishment mirrored the male breadwinner economic redistribution model. This method of meting out punishments forced tirailleurs sénégalais to reprimand mesdames tirailleurs for offenses judged egregious by the French military but not necessarily by their husbands. Tirailleurs sénégalais and mesdames tirailleurs had little alternative but to comply with French directives because their homes were a long walk south across open Sahara. If inclined to desertion, their physical and linguistic differences from the bulk of Moroccan populations would have hampered integration into local communities and may have led to their enslavement by trans-Saharan traders.[47]

Conclusion

These complex and paradoxical French colonial military representations of mesdames tirailleurs as remedies to and causes of social conflict in Morocco were informed by a diverse set of ideas about race, gender, and power relations among populations living north and south of the Sahara. The production of images and information about the families of tirailleurs sénégalais in Morocco provides historians with a blurry snapshot of French military thought concerning race, gender, and the legacies of the trans-Saharan world in colonial Morocco. French military officials drew upon and manipulated Moroccan imperial history, the legacies of the trans-Saharan slave trade, and Moroccan assumptions concerning race and social status in order to advocate for the presence of the wives of tirailleurs sénégalais in Morocco. In the expansion of the Alawi and French colonial empires, West African women and women with sub-Saharan African diasporic identities played integral roles in completing the image of racially distinct, loyal and obedient soldiers.

When the Senegalese woman at the well in Zahiliga leaped on the Moroccan woman and wiped her face with a bit of cloth to prove her uncleanliness, Pierre Khorat framed this incident through the dominant military discourses of his day. At the beginning of the twentieth century the debates surrounding the troupes noires racialized the tirailleurs sénégalais and mesdames tirailleurs in ways that were useful for short- and long-term military strategies. Charles Mangin's *La Force Noire* manipulated the legacy of the Abid al-Bukhari in order to convince military and civilian administrations to invest in a permanent West African colonial fighting force. The process of locating a "usable" indigenous Moroccan history to justify French colonial conquest coincided with the rapid assembly of a colonial archive of knowledge on Morocco. Thus, abridged versions of Moroccan history and imperial Morocco's trans-Saharan relationships aided in a systemic shift in how military officials racialized the tirailleurs sénégalais and substantiated fixed racial differences that they perceived as social fact in North Africa.

NOTES

1. Pierre Khorat, *Scènes de la Pacification Marocaine* (Paris: Perrin et Cie, 1914), 179–80.
2. Patricia M. E. Lorcin, *Imperial Identities: Stereotyping, Prejudice and Race in Colonial Algeria* (London: I. B. Tauris, 1995); Hélène Claudot-Hawad, *Berbères ou Arabes: Le Tango des Spécialistes*, (Aix-en-Provence: Institut de recherches et d'études sur le monde arabe et musumalman, 2006); Albert Memmi, *Juifs et Arabes* (Paris: Callimard, 1974); Joshua Schreier, *Arabs of the Jewish Faith: The Civilizing Mission in Colonial Algeria* (New Brunswick NJ: Rutgers University Press, 2010).
3. Allan G. B. Fisher, *Slavery and Muslim Society in Africa; The Institution in Saharan and Sudanic Africa and the Trans-Saharan Trade* (Garden City NY: Doubleday, 1971); John Ralph Willis, ed., *Slaves and Slavery in Muslim Africa* (London: F. Cass, 1985); Humphrey J. Fisher, *Slavery in the History of Muslim Black Africa* (New York: New York University Press, 2001); Bruce S. Hall, *A History of Race in Muslim West Africa, 1600–1960* (Cambridge: Cambridge University Press, 2011).
4. Mohammed Ennaji, *Serving the Master: Slavery and Society in Nineteenth-Century Morocco*, trans. Seth Graebner (New York: St. Martin's, 1999); Chouki El Hamel, *Black Morocco: A History of Slavery, Race, and Islam* (New York: Cambridge University Press, 2013).
5. E. Ann McDougall, "Discourses and Distortion: Critical Reflections on Studying the Saharan Slave trade," *Revue française d'histoire d'Outre-Mer* 89 (2002): 195–227.
6. William Cohen, *The French Encounter with Africans: White Response to Blacks, 1530–1880* (Bloomington: Indiana University Press, 1980), 2–3.
7. Edmund Burke was particularly interested in portraying these processes in the "invention" of Moroccan Islam. This chapter follows his lead but applies them to racial difference and soldiering. Edmund Burke III, *The Ethnographic State: France and the Invention of Moroccan Islam* (Oakland: University of California Press, 2014), 9.
8. For further thoughts on the dialogic production of history and knowledge, see Eugene Irschick, *Dialogue and History: Constructing South India, 1795–1895* (Berkeley: University of California Press, 1994), 8.

9. I translate *nègre* as negro, although this is a word whose connotation has shifted toward "n——" in contemporary France. Aboulqasem Ben Ahmed Ezzaini, *Le Maroc de 1631 à 1812: Extrait de l'Ouvrage Intitulé l'Interprète qui s'Exprime Clairement sur Les Dynasties de l'Orient et de l'Occident de Aboulqasem Ben Ahmed Ezzaini*, trans., Octave V. Houdas (rpt. Amsterdam: Philo, 1969), 29.

10. Ezzaini, *Le Maroc*, 30.

11. Lieutenant-Colonel Mangin, *La Force Noire* (Paris: L'Harmattan, 2011), 105.

12. John Hunwick and Eve Trout Powell, *The African Diaspora in the Mediterranean Land of Islam* (Princeton NJ: Marcus Wiener, 2002), xix.

13. Chouki El Hamel, *Black Morocco: A History of Slavery, Race, and Islam* (Cambridge: Cambridge University Press, 2013), 160–66.

14. Chouki El Hamel. "Blacks and Slavery in Morocco: The Question of the *Haratin* at the End of the Seventeenth Century," in *Diasporic Africa: A Reader* (New York: New York University Press, 2006), 194; Mohammed Ennaji, *Serving the Master: Slavery and Society in 19th Century Morocco*, trans. Seth Graebner (Houndsmills UK: Macmillan, 1999).

15. Mangin, *La Force Noire*, 111–28.

16. Joe Lunn, "Les Races Guerrières: Racial Preconceptions in the French Military about West African Soldiers during the First World War," *Journal of Contemporary History* 34 (1999): 521; Daniel Rivet, *Lyautey et l'institution du protectorat français au Maroc, 1912–1925* 2 (Paris: L'Harmattan, 1988), 17.

17. Myron Echenberg, "Slaves into Soldiers: Social Origins of the *Tirailleurs Sénégalais*," in *Africans in Bondage: Studies in Slavery and the Slave Trade*, ed. Paul E. Lovejoy (Madison WI: University of Wisconsin Press, 1986) and Martin Klein, *Slavery and Colonial Rule in French West Africa* (Cambridge: Cambridge University Press, 1998), 104.

18. "Note sur le recrutement des Troupes Noires en Afrique Occidentale Française," signed by William Ponty, 1910, 10N104, Archives Nationals du Sénégal (hereafter ANS).

19. Correspondence from the Lieutenant-Governor of French Guinea to the Governor-General of AOF, William Ponty, October, 19 1907, 4D30, ANS.

20. Charles Mangin authored "Sommaire" for William Ponty, folder dated 1909–10, 4D31, ANS.

21. Report on the subject of Black troops from Lieutenant Lautrou in Fez, August 29, 1913, 3H692, Service Historique de Défense, Terre (hereafter SHD-T).

22. "Extraits et Commentaires de la "Force Noire" du Colonial Mangin," by Capitaine Voland, undated, 4D31, ANS.

23. Report from Lieutenant LeJeune, August 5, 1913, 4D103, ANS.

24. A point emphasized in L. Arnaud, "Étude anthropologique de la Garde Noire du Sultan du Maroc," *Bulletin d'Institut d'Hygiene du Maroc* 10 (1940): 44.

25. Rita Aouad Badaoul, "'Esclavage' et la situation des 'noirs' au Maroc dans la premrière moitié du XXe siècle," in *Les Relations Transsahariennes à l'époque*

contemporaine: un espace en constante mutation, ed. Laurence Marfaing and Steffen Whippel (Paris: Karthala, 2004), 353.

26. Lunn, *"Les Race Guerrières,"* 523.

27. Chief of Battallion Mouveaux's Report from Colomb-Béchar, December 1, 1910, 4D32, ANS.

28. Capitaine Cornet, *A la Conquête du Maroc Sud Avec la Colonne Mangin, 1912–1913* (Paris: Plon-Nourrit et Cie., 1914), 77–78.

29. H. Dugard, *La Conquête du Maroc: La Colonne du Sous (Janvier-Juin 1917)* (Paris: Perrin et Cie., 1918), 150. The *spahis* were light cavalry regiments recruited in France's colonies north and south of the Sahara.

30. Claude Meillassoux, "Female Slavery," in *Women and Slavery in Africa,* ed. Claire C. Robertson and Martin A. Klein (Madison: University of Wisconsin Press, 1983), 49–65.

31. Ezzaini, *Le Maroc,* 30–31; Mangin, *Force Noire,* 107.

32. El Hamel, *Black Morocco,* 203.

33. El Hamel, *Black Morocco,* 190.

34. Sur les troupes sénégalaises du Maroc Occidental," signed by Franchet d'Esperey, September 1913, 3H692, SHD-T and "Extraits et Commentaires de la 'Force Noire' du Colonel Mangin," by Capitaine Voland, undated, 4D31, ANS.

35. Report from Capitain Causette in Casablanca, September 1, 1911, 3H392, SHD-T.

36. Postcard entitled, "Casablanca.–Au Camp Sénégalais: Les Futurs Tirailleurs," 2K 148 Michat Album Maroc/Algésiras/Chaouia/ Casablanca 32, Service Iconographique, SHD.

37. General de Torcy, *La Question des Troupes Noires en Algérie: Devant la "Réunion des etudes algériennes,"* (Paris: Augustin Challamel, July–October 1910), 21.

38. Letter from the Head of the Military Office in Bofosso, Guinea, February 3, 1910, 3N44, Archives Nationals du Guinée (hereafter AGS), and "Sur les Troupes Sénégalais du Maroc Occidental," signed by Franchet d'Esperey, September 1913, 3H692, SHD-T.

39. Barton C. Hacker, "Women and Military Institutions in Early Modern Europe: A Reconnaissance," *Signs* 6 (1981): 645. See also Thomas Cardoza, *Intrepid Women: Cantinières and Vivandières of the French Army* (Bloomington: Indiana University Press, 2010), especially chapters four through six.

40. Michel Serge Hardy, *De la morale au moral des troupes au l'histoire des B.M.C, 1918–2004* (Panazol: Lavauzelle, 2004).

41. "Rapport au Ministre sur l'utilisation des troupes noire en 1910–1911," Casablanca, September 22, 1911, 3H152, SHD-T.

42. Report from Chief of Battalion Mouveaux in Colomb-Béchar, Algeria to the Governor-General of AOF, December 1, 1910, 4D32, ANS.

43. "Rapport au Ministre sur l'utilisation des troupes noires en 1910–1911," Casablanca, September 22, 1911, 3H152, SHD-T.

44. "Note pour l'État-Majeur de l'Armée," November 5, 1909, 7N80, SHD-T.

45. Report from Captain Causette in Casablanca, September 1, 1911, 3H692, SHD-T.

46. Letter from General Moinier to the Minister of War, November 12, 1909, 3H152, SHD-T. As late as 1944, a former slave named Griga spoke of the possibility of enslavement in the Sahara. F. J. G. Mercardier, *L'Esclave de Timimoun* (Paris: Éditions France-Empire, 1971), 175.

47. Burke, *Ethnographic State*, 8–9.

3

Returning from France after World War II

African Soldiers and the Reshaping of Colonial and Racial Categories in French West Africa

RUTH GINIO

When William Holmes Dyer, an African American practicing physician and a first lieutenant in the Medical Reserve Corps of the American army, returned from France at the end of World War I, he noted in his memoirs the respectful treatment he had witnessed of Africans in France: "Many colored men in civilian dress, not Americans, are employed in Marseille and seen on the streets daily. We found they are welcome in the best hotels, cafes, theaters, in fact, everywhere for the French have no prejudice."[1] One of Dyer's African American comrades shared his view of France as a "color-blind" nation and the strong sentiments he had acquired for this country during his service: "I love France, and would deem it an honor to die in defense of her beautiful country. Here I am not a savage, nor a mere educated dog, but a human being capable of having a soul like any other man."[2]

These two views are far from isolated. As Chad Williams has shown, African Americans who returned from France after World War I saw France as an egalitarian heaven. Many of them decided to turn this country into their permanent home or at least spend some time in it after their demobilization.[3] Yet France, which ruled over vast territories in Africa at the time, was in fact far from being a color-blind nation. The perspective of these African Americans only demonstrates that racism is relative. Compared with their experiences of racism in the U.S. and within the American army, it is no wonder that African Americans held such good memories from their encounters with French society.

As I will demonstrate in this chapter, African colonial soldiers who served in France during World War II underwent a similar experience. Coming from a colonial racist reality, their encounters with French civilians during the war made this reality no longer acceptable. After they fought for France and in some cases fell into German captivity, they resolved upon demobilization to protest against their ongoing discrimination. World War II should be regarded as a turning point on this matter; while Africans also served in World War I, the different political circumstances after the Second World War and the relative weakness of French colonial power at this time made a huge difference. The experiences of Africans serving in this war were much more effective and meaningful as a catalyst for their aspiration to challenge colonial convictions and regulations.

While the changes described above are a direct result of World War II and the soldiers' experiences in metropolitan France, this chapter will focus on the postwar years in the federation of French West Africa (FWA), from which most soldiers had originated, and the struggle of the demobilized soldiers to achieve equality with their metropolitan comrades after the war.[4] My aim is twofold: first, I wish to demonstrate the fluidity of colonial categories and convictions, which can change according to time, location, and context. I will therefore show how the encounters between African soldiers and French civilians in France during World War II transformed the way in which the soldiers saw their relations with the French officials, commanders, and comrades in the colonies. Second, I will examine how African veterans used the concept of racism as an effective tool in their organized struggle for equality in the postwar years. The war experiences of the African soldiers were followed by the years of decolonization and should be examined within the wider colonial context. Thus, this chapter will also emphasize the agency of African soldiers and veterans, who far from being merely victims of colonial racism, were men who were often able to affect their destiny and to shape it to their own advantage by evoking their experiences as soldiers serving France. In fact, as I will show, the soldiers' and veterans' struggle for equality during the postwar period was far more successful than that of any other sector in colonial French Africa. Their military service became an asset, providing them tools to ameliorate their situation as colonial subjects. Race and racial discourse were not only French tools of repression and marginalization—at a time when racism was attributed to those who had lost the war, the African soldiers could use them to achieve victories in the struggle for equality.

I will begin by examining the army service of Africans in World War II and especially the encounters between African soldiers and French civilians during the war. My main source is letters written by French women to colonial administrators in FWA at the end of the war, asking to be reunited with the African lovers they had met during the war. Relying mainly on colonial and military reports, I will then discuss the protests of African soldiers upon demobilization as a struggle between the soldiers' challenge of racial boundaries and the colonial attempts to maintain them. Finally, I will follow the discussion of French racism in the main African veterans' journal—*La Voix des Combattants et des victimes de guerre* (The voice of the combatants and the war victims)—from its inception in 1948 until the end of French colonial rule over a decade later.

I will thus demonstrate the use African veterans made of French racism in their struggle for equality and how their major achievement—the equalization of military pensions of metropolitan and colonial soldiers—transformed the discourse of African veterans regarding racism within the military and colonial systems.

African Soldiers in World War II

Between the outbreak of the war in September 1939 and the fall of France in 1940, approximately one hundred thousand soldiers from FWA were recruited into the French army, and three quarters of them served in Europe. At the time of the signing of the armistice agreement with Germany in June 1940, as many as twenty-eight thousand Africans were declared missing. Of them, over half had fallen into German captivity. Approximately seventeen thousand Africans had perished in the war.[5]

During their service in France, Africans fought in the battles of May–June 1940, witnessed France's defeat and the German occupation of its soil, spent considerable time in German POW camps and, finally, took part in the liberation of France within the ranks of the Free French Forces. In the process they often came into close contact with French civilians whose attitudes toward them and views on French colonial rule were often quite different from those of the French officials the soldiers had encountered in the colonial arena. Their experiences on and off the battlefields reshaped their views of French colonialism and enhanced their resentment toward the racial discrimination they faced within the army and in their civilian lives in West Africa.

As noted above, I would like to focus here on the encounters between African soldiers and French civilians—both men and women—during the war. These encounters were mostly spontaneous and were not controlled by the military authorities. African soldiers were often invited into French homes. They forged relationships with French women on various occasions, and women came to POW camps to bring food to African prisoners. In part these encounters were organized by French local organizations that arranged a service comprised of young women, called *marraines de guerre*, who accompanied African soldiers, sent them letters, and invited them to their homes during their leaves. Some of these relationships remained nonsexual, while others developed into intimate relations, leading sometimes to pregnancies.[6]

African soldiers who were involved in serious relations with French women and wanted to formalize these relationships had to apply for permission from their commanders. In fact all soldiers—French or others—who wished to get married during their service had to ask their commanders for approval. When the African soldiers were demobilized after the war, however, they were sent back to the colonies without their wives, even though many of these marriages had been approved.

Eventually some of the French women who were left behind, often with children, wrote to the colonial authorities in FWA asking to be reunited with their husbands. Their letters offer us some insights into these encounters and the ways that the colonial administration perceived them.[7] Many of these requests were approved on the condition that the couples unite on French soil and not in the colonies. The fear of blurring colonial and racial boundaries in the colonies was too great and the colonial authorities believed that the damage such relationships would cause would be more limited in France.[8] Here we can see the importance of location within the context of examining racial relations. While in France there was some tolerance toward relations between African soldiers and French women, such tolerance completely disappeared when the mixed couple expressed its intentions to reside in the colonies among other colonial subjects.[9]

Location was not the only factor that determined the perception of such bonds. The relative tolerance toward interracial relationships in France was limited to Africans serving as soldiers. African workers who came to France in World War I and later in World War II did not enjoy such tolerance. Tyler Stovall asserts that the racism in France from World War I onward was directed mainly against African colonial workers who were brought there during the war to fill the ranks of French workers sent to the trenches. These men were seen as dangerous because they settled in France and competed with French men over both employment and women.[10] African soldiers, on the other hand, were in a different and much more advantageous position. They did not come to replace fighting French men in their place of employment, nor did they work side by side with their wives. They came to fight with these men, and toward the end of the war they also came to liberate French civilians. This is not to say that their presence in France did not provoke some hostility in certain cases, but in general they were looked upon as liberating soldiers and their special position blurred racial categories and allowed a certain tolerance and tacit acceptance, even regarding their relations with French women.

While the African soldiers in France did enjoy positive experiences, they also encountered racial discrimination during their service. The multiple protests, often quite violent, initiated by African soldiers in France toward the end of the war show that discrimination was quite rampant within the army. Nevertheless, the references to soldiers' complaints in colonial and military reports about such protests demonstrate that they often compared their positive experiences during their stay in France to the ongoing colonial racism at home. Witnessing the French defeat at the beginning of the war and being part of the liberating forces at its end also enforced most soldiers' wishes to challenge the way in which they were treated in the army and in their everyday experiences in the colonies. It is with these aspirations that many of them returned home after a long and difficult stay in Europe. The very same aspirations terrified the colonial and military authorities awaiting them in French West Africa.

The experiences of African soldiers in France during the war concerned the military and colonial authorities when these soldiers began returning home. African soldiers who had witnessed the fall of France and were later in German captivity concerned the authorities because of their exposure to the Germans' anti-French and anticolonial propaganda. The Africans' experiences as the liberators of France were no less troubling for the colonial administration. From the colonial perspective, having African subjects as part of the heroic forces of liberation to which the civilian metropolitan population owed its gratitude was mostly disadvantageous. This was in fact the main motive that pushed De Gaulle to order the "whitening" of the liberating forces that had entered Paris in August 1944. African soldiers were not allowed to march into Paris so as not to cause demoralization to the civilian liberated population. This decision enraged African soldiers and contributed much to their deep resentment of their French commanders.[11]

These fears were only reinforced following a series of soldiers' protests in France, even before they boarded the ships back to West Africa. The chaos that reigned in France right after the liberation and the preference the military authorities gave to returning British and American soldiers home caused delays in sending African soldiers back to their colonies. This made the soldiers restless and impatient. The conditions in the camps where African soldiers waited to be repatriated were terrible. The food, for example, was very limited. Some soldiers claimed that even the conditions in the German prisoner of war camps had been better. In 1944 and the beginning of 1945 several incidents and mutinies occurred in various cities in France where African soldiers were stationed, such as Morlaix, Versailles, and Fréjus. African soldiers disobeyed orders, marched in protest, and occasionally were violent toward French soldiers and civilians. In some cases they demanded to receive their groceries for free. Revolts also erupted among African soldiers serving in Syria.[12] It is no wonder, then, that by the time the soldiers arrived in FWA the colonial authorities were extremely concerned regarding their rebellious state of mind.

Turbulent Demobilization and Racial Boundaries

In 1943, right after the Free French Forces took over the federation of FWA, Secretary General Léon Geismar reported on demobilized soldiers who were causing disturbances in Senegal. He reminded the governors of the problems caused by demobilized soldiers after the previous world war due to their difficulties readjusting to their former lives. He asked that the military authorities inform the administration upon the arrival of demobilized soldiers at FWA and requested that the governors do all in their power to prevent undesirable incidents.[13] In spite of the vigilance of the colonial administration and their concern that the demobilized African soldiers might cause instability to the colonial rule, it seems that no one in the French colonial administration or in the colonial army could have predicted the scope of the African soldiers' discontent and the tragic results that their mistreatment in France and in FWA would entail.

The most prominent protest by African soldiers was the revolt that erupted on December 1, 1944, in Camp Thiaroye near Dakar. Around 1,200 ex-POWs had been waiting in this camp for demobilization. The poor conditions in the camp along with the refusal of their French commanders to grant them the payment they justifiably demanded led the soldiers to protest. When a group of soldiers took a French general hostage, the French declared their actions a mutiny and brought in other African soldiers, ordering them to shoot the rebels. Thirty-five soldiers were killed according to official estimations, though the actual number was probably considerably higher.[14]

The soldiers' protest in Thiaroye ended in an especially tragic manner, but this was not the only case in which African soldiers responded with rage to what they perceived as an intentional discrimination against them. My aim here is not to merely describe these protests and the military and administrative response to them, but rather to look at these clashes between disgruntled soldiers and apprehensive colonial authorities as a struggle over the redefinition of colonial and racial boundaries.

An examination of administrative reports about soldiers' protests and the means to prevent them shows that those who had formulated policy attributed great importance to the experiences of African soldiers in France and the supposed contribution these experiences had to their unruly behavior. A month before the revolt in Thiaroye, Minister of the Colonies Paul Giacobbi revealed that he anticipated some kind of trouble due to the long absence of the soldiers from their homes and the new habits and mentality they had acquired. These factors turned them, according to the minister, into a "very special element." He pointed out the confusing situation that they had lived in since the liberation of France, which contributed to their becoming extremely demanding, especially regarding material comforts such as better clothes and food. The best solution to the problem, he felt, was to send the soldiers as quickly as possible to their villages.[15]

The attempts to analyze and understand the motives behind the soldiers' protests intensified after the Thiaroye rebellion and its repression. It is quite clear from these reports that the French administration and military command were surprised at the level of the African troops' discontent. Although the reports express no regret about the decision to shoot at the soldiers, they do try to understand their motives and suggest ways to prevent such occurrences in the future. Thus the authorities offered several ideas regarding the grounds for the soldiers' behavior that were related to their sojourn in Europe during the war. One was the negative influence of German propaganda. Another was the close relations African soldiers developed during their stay in France with naïve civilians who did not understand the complexity of the colonial situation and, even worse, with irresponsible and loose French women who made the soldiers lose all respect toward the white man. In order to prevent future revolts, the military and administrative authorities suggested that the African soldiers awaiting demobilization be subdued by supplying them with all sorts of material goods such as biscuits, cigarettes, and fabric, a practice that had been effective in the past. In addition, as the minister of the colonies had advised even before the revolt in Thiaroye, the soldiers should be sent as quickly as possible back to their villages so that they could resume the routine of their lives and forget the marvels of the *metropole* and its women.[16]

These measures were not sufficient to reduce the soldiers' discontent, as described in a report addressing the situation in Thiaroye more than a year after the revolt. According to this source, the 2,700 African soldiers who had just arrived in the camp were in a very bad state of mind. They were aggressive toward the European personnel and did not respect their officers, refusing to salute them. European women, the report emphasized, had lost all esteem in their eyes.[17] Here again, this mention of the loss of respect for French women reflects the connection established by the French administrators between African soldiers' disobedience and their intimate relations with French women, which according to these administrators' logic caused this loss of respect toward all Europeans.

The military and colonial authorities also tried to monitor the morale of African soldiers by sending agents to listen to their conversations in public venues, such as trains. The object of such surveillance was to understand the soldiers' state of mind following their experiences in the war and especially to analyze their political views regarding the French, Germans, Americans, and Russians. One such report mentioned several ex-POWs from among the *originaires* who had been returning by train to their homes in Saint Louis and were overheard during their journey.[18] They were reported to be anti-Russian and deeply pro-French. It turned out that they were delayed in Russia after their release from German captivity and claimed that the Russians treated them even worse than the Germans. They told the other passengers that the French in France opposed the current colonial policy and many of them worked to improve life in the colonies.[19] Another report stated that originaires who returned from France commented on the difference between the way the French and the Germans treated them. According to the report, the former soldiers recognized the importance of a continued French tutelage without which they openly admitted the colonies would not have advanced. Race relations were crucial for them when comparing the French to the Americans. They did not favor the Americans because they knew that they would never sit at the same table with a Black man, while French fraternity allowed the Blacks and whites to study and work together. None of the demobilized soldiers was in favor of Nazism and they all had bad memories from the Germans.[20]

In spite of the limited reassurance that such reports gave French colonial administrators, they also indicated continued threats. The ostensible love for the French in France, for example, contained hostility to the French of the colonies. The French civilians Africans had met during the war were respected for their opposition to colonial rule and equal and respectful treatment of African soldiers. In one case, demobilized soldiers from Dahomey expressed their excitement about the warm welcome they were given by French families.[21] Other soldiers from Dahomey that demobilized two months later spoke about their regret at leaving France, where they had worked as builders and mechanics, earning between six thousand and nine thousand francs, which was considered quite a good salary.[22]

This semblance of equality only reinforced African soldiers' expectations when they returned home. Their experiences in France during the war encouraged them to reject the racial and colonial categories the French administration and military authorities had tried to restore upon their return to FWA. Colonial officials, on the other hand, did not accept the possibility that the soldiers were becoming politically aware on their own and accused the Germans and civilians in France of destabilizing the soldiers, either on purpose in the German case or out of gullibility in the French case. These officials refused to see the soldiers' protests as reflecting a deep change in their perception of the colonial situation and the inherent inequality within it. This is probably the motive for the official refusal to allow Madame Jane Vialle to visit Dakar eight months after the events in Thiaroye and meet with African ex-POWs.

Born in 1906 to a French father and a Congolese mother, Vialle was the representative of Ubangui-Shari (now the Central African Republic) in the French parliament. She graduated from Jule Ferry High School in Paris and during the war joined the resistance movement in Marseille, where she was arrested in 1943. She spent a year in a concentration camp and was later awarded the Medal of the Resistance for her activities. Vialle entered politics following a tour she made in Senegal with Léopold Sédar Senghor, a member of the French parliament who served as the colony's deputy, in 1945.[23] In August of that year the minister of the colonies asked High Commissioner Pierre Cournarie to allow Vialle to meet with African ex-POWs within the framework of this tour. The minister noted that Vialle had already worked with African POWs in France before they were sent back to FWA. [24] Cournarie's outright rejection of this suggestion, accompanied by an obviously false description of his total control over the situation in the colonies, reveals the threat a figure such as Vialle posed for the administration. After all, the administration was attempting to present the soldiers' protests as a temporary outrage influenced by their uprooting from their so-called natural environment rather than a real and permanent change in their perception of the colonial and racial relations in FWA. As a mixed-race woman, a hero of the resistance, and a politician fighting for Africans' rights and equality, Vialle had crossed both racial and gender boundaries. Such a figure was not someone the High Commissioner wanted African ex-soldiers to meet.

Changing Discourse of Veterans—La Voix des Combattants

Until 1948 African soldiers' flare-ups were spontaneous and stemmed from rage and ongoing frustration. In time, when African veterans began to establish organizations, these outbursts of fury were enlisted into a well-calculated struggle for equality. In order to examine the place racial issues occupied in the veterans' struggle for equality, I will review the official discourse of the main veterans' organization of FWA, situated in Dakar, as reflected in the organization's journal: *La Voix de Combattants et des Victimes de Guerre*. This organization's general secretary, and the force behind it until his retirement in 1957, was Papa Seck Douta. Seck was born in Saint Louis in 1887 and therefore held French citizenship. A teacher at Malic Sy School in Dakar, he began a political career in 1946 within the framework of the first African federal political party, the Ressemblement Démocratique Africaine (RDA). His political opinions, however, became more moderate and he began to support the African section of the Socialist French Party (SFIO) and its leader Lamine Guéye.[25] While serving as the association's general secretary he tried to maintain political neutrality so as to represent all veterans. It is important to bear in mind, though, that African veterans did not speak in one voice. There were differences in the political views of veterans from different territories and between those who were close to the urban centers and took part in veterans' politics and those who lived in rural areas and were therefore distanced from any political activity. The so-called apolitical stance of Seck's organization was not supported by all veterans' and territorial associations; the organization in French Sudan, for example, often diverged from this line and adopted the RDA's political positions.

Despite some different modes of thought, it can be argued that most veterans adopted a so-called apolitical approach during the postwar years and attempted to further improve their conditions within the existent colonial framework. Therefore, the veterans' use of the issue of race as seen in the journal reflects, to a large extent, their general position on the subject.[26] This strategy and the place antiracist discourse had occupied in it is best understood through an examination of the veterans' main journal in this period.

The journal's first issue was published on April 1, 1948, and its last one on January 2, 1959. In other words, it was introduced around the same time that the spontaneous protests of demobilized soldiers were beginning to die out. The journal was first published at the Malic Sy School, where Seck had worked as a teacher, and later moved to better lodgings in Dakar. It was financed by the main veterans' organization mentioned above, while the organization's budget consisted of membership fees only, which covered just above half of its expenses and administrative support.[27]

The journal's main aim was to provide its readers with practical information. It therefore included updates regarding veterans' rights and published, for example, charts showing the amounts they should receive as pension, reports regarding the achievements of the federations of veterans and their ties with the French veterans' organization, and information regarding the actions and debates of African parliamentarians on behalf of veterans. In addition, the journal used its articles and reports, notably commemorative articles dealing with the two world wars, to advance veterans' claims for partnership and equality vis-à-vis their French comrades.

From its very first issues the journal's articles used two main discourses. One was that of "brotherhood in arms," demanding equal rights for the veterans based on the soldiers' sacrifices during the two world wars. The other pointed an accusing finger toward French officials in the army and the colonial administration who had treated veterans in a racist manner. The journal's various reports emphasized that racism was against the spirit of what was termed as the "true France," explicitly alluding to the Vichy episode in French history. The journal's reporters attributed all cases of discrimination and racist behavior toward African soldiers and veterans to people who acted against the principles of an ostensibly "true France," which was represented during World War II by De Gaulle and the Resistance.[28]

In one of the first issues, the journal published a letter from the president of the federation, Douta, to the high commissioner of FWA. Douta protested about a decorated veteran from Côte d'Ivoire who had been sentenced to eight months imprisonment for failing to salute a European civilian. A veteran who referred to this incident wrote to the journal that he could not imagine that those who had saved France would be attacked not by Germans but by their own countrymen. The administration's quick response to this publication arrived in time to be included in the same issue as the story itself and is very revealing. The high commissioner assured the veterans that an investigation regarding this case was already under way and that some conclusions had been drawn. He noted that the veteran was not arrested for failing to salute a European but rather for unlawfully donning a uniform and decorations. The case was transferred to the appeals court in Dakar but in the meantime the veteran in question had been released.[29]

In this case, as in other complaints against discrimination and racism, the journal distinguished between those individuals who were responsible for the discrimination and the general French approach. Colonial administrators who opposed the rights accorded to veterans were labeled by the journal as non-French, thus making it clear that a "true Frenchman" could not be a racist.[30]

In its discussions regarding cases of discrimination, the journal emphasized the heroism of the veterans in question. Often, this emphasis was made by publishing an article about Africans' participation in one of the world wars in close proximity to a report on racist attitudes toward soldiers and veterans.[31] The protests about discrimination were often accompanied by the main demand of the veterans' organization—the need for equating African soldiers' pensions to those of French soldiers.[32]

This demand was finally met in 1950 in the framework of the military reforms that completely transformed the French army's relations with its African soldiers and were a direct result of the soldiers' postwar protests. In that year a new era had begun in the relations between the French army and its African soldiers, both past and present. The military authorities took several steps to render military service more attractive to Africans. They augmented the percentage of volunteers in the army, improved pay and service conditions, offered professional education to soldiers, and encouraged African soldiers to become officers.[33] But more than anything else it was the decision of the French government to subscribe to the principle of paying equal pensions to veterans in the metropole and in the colonies that marked the end of the previous period, which had been characterized by anger and mistrust.

Following these reforms the journal's tone softened considerably and accusations against military and administrative authorities regarding racism and discrimination diminished significantly. The journal still complained about the bureaucratic obstacles that veterans living in remote areas had to tackle in order to receive their pensions, but it no longer accused the authorities of deliberate discrimination.

The reason race was no longer an issue in the veterans' discourse after 1950 is that the veterans who struggled for equality felt that they no longer needed it. The aim of equality was achieved through the soldiers' spontaneous protests and later by an organized campaign. The veterans' leaders knew that the key to achieving equality was to stress what the African workers in FWA fighting for the same cause could not stress: the concept of brotherhood in arms, of shared sacrifices and glory; of companionship and cooperation rather than division and resentment. Therefore, even when accusations of racism were used as a weapon, veterans made sure to make a clear distinction between racist French people who represented the beaten Vichy regime and "true" Frenchmen who could never be racist. One can assume that most veterans did not really believe in this distinction. Nevertheless, it was certainly useful to them. It was this strategy of defining racism as outside the norm that won the veterans' struggle in the 1950s.

Conclusions

The approaching independence of the territories of FWA brought with it a blow to the successful veterans' struggle for equality. Article 71 of a law from 1960 redefined French obligations toward veterans living in countries that had left the French community, freezing their base pension rates. It did so in such a way that the pensions of veterans in the newly independent states would decline steadily in years to come. The consequences of this article began to be felt only years later, when the freezing of the pensions became the focus of a renewed veterans' struggle against the French government.[34]

In one of my research trips to Dakar I was looking for African veterans that would be willing to talk to me about their experiences in the French army. The Gueule Tapée neighborhood Imam directed me to a veteran he knew that lived close by. The veteran agreed to talk to me, but after a few minutes he could no longer contain his anger and snapped at me: "You stole my pension, you have to return it." Surprised by this attack, I found myself mumbling in my defense: "I am not French." The veteran was not confused by my response and said: "It does not matter if you are French or not, you are white." This specific veteran insisted, then, on a direct link between racism and the French decision to freeze his pension years before. The response of the people in the Imam's house when I told them this story revealed that they did not see eye to eye with the veteran on this matter. Some of them just shrugged, saying that although ex-tirailleurs gained much from the French they did not stop complaining about them, thus rejecting the veteran's accusation of racism.

It is important to note that most of the veterans I talked to served after World War II and did not raise the issue of race or complain about racist attitudes toward them during their service. Some of them noted the good relations they had with French metropolitan soldiers.[35] Therefore, even if the renewed struggle for equality drove some veterans to use racism again as a weapon to achieve equality, this does not necessarily reflect veterans' perceptions in the period under consideration here.

As I have shown in this chapter, World War II and the prolonged presence of African soldiers on French soil transformed their perceptions of the racial and colonial categories and boundaries that had existed before the war. Soldiers' encounters with French civilians and other experiences they went through during the war made them successfully challenge these categories, which the colonial authorities wished so deeply to maintain.

When discussing the concepts of race and racism within the French army we have to remember that African soldiers and veterans were not only helpless victims of racism. They had also experienced respect and kindness during their presence in France. Even more importantly, they knew how to struggle against racism when they returned home and how to use it as a tool to achieve equality and change their destinies.

NOTES

The research leading to this publication was supported by the Israel Scientific Foundation, grant no. 882/09.

1. William Holmes Dyer memoirs, 1917–18, Schomburg Center for Research in Black Culture, New York Public Library.

2. Berry Family collection, Sc MG 483, Manuscripts, Archives and Rare Books Division, Schomburg Center.

3. Chad L. Williams, *Torchbearers of Democracy: African American Soldiers in the World War I Era* (Chapel Hill: University of North Carolina Press, 2010), 145–84.

4. French West Africa was the more strategically and economically important of the two French federations in sub-Saharan Africa. It included eight colonies: Senegal, in which the city of Dakar was the federation's capital, Côte d'Ivoire, French Guinea (today Guinea Conakry), French Sudan (today Mali), Niger, Mauritania, Upper Volta (today Burkina Faso), and Dahomey (today Benin), as well as the mandate territory of Togo.

5. Myron Echenberg, *Colonial Conscripts: The Tirailleurs Sénégalais in French West Africa, 1857–1960* (Portsmouth NH: Heinnemann, 1991), 88.

6. Raffael Scheck, *French Colonial Soldiers in German Captivity during World War II* (Cambridge, UK: Cambridge University Press, 2014), 234–39.

7. The letters are held in the National Archives of Senegal (ANS), dossier 4D 61 (89).

8. See for example a letter from the governor of French Sudan to the high commissioner rejecting the request of a French woman to join her African lover in French Sudan and suggesting that the ex-soldiers be sent to France instead, June 26, 1945, 4D 61 (89), ANS, Dakar.

9. For a more detailed discussion of the specific cases which appear in these letters, see Ruth Ginio, "African Soldiers, French Women, and Colonial Fears during and after World War II," in *Africa and World War II*, ed. Judith A. Byfield, Carolyn A. Brown, Timothy Parsons, and Ahmad Alawad Sikainga (Cambridge, UK: Cambridge University Press, 2015), 324–38.

10. Tyler Stovall, "The Color Line behind the Lines: Racial Violence in France during the Great War," *American Historical Review* 103, no. 3 (June 1998): 737–70.

11. On the whitening of the army, see Jean-Yves Le Naour, *La honte noire—L'Allemagne et les troupes coloniales françaises, 1914–1945* (Paris: Hachette, 2004), 247–48; Eric Jennings, *La France libre fut africain* (Paris: Perrin, 2014), 166–70.

12. Julien Fargettas, *Les Tirailleurs sénégalais: Les soldats noirs entre légendes et réalités, 1939–1945* (Paris: Tallandier, 2012), 267–82.

13. ANS 4D 60, Dakar, October 15, 1943.

14. The most recent and updated account of the events is Martin Mourre, *Thiaroye 1944: Histoire et mémoire d'un massacre colonial* (Paris: PUR, 2017). More on the tragic events at camp Thiaroye, see Myron Echenberg, "Tragedy at Thiaroye: The Senegalese Soldiers' Uprising of 1944," in *African Labor History*, ed. Peter Gutkind, Robin Cohen and Jean Copans (Beverly Hills CA: Sage, 1978), 109–27; Fragettas, *Les Tirailleurs*. 288–92; Armelle Mabon, *Prisonniers de guerre "indigènes": Visages oubliés de la France occupée* (Paris: La Découverte, 2010), 193–211.

15. ANS, 4D 60, October 31, 1944, letter from the minister of the colonies to the governor-general of FWA.

16. ANS, 4D 60, Conakry, December 18, 1944; Dakar, January 4, 1945; December 6, 1945; November 13, 1946.

17. ANS, 4D 60, November 13, 1946.

18. The *originaires* were the descendants of Africans who lived in the four communes of Senegal—Dakar, Gorée, Rufisque and Saint Louis—and were granted citizenship rights in 1848. They served in French metropolitan units. On the special service conditions of the originaires during World War II, see Jaqueline Woodfork, "It Is a Crime to Be a Tirailleur in the Army: The Impact of Senegalese Civilian Status in the French Colonial Army During the Second World War," *Journal of Military History* 77, no. 1 (January 2013): 115–39.

19. ANS, 4D 60, January, 28 1948, information report.

20. ANS 4D 60, 26 June, 1946, a report of the military cabinet.

21. ANS, December 6, 1945.

22. ANS, Dahomey, February 1946.

23. "Senator Jane Vialle," *Crisis* 57, no. 4 (April 1950): 208.

24. ANS, 4D 60, August 23, 1945, letter from the high commissioner of FWA to the minister of the colonies.

25. The RDA was the first African political party that was established after the war and was not limited to the originaires. Its leader was Félix Houphouet-Boigny. It was a federal party with sections in all of the territories of FWA and was considered by the French, especially in its earlier years and because of its alliance with the French Communist Party, as radical and dangerous to colonial stability.

26. Echenberg, *Colonial Conscripts*, 138–39.

27. Echenberg, *Colonial Conscripts*, 132.

28. On the idea of "two Frances" in FWA, see Ruth Ginio, "Vichy Rule in French West Africa: Prelude to Decolonization?" *French Colonial History* 4 (2003): 205–26.

29. "Ils ont des droits sur nous!," *La Voix des combattants*, no. 3, May 13, 1948, 1.

30. *La Voix des combattants* 5 (May 29, 1948): 1–2.

31. For example, a story about an African officer who fought bravely to his death on the Somme in 1940 was published next to a circular addressed to Coste Flore,

minister of Overseas France, dealing with racism in the colonies. *La Voix des combattants* 15 (November 17, 1948): 3.

32. See for example *La Voix des combattants* 22 (February 15, 1949): 1.

33. Echenberg, *Colonial Conscripts*, 105; Gregory Mann, *Native Sons: West African Veterans and France in the Twentieth Century* (Durham NC: Duke University Press, 2006), 124–29, 171–74.

34. Mann, *Native Sons*, 141–44. Mann notes that although this was certainly an unjust measure, it was not vindictive but rather part of move that began the year before to diminish payments to veterans in general, including French metropolitan ones. This decision affected half a million veterans, who represented one third of all French veterans.

35. Interviews with Sadibou Badji (born 1937), Marc Guéye (born 1934), Papa Figaro Diagne (born 1932), Dakar, March 2011, and with Sadiq Sall (whose father served in the French army and was born in 1921), January 24, 2014. Although, according to his son, Sall's father deeply disliked the French, he had maintained relations with some of his French comrades and even took his children to France to meet them.

PART 2

Blacks in Metropolitan France

4

Black Families in France (Eighteenth–Nineteenth Centuries)

Some Cases

PIERRE H. BOULLE

Color Prejudice and the Marriage Ban of 1778

In 1778 the French government, which a year earlier had passed a law prohibiting "Blacks, Mulattoes and other people of color of one or the other sex" from entering France, issued a second law to deal with those who already resided there.[1] White subjects were prohibited from marrying them, on pain of both partners being exiled to the colonies.

Concern about mixed marriages had not been expressed in the first years of Louis XV's reign. An edict was promulgated in October 1716 that allowed colonials to bring their slaves to France for religious instruction or for learning a trade without fearing that the "freedom principle," which stipulated that there could be no slaves in metropolitan France, would cost them the loss of their property.[2] Article VII of the edict allowed these slaves to marry while in France so long as they obtained their master's permission to do so, which authorities deemed the equivalent of manumission. The expectation of the authorities seems to have been that only a few slaves would be brought to France under the 1716 rules and that those few would remain only a short time. It was believed that even fewer would be allowed to marry, so no concern was expressed about these few.

Things began to change around midcentury, as the number of nonwhites in France began to rise, in part because the 1716 law had failed to specify any limit to the slaves' "visits" and because a 1738 law that placed a limit of three years to their residence was poorly enforced.[3] Estimates of the nonwhite population in France are particularly unreliable, but the two figures given by contemporary sources—four thousand Blacks in 1738 and approximately twice that number in 1782–suggest a gradual increase.[4] Although the total number of Blacks represented only an insignificant fraction of the French population (at most, 0.04 percent), the fact that a substantial number served as domestics or artisans in the aristocratic sectors of Paris made their presence more visible to the elite than their true number would suggest. An even more significant factor was the introduction into metropolitan France of attitudes transferred from the colonies, where color prejudice functioned as a means of ensuring the dominance of a small class of white proprietors over a much larger group of servile workers of African descent. Starting in midcentury, an increasing number of West Indian proprietors came to reside in France and, along with returning colonial officials, entered into the circles of the governing elite, and transmitted their prejudices to it.[5] Thus we see expressions of concern about the effect of Black residents in France starting in the 1750s, notably about their alleged role in the degeneration of the French nation. In 1762 the King's *procureur* at the Admiralty of France, Guillaume Poncet de la Grave, argued that France was being "deluged" with Blacks and warned that "we will soon see the French nation disfigured if such an abuse continues to be tolerated."[6] A year later the minister of the marine, Etienne François, duc de Choiseul, who had family connections with West Indian planters, ordered all Black slaves out of France so that, among other things, they would "cease the disorders they have introduced in France by their communications with whites, from which results a mixture of the blood which increases daily."[7] A successor, Antoine de Sartine (a former lieutenant-general of police in Paris who was thus familiar with the "colored" situation there), stated in his background paper for the 1777–78 laws against Black residents that "each day in France, Blacks increase in numbers . . . ; their marriages to Europeans are encouraged and public houses are infected by them; colors are mixed; blood is altered."[8] The most extreme statement of this prejudice is found in the *Mémoire sur l'esclavage des nègres* (1788), written by Pierre-Victor Malouet, a Marine administrator and colonial planter who later served as minister of the Marine and Colonies under the Restoration:

> Blacks can never become a part of our society. For no-one surely will make us desire the incorporation and the mixing of races. But, in order

to avoid this, slavery is necessary, for the nation owes its own filiation to the shame attached to a marriage with a Black slave. If this prejudice is destroyed, if the Black man is assimilated to whites amongst us, it is more than probable that we will very soon see mulatto nobles, financiers and merchants, whose wealth would then procure spouses and mothers to every order of the State. It is thus that individuals and nations are altered, degraded and dissolved.[9]

The Effects of the Marriage Ban

Even before the 1778 marriage ban some priests had hesitated marrying not only mixed couples but also Black ones, suggesting that the prejudices expressed at the center of the realm could in certain circumstances spread beyond the limits of Parisian society. In early 1777 the parish priest of Moncontour, Brittany, had rejected the request of two local Blacks to marry. Obviously they or someone close to them had appealed to the bishop, and when not obtaining satisfaction wrote to his well-connected predecessor, who appealed to the minister of the marine. Sartine, who was already preparing the 1777–78 legislation, responded that matters of marriage were not within his purview but were instead the domain of religious authorities and the courts. He suggested that a proper appeal should thus go the Parlement in Rennes.[10] A subsequent document indicates that the potential groom was living alone in Nantes and working at the local earthenware manufacture, suggesting that the marriage had fallen through.[11] Even sadder was the case of Joseph Maria, a Black in Châteauroux, a city in Berry. Involved with a white girl whom he had impregnated in early 1778 (prior to the marriage prohibition), he sought to regularize the situation but encountered the oppositions of the priest and of the local *procureur*.[12] Ultimately all he could do was recognize his illegitimate son at his baptism.[13]

Appeals to a Parlement could succeed on occasion. A number of cases exist in Provence of priests who were ordered to perform such marriages by order of the Aix tribunal. The most interesting is that of Alexis Brémont, a mulatto of Cassis who had married a local girl in August 1778, after the passage of the law prohibiting mixed marriages. The marriage was denounced, which led the minister to inquire whether Brémont should be expulsed to the colonies.[14] The local community successfully fought on Brémont's behalf. According to the report made by the intendant's subdelegate, not only had the marriage occurred at the specific order of the Parlement, which the local priest felt he couldn't disobey, but also Alexis had "never been a slave," and was, rather, the illegitimate son of a member of an important local family, from whom he had inherited "a considerable sum." Well established, he was "an *honnête homme*, fulfilling his duties with exactitude, generally loved and esteemed; his relatives . . . are not ashamed to have him bear their name. . . . He had anticipated on the rights of marriage with his wife, before their union was allowed and much before the royal edict. As a gallant man, he thought he should repair his fault; the two families agreed readily to these dispositions." And the subdelegate added that, "as for his color, the said Alexis is very close to European blood."[15] The minister did not insist.

In fact, no case has been found of an expulsion as a result of the 1778 law. Even though expulsion was recommended to Sartine's successor in one 1782 case from Toulouse, the *maréchal* de Castries took no action and the individual in question was still in Toulouse in 1790, when he witnessed the baptism of a new daughter.[16] Castries even recommended and the king approved such a marriage in 1785, probably because the king's sister expressed an interest in the affair.[17] Marriages continued to be performed, though perhaps less frequently than previously, because to do so required ignoring the law.

In the next sections I will examine the construction of three families that resulted from mixed marriages. Having been started earlier than 1778 and the children having married later than 1789, two of these families had no occasion to experience the administrative difficulties that mixed couples had to overcome in the last years of the Old Regime. Only one ancestor married at the time of the marriage ban, and he too, for reasons I'll attempt to explain, faced no problems. However, their stories can be used to test whether or not prejudice affected their progress.

The Guizots of Saint-Geniès-de-Malgoirès (Gard)

Saint-Geniès-de-Malgoirès is a small village north of Nîmes with a mixed population of Catholics and Protestants. The Guizots were Protestants involved in the local textile trade, in landowning, and in land management. Some were also trained in law, as was a cousin of the Guizot who interests us, a lawyer in Nîmes who was the father of Louis-Philippe's prime minister, the historian François Guizot.[18]

Paul Guizot was a younger son who, in 1726, sought his fortune in the West Indies. At the death of his father, who had squandered the family's assets, Guizot returned to his native village, where he worked to reconstruct the family fortune with what he had earned on Saint-Domingue. Soon after his departure from the island his illegitimate mulatto son, Louis Ferrier, was born on his ex-plantation, near Fort-Dauphin. Two years later, in 1742, Guizot brought the mother and the child to France. The mother soon returned to Saint-Domingue, leaving her son Louis with his father.[19]

Besides reconstructing the family business and supporting his older brother and unmarried sisters, as well as his brother's family, Paul Guizot spent most of his energy making sure that his illegitimate son would succeed. He provided him with a good education, had him trained as a lawyer, established him in Saint-Geniès as a silk stocking manufacturer, and had him appointed as the duc d'Uzès's local *viguier*, the seigniorial judge. [20] When it came time to see him married, the father found a good prospect in Marie Boisson, the daughter of another local silk stocking manufacturer, who gave his son six children.[21]

Mostly Paul Guizot sought to make sure that Louis Ferrier, despite having been born illegitimate, would receive an inheritance from him. This was something that was not legally possible in the presence of legitimate heirs, however remote. Legitimizing the son of an unmarried father was expensive, since it required a royal act, but it did not normally prove too difficult. However, the procedure was started in 1764, just as color prejudice was becoming rampant in government circles. More to the point, Ferrier, now renamed Louis Guizot by an act of the Parlement of Toulouse, had been born a slave and had never been officially manumitted.[22] Despite convincing the local Catholic priest to have Louis "rebaptized" as an adult, thereby avoiding the need to provide a certified copy of the Saint-Domingue baptismal record that was found in the slaves' register, the procedure dragged on for years.[23] One factor was a confrontation with Louis's cousin Jean-Antoine Guizot, a trained lawyer who, as the legitimate heir, put every possible obstacle in the way.[24]

Finally, Paul Guizot abandoned his efforts at legitimating his son and adopted a strategy frequently used by Protestants after the 1685 Revocation of the Edict of Nantes: the transmission of property to a legally acceptable individual with the understanding that the beneficiary would pass the assets on to the desired but illegal heir or heirs.[25] In a first testament that Guizot signed in 1758, he made his two sisters his sole legatees with the understanding that they would transmit the inheritance to their nephew. Fifteen years later, perhaps not sufficiently sure of his sisters' devotion to their nephew and perhaps also because their status as Protestants could be used by Jean-Antoine to challenge the will, Guizot signed another will giving his fortune to a Nîmes acquaintance with the proviso that the said acquaintance, "as soon as he can safely do it, will deliver to my natural son Louis Guizot, viguier of the barony of Saint-Geniès, my total inheritance in whatever form it consists or can consist." The Nîmes acquaintance having died, Paul made yet another will in 1780 that entrusted his fortune to a parent of his notary, the Catholic priest Jacques Rivière, with the request that Rivière provide half of the assets to Louis "*à titre d'aliment*" (as usufruct).[26] At Paul's death in 1785 the 1780 testament was opened and its clauses observed. Louis inherited, if not his father's properties, at least their use and became one of the richest and most influential members of the village community.[27]

The story could end there were it not for the Revolution, in which Louis Guizot took an active part. He was named by the village community one of their representatives to the Uzès *sénéchaussée* meeting, where the local *cahier* was drafted and the representative to the Estates-General was chosen. During the Great Fear of 1789 he served as commander of the local National Guard and in 1790 he was elected mayor of Saint-Geniès, becoming the first nonwhite mayor in France. He then was elected district administrator and finally to the new department's executive.[28] It is there that problems arose, for the politics of the Gard replicated in 1793–94 those of the capital, with its struggle between the Girondins and the Mountain. The departmental directorate was fully engaged in the Federalist struggle, and when the movement was defeated in 1794 the whole directorate was brought in front of the local Revolutionary Tribunal. There, all but one (not Louis Guizot) were condemned to death for "having attempted to break the unity and indivisibility" of the Republic and guillotined on June 3, 1794.[29] Two weeks earlier Louis Guizot's cousin André, the father of Louis-Philippe's minister, had suffered the same fate.[30]

The tribunal's sentence included the confiscation of all the goods of the condemned. Seals had already been put on Louis's house and warehouses in Saint-Geniès at the time of his arrest and his family had been kicked out. It was pointless to claim that Louis had only enjoyed the usufruct of the house, as the priest Jacques Rivière, who had refused the civil constitution of the clergy, emigrated and also had his property confiscated.[31] Although Louis's children were adults and ran their own affairs, the loss was a severe blow.

The family was saved by the discovery of a fourth will, dated 1784, that had been entrusted "secretly" by Paul Guizot to a certain François Boisson, undoubtedly a parent of Louis's widow. The new will disinherited Jacques Rivière in favor of Pierre Guizot of Nîmes. The latter having died, as had his son, the heir was Jeanne Guizot, one of the witnesses to the marriage contract between Louis Guizot and Marie Boisson in 1760. Despite the peculiar circumstances of its discovery and the suspicious family relationship between François Boisson and Louis Guizot's widow, the new will was finally accepted. With Rivière no longer being the legitimate heir and the guillotined mayor and developmental director having no right to the properties the priest had left him to enjoy, the confiscation of the estate was lifted and Jeanne Guizot was declared the legitimate heir of Paul Guizot.[32] In an arrangement with the latter's grandchildren, she transmitted her property to them in exchange for a sixty thousand franc settlement, ten thousand of which were reserved for the surviving sister of Jean-Antoine Guizot.[33] Thus Louis Guizot's children returned to their status as village and departmental notables. They were described in various acts as "bourgeois" or "landowners" and assumed a number of positions under the Directory, the Empire, and the Restoration, when Louis II became mayor of Saint-Geniès.[34]

I haven't studied the next generations, but in 2012 when I was kindly allowed to take a look at the family archives, at least one descendant remained in the village, retired in the large house that Paul Guizot had built outside the village's walls.

The Almoradins of Bû (Eure-et-Loir)

Though somewhat conflicting about his early life, documents suggest that Pierre Almoradin came to France directly from Guinea on a naval vessel at a very young age, landing in Lorient in the 1730s.[35] The first direct evidence finds him baptized in Versailles in 1745, aged eleven to fourteen, as the slave of the marquise de Flavancourt, a lady-in-waiting to the Queen.[36] Already rather old to be one of those turbaned "little Blacks" so prized by the ladies at court, he soon was transferred, probably as a free man, to the hunt of the Prince de Dombes, one of Louis XIV's grandchildren, where he served as a "*piqueur*" helping run the pack of hounds at the prince's castle in Sceaux. When the prince died in 1755 and his brother, the comte d'Eu, inherited the castle, Almoradin continued his services there. In 1760 he married the daughter of a local boilermaker, Marie-Anne Geneviève Fabre, with whom he ultimately had seventeen children, born between 1761 and 1784.[37] The first two were born at Sceaux, but two years after their marriage the couple moved to Bû near Anet, Diane de Poitiers's famed castle, and Eu's property, where the nearby forests were particularly suited for the count's predilection for hunting.[38] Eu used the castle at Bû, which he also owned, as a residence for some of his large retinue.[39] And there, then in the village itself, the Almoradins stayed until their death, he in 1805 and she in 1818.[40]

Two factors are revealed from the numerous mentions of Pierre Almoradin in the Bû parish registers. One is his easy, flowing signature, unchanging throughout his years there, suggesting a reasonable level of literacy. His wife's signature, on the other hand, appears somewhat awkward as do those of his children. The second factor revealed by the registers is his fairly good integration into the community, represented by the numerous occasions when he signed as "neighbor" or even "friend" for the baptism and marriage of villagers; similarly, among the godparents of his children are not a few drawn from nearby merchant and *laboureur* families.[41] His connection to the royal family and the fact that, in a rural community, he was able to live off a pension must have trumped any possible reservation about his color. [42] Indeed, as seems to have been the case that in regions where Blacks were rare oddities, away from ports or Paris and the court, his color may have given him a certain cachet.

His pension undoubtedly stopped with the sequestration of royal properties during the Revolution, for he resumed work in his sixties, taking on a number of petty jobs for the municipality—*garde bois* (woods warden), *concierge* (porter), and perhaps also *commissionnaire* (messenger). By 1801, however, he is described again as being on a state pension he enjoyed until his death four years later.[43]

Out of the seventeen Almoradin children, two disappear from the records before adulthood and only four—two boys and two girls—survived to be married. Their mortality rate of 65 percent (if we count among the survivors the two for whom we have no information) is above the period's norm of one in two children reaching adulthood, but not altogether exceptional.[44] The two girls married quite late (aged thirty-five and forty-one), after the death of their father, the first to an ex-Polish prisoner taken by the French in the Revolutionary wars turned day-laborer and the second to a shoemaker from Anet.[45] Neither of them had children. The younger of the boys had a quite undistinguished career, described as a commissionnaire, a day laborer, and then a gardener in the various birth records of his children. Poorly educated—his signature is awkward and drawn in imitation of his brother's—he married at age thirty-four and had six children, all of whom died in infancy, four of them born dead or dying less than a day after their birth, suggesting a genetic incompatibility between he and his wife.[46] It is, therefore, through the oldest of the boys, Jacques, who lived eighty-one years (1763–1845), that the Almoradin lineage survived, though under other names as the male line stopped at his great-grandchildren in the last half of the nineteenth century.

If we take signatures as evidence, the oldest boy and the elder of the two sisters were the better educated children. Indeed, Jacques Almoradin, who after service in the Revolutionary Army became Bû's *garde champêtre* (rural policeman), must have been sufficiently educated to be able to perform one of the tasks of that office, which was to announce municipal decisions by reading them aloud at various sites within the community.[47] He married twice and had seven children.[48] For a while during the Restoration he resumed the family tradition by working for the duc de Penthièvre's daughter as *garde forestier* (forest warden) in one of the properties that had been returned to the family.[49] But he eventually returned to Bû as a day laborer and finally resumed his role as *garde champêtre* in Bû and nearby Rouvres.[50]

It would be too tedious to go through the four succeeding generations. Let me simply state that for the most part Pierre Almoradin's grandchildren (born between 1797 and 1824), great-grandchildren (born 1827–67) and great-great-grandchildren (born 1855–97) and their spouses remained in humble occupations; even his daughters were poorly educated, took on menial jobs, and married poorly.[51] For the most part members of the next generations were and remained rural day laborers, domestics, and needleworkers and settled generally in or within walking distance of Bû. After the first generation and until the 1880s, when rural education spread, the majority had become illiterate and married illiterate spouses. If movement occurred for the family in the nineteenth century it was downward, a trend that probably was initiated by the reduced situation of the patriarch as a result of the Revolution. The change of names from Almoradin and the fact that *état civil* records can now only be consulted until 1902 makes it difficult to pursue the family beyond the nineteenth century, but genealogical sites, when consultable, as well as marginal notes in the late-nineteenth century records suggest that it is only in the twentieth century that some descendants of Pierre Almoradin made a move to the urban middle class.

The Chandernagors of Civray (Vienne)

As with Pierre Almoradin, the first document we possess concerning Charles Louis Chandernagor dit Bengale is his baptismal record, signed in the small parish of Plou in Berry. It is a remarkable document:

> On the 26 of October 1760, by permission of M. Caraton, vicar-general [of the bishopric of Bourges], was baptized by the undersigned under the condition *si non est baptisatus* [that he is not yet baptized], Charles François Chandernagor, nicknamed Bengale, an Indian aged twelve or thirteen, taken in, in Paris, by the charity of Messire François Dumersan and Demoiselle de Bussy, as a poor orphan who doesn't know the names of his father or mother, a catechumen for the last fifteen months. His godmother was Honorable Demoiselle Madeleine de Bussy, sister of

Messire Charles Joseph de Bussy, marquis de Castelnau of this parish, who signed with the baptized and ourself. [Signed] Charles Fransois Chandernagor [in large child-like letters]; de Bussy; Camus, *curé*.[52]

It is not the conditional aspect of the act that is unusual, as it was standard policy to indicate the possibility of an earlier baptism in the case of all but the very young slaves baptized in France, and this did not require a special permission from the bishop. What is unusual is that permission was deemed necessary at all and that only one godparent was mentioned. It is only one of two such baptismal records I have encountered among the many I have seen (the other is that of a slave whose sole godparent was his male master), so perhaps the two phenomena are connected.[53] What is particularly odd is that a potential godfather, François Marion Dumersan, is mentioned in the text and that we know that he was usually present at the castle of the marquis de Castenau with Mlle de Bussy. It is also noteworthy that the Christian names given to Bengale are those of Mlle de Bussy's brother and that of Dumersan, a traditional practice when godparents named their ward.

The story of how Bengale came under the protection of the two is equally intriguing. The baptismal record makes it sound as if Mlle de Bussy and Dumersan found him abandoned on the streets of Paris in or around the year 1758 and had him instructed in Catholicism and baptized. But who were these two benefactors? Mlle de Bussy was the younger sister of Charles Joseph Patissier de Bussy, the lieutenant of Joseph François Dupleix and then Thomas Arthur Lally-Tollendal, commandants of the French establishments in India. Bussy was the man who conquered the Dekkan only to be taken prisoner by the British in the Seven Years' War.[54] While occupied in the Dekkan following Dupleix's recall, Bussy had prepared his return to France by purchasing the castle of Castelnau with the title of marquis. This was his sister's first visit to the region. Bussy had also a residence in Paris on the rue de Richelieu, where his sister and Dumersan usually lived. As to Dumersan (or du Mersan), he was Bussy's aide in India and returned to France in 1754 to become his business agent in Paris.[55] He and Mlle de Bussy remained close throughout their lives.

The names Bengale and Chandernagor as well as his indicated ethnic origins suggest that he came from India. It is quite possible that he was bought by de Bussy there and then shipped to France with Dumersan.[56] However, when Bengale died in 1821 his son told the recorder that his father had been born on Île Bourbon (present-day Réunion). It may be that, indeed, Dumersan and Mlle de Bussy acquired Bengale, who may have been an Indian, an African, or even a Malgache, in Paris either as a "poor orphan" found on the streets or more likely by purchasing him from someone else. This may explain why they chose Plou for the baptism rather than having it performed in Paris. Under the law then in effect only planters were allowed to bring slaves into France and only for three years. Furthermore, manumission in France had been prohibited in 1738 and the penalty for noncompliance was the confiscation of the slave by the Crown, "to be employed in the colonies for work the King would order." A baptism in Paris, therefore, could have been risky, whereas being tucked away in a small parish where the priest was dependent on the local seignior was a safe way to provide Bengale with a new identity as a free person.[57] The names chosen may have been part of the subterfuge.

Bengale remained at Mlle de Bussy's service for the following fifteen years as she moved back and forth between Castelnau and Paris. From 1764 onward he was listed in the castle's accounts as paid to serve his mistress as her "*laquais*."[58] Sometime in the 1770s, probably after 1777, he left the Bussy household and became a cook at the castle of the Maron de la Bonnardelière near Civray (Vienne). We find him there at his marriage to Marie-Anne Pontenier, the daughter of a *garde-traversier* (ferryman) with the administration of Eaux et Forêts.[59] The marriage date is interesting, for it is only two years after the 1778 law that prohibited such unions and yet there's no evidence anyone opposed it. Did the fact that Bengale was reputedly of Indian rather than African origins that play a role? In any case, no one seems to have denounced him to the authorities.

He remained in the La Bonnardelière's service until the Revolution, when the family emigrated and he established himself in Civray as "*traiteur*" (caterer), "*cabaretier*" (bar owner; publican), and finally "*aubergiste*" (innkeeper). The different names given to his occupation in état civil registers do not suggest a progression in wealth and status. He remained throughout his life a petty artisan, offering food and drink to modest Civray residents at a back-alley shop in the poorer section of town.[60]

Bengale and his wife, who survived him, had six children, three of whom (one girl, two boys) reached adulthood and married. The eldest, Anne, married Charles Michel Cabaret, a *tisserand* (weaver) who later established himself as an innkeeper.[61] His address on rue Nationale at Civray, suggests he had more success than his father-in-law had achieved in that occupation during his lifetime. The couple had five children, one of whom became a weaver and married the daughter of a house carpenter,[62] another who married a gardener.[63] The second surviving child of Charles François, Antoine Marcellin, worked as an *ouvrier menuisier* (journeyman carpenter) and married the daughter of a *fournier* (a mason specializing in the construction of bread ovens); they had two children who died in childhood.[64] Having later become a *pâtissier* (confectioner), Antoine Marcellin married a second time to a widowed *lingère* (seamstress), the daughter of a *gendarme*, from whom he had no children.[65]

It is the third child of Bengale, named simply Antoine, who had the most interesting life. Trained as a *coutelier* (cutler) he left home in his late teens to join the Napoleonic Army and was wounded at the battle of Smolensk in 1812, losing a finger of his right hand.[66] Having returned to Civray, in 1814 he married the daughter of a weaver who earned her living as a *ravaudeuse en bas* (stocking mender).[67] The couple had thirteen children over the fifteen following years. Antoine took up again the cutler's craft, but his handicap must have made the work difficult for him.[68] We later find him engaged in petty official jobs as *piéton* (messenger), *garde champêtre* (rural policeman), and *facteur* (postman).[69] He couldn't keep these positions—tradition says because of his foul temper—and became indigent (the need to feed thirteen children must not have helped).[70] He was finally taken on as a *garde particulier* (guardian of private properties) by some charitable Civray residents, including the mayor who unsuccessfully sought to obtain a pension for him during the Second Empire. He died in 1865.[71] Those of his children who survived childhood and whose life we've been able to follow continued in the artisan class or below, working as day laborer, messenger, tailor, cutler, chair repairer, postman, and wheelwright (some of these occupations were taken up serially by the same individual). Those that married also did so within the petty artisanal class—seamstress, tailor, *cordier* (rope maker)—while unmarried daughters are indicated without occupation but probably did needlework.

This remained the case for the next generations until the twentieth century, when Bengale's great-great-grandson, André Chandernagor, born in 1921, obtained an education at the prestigious Lycée Henri IV in Paris, won admission to the École Nationale d'Administration (ÉNA), and was appointed to the Conseil d'État. He then entered politics first as mayor of his wife's family town in the Creuse and went on to be elected as deputy for the department and as president of the department's *conseil général*. After becoming minister-delegate for European Affairs under the Socialist governments of Pierre Mauroy, he finished as first president of the Chambre des comptes, appointed by President François Mitterand.[72] His daughter, Françoise Chandernagor, started in his footsteps, becoming the first woman major of the ÉNA, and then was attached to the Conseil d'État, as her father had been. As an aside, she began writing historical novels and has become a major French literary figure, having published a dozen novels, and is a member of the jury of the prestigious Prix Goncourt.[73]

Conclusion

As with the Almoradins, the Chandernagors became integrated in France's provincial community. They benefitted, as did others, from the Republican opportunities provided to talented provincials in the late-nineteenth century and throughout the twentieth century, but they did so in a much more spectacular way. With these opportunities, they tended to move away from the countryside to the capital and other large cities. By then, of course, their color had been substantially diluted so that, except for memories within their families and, in the case of the Chandernagors, their exotic family name, few people probably noted them as different from their neighbors. The Guizot family remains the exception here, no doubt as a result of the good education and support that a well-established father provided his illegitimate son, permitting him and his descendants to establish themselves quickly into the local bourgeoisie.

Two further reflections should be taken into consideration at the end of this narrative. For one thing there seems to have been no particular official difficulty placed on the marriages of our three families during the nineteenth century, despite the fact that slavery and the Old Regime laws against nonwhite residents, including the ban on mixed marriages, were reestablished by Bonaparte in 1802 and remained in effect until the late 1810s and early 1820s.[74] However, as early as the First Empire it was decided that the law against marriage should not be applied to those individuals of mixed origins. By then all the Guizot, Almoradin, and Chandernagor children were regarded as such. It may be as well that, despite the increased efficiency and centralization of public administration after the Revolution, living in the provinces still provided some sort of protection against state interference.

The second point is that, in the absence of état-civil records for Paris (they were burned along with the Tuileries Palace during the 1871 Commune), I have been unable to provide any comparative case study from the capital. Thus it has proven impossible to follow Parisian families of humble origins, so we must depend of the story of more atypical ones such as that of Thomas-Alexandre Dumas, the mulatto son of a nobleman who joined the royal army as a private, reached the rank of general during the Revolution, and was the father of the novelist Alexandre Dumas.[75] If, as I have argued, color prejudice was particularly rampant among the Parisian elite in the eighteenth century, would lower-class nonwhite families have had different experiences in Paris from those I have described? Given official prejudices against mixed marriages, could such families have even been constructed? Some indications from the early nineteenth century, notably difficulties placed by civil officers on marriage requests, suggest such differences. Eighteenth-century evidence concerning the white laboring and artisanal classes, on the other hand, do not at all reflect the color prejudices of the upper class even in Paris. It is true that those prejudices (let's call them racial) were fairly exclusive to the elite before the Revolution and tended to spread beyond that class in the nineteenth century as a result of the democratization of literacy, the popularization of pseudosciences and, ultimately, the appearance of the yellow press.[76] But much of this occurred in the second part of the nineteenth century in the context of the second colonial empire and when mixed families issued from the eighteenth century were practically indistinguishable from the general population.

It is also true that, at the time of the first abolition of slavery in 1794, a police *commissaire* reported a complaint from a common Parisian woman to the effect that with the new law she and others would be burdened with Black sisters-in-law.[77] And it is true as well that the ill-tempered Antoine Chandernagor of Civray was still recalled in the early twentieth century as "this swarthy man who took out his saber at the first occasion [*ce basané qui sortait son sabre pour un oui, pour un non*]," but this reference to his physical appearance had probably more to do with his character than with any racial rejection.[78] If Louis Chevalier's "laboring classes," at least in the first part of the nineteenth century, were not colorblind, they do not appear to have been particularly exercised about nonwhites in their midst.[79]

NOTES

1. "Déclaration du Roi, du 9 août 1777, concernant la Police des Noirs" and "Arrêt du Conseil d'État, du 5 avril 1778, concernant le mariage des Noirs, Mulâtres ou autres gens de couleur," in *Le Code Noir ou Recueil de Reglemens Concernant [. . .] les Negres dans les Colonies Françoises* (Paris: Chez Prault, 1788), 489–500, 518–20.

2. "Édit du Roi concernant les esclaves nègres des colonies," October 1716, *Le Code Noir*, 169–81.

3. "Déclaration du Roi concernant les Nègres esclaves des colonies," December 15, 1738, *Le Code Noir*, 382–95.

4. For the 1738 figure see [François Gayot de Pitaval], "Liberté réclamée par un Negre, contre son maitre qui l'a amené en France," *Causes célèbres et intéressantes, avec les jugemens qui les ont décidées. Recueillies par M.***, avocat au Parlement*, vol. 13 (Paris: Chez la Veuve Delaulne, 1739), 573. The actual number given in 1782 is of four to five thousand slaves ("Avis" of the Comité de législation coloniale, Archives nationales d'outre-mer, Fonds ministériels, Colonies [hereafter ANOM, FM, COL], F/1B/4, fol. 316). Given that, at the time, slaves represented approximately 60 percent of the nonwhite population (Pierre H. Boulle, *Race et esclavage dans la France de l'Ancien Régime* [Paris: Perrin, 2007], 190), the number of nonwhites, slaves and free, would be approximately 6,700 to 8,300 individuals.

5. A particularly good example is that of Jean-Baptiste Dubuc du Ferret, Martinique planter and the deputy of the colony on the Conseil du commerce, who became Choiseul's *premier commis* at the Ministry of the Marine. On Dubuc, see Jean Tarrade, *Le commerce colonial de la France à la fin de l'ancien régime. L'évo-*

lution du régime de l'"Exclusif," 2 vols. (Paris: Presses universitaires de France 1972), ch. 7.

6. Poncet's address as *procureur* in "Ordonnance" of the Admiralty of France, March 31 and April 5, 1762, in *Le Code Noir*, 458–59 (unless otherwise stated, translations throughout this essay are my own).

7. Circular letter to the *intendants* and *commissaires des ports*, June 30, 1763, ANOM, FM COL, F/3/90, fol. 104.

8. Report to the *Conseil des Dépêches*, [August 9], 1777, ANOM, FM COL, F/1B/3, fol. 380v.

9. *Mémoire sur l'esclavage des Nègres, Dans lequel on discute les motifs proposés pour leur Affranchissement, ceux qui s'y opposent, and les moyens praticables pour améliorer leur sort* (Neufchatel: n.p., 1788), 40.

10. Sartine to the bishop of Verdun, March 7, 1777, ANOM FM COL, B161, fol. 75v.

11. Louis René Hippolyte's declaration, March 27, 1777, Archives départementales (AD) de la Loire-Atlantique., B4558, fol. 123v.

12. King's *procureur* at Châteauroux, to Joly de Fleury, *procureur général* at the Paris *parlement*, March 5, 1778, Bibliothèque nationale de France, département des manuscrits, Joly de Fleury 485, fol. 459.

13. Archives municipales (AM) de Châteauroux, GG31 (Registres paroissiaux, paroisses [RP] St-Denis, and St-Martial, Baptêmes, mariages, sépultures [BMS] 1775–1778), vue 64 online, June 9, 1778.

14. The correspondence between the Minister and La Tour de Gléné, intendant of Provence, September–December 1778, is found in AD Bouches-du-Rhône, c4621.

15. Payan, subdelegate at Cassis, to La Tour de Gléné, October 25, 1778, AD Bouches-du-Rhône, c4621.

16. Internal ministerial memorandum, [1782], ANOM, Instruments de recherche en ligne (IREL), E358, 266–67; Baptism of Jeanne-Marie Alexis, January 26, 1790, AD Haute-Garonne, E/1/M 8454 online, view 9 (Toulouse, R.P. St-Etienne: BMS 1790, fol. 8v).

17. Castries to Aubert, *valet de chambre* of Madame, April 21, 1785, ANOM, IREL, E396, dos. 12, 113–14.

18. The story of the Guizots has already been treated by authors who have inspired me, notably Camille Hugues, "Deux colons gardois au XVIIIe siècle: Louis et Paul Guizot," *Cahiers du Gard rhodanien* no. 18 (1980): 115–23. See also Roger Little, "Un maire noir sous la Révolution," *Africulture* no. 64 (July–September 2005): 67–77. Just as Camille Hugues and Roger Little, I have benefitted from consulting the private papers [hereafter: AP Guizot] which were kept in Saint-Geniès by a descendant of Louis Guizot, Madame Astrid Sauvage, now deceased, to whom I wish to express here my gratitude. These documents have since allegedly been transferred to the Departmental archives of Gard. Sur la famille de François Guizot, voir Charles H. Pouthas, *Une famille de bourgeoisie française de Louis*

XIV à Napoléon (Paris: Félix Alcan, 1934); Laurent Theis, *François Guizot* (Paris: Fayard, 2008).

19. "Mémoire pour sieur Paul Guizot, Bourgeois de St geniéz de Malgoirés en Languedoc," [1775?], AP Guizot, no. 154, fol. 2 ; Paul Guizot, "Déclaration" confirming the manumission of Catherine Rideau *dite* Catin, September 1, 1747, AP Guizot, no. 14.

20. Louis is indicated as *négociant* and *marchand-fabricant* in an act dated 1766 (AP Guizot, no. 33), as *bachelier ès droit* and *viguier* in another (AP Guizot, no. 43, 1768).

21. The couple was married by a Protestant minister and the act hasn't been found, but the marriage contract, signed on January 15, 1760, is in AD Gard, Étude Cherveau, 2E54/258, fols 311v-313. The children were also baptized as Protestants and I have only found the acts for two of them, in the registers of Minister Theyron, December 7, 1765 (AD Gard, 5 Mi 11–38) and 15 August 1769 (5 Mi 11–37). However, the existence of all the others is confirmed in other parish records and in documents from AP Guizot.

22. Sentence of July 9, 1771, AP Guizot, no. 47.

23. Certified copy of baptismal act, June 10, 1767 (baptism, January 13, 1766), AP Guizot, no. 35.

24. Jean-Antoine went so far as to force Paul to prove that he was not senile (AP Guizot, no. 45, 1771). He only abandoned his fight on the eve of the Revolution, signing a "désistement" on March 30, 1788, in exchange for what family assets were left on Saint-Domingue (AP Guizot, nos. 254–55).

25. Pouthas, *Une famille de bourgeoisie française*, 6.

26. The three wills are dated August 29, 1758, March 5, 1773, and August 23, 1780 (AP Guizot, nos. 29, 281, and 271, respectively).

27. His *capitation* is among the highest in the village (Pouthas, *Une famille de bourgeoisie française*, 8).

28. Camille Hugues, *Les révolutionnaires de Saint-Geniès-de-Malgoirès* (Saint-Geniès de Malgoirès: Association Pont de l'Esquille, 2008), 5–17; François Rouvière, *Histoire de la Révolution française dans le département du Gard*, 4 vols. (Nîmes: Librairie ancienne A.Catéla, 1887–89; repr. Marseille: Lafitte, 1977), 1:132 and 3:341n.

29. Rouvière, *Histoire de la Révolution dans le Gard* 4:264–71; Hugues, *Les révolutionnaires de Saint-Geniès*, 22–23.

30. Rouvière, *Histoire de la Révolution dans le Gard*, 4:232–34.

31. AP Guizot, no. 160, 2–3.

32. "Extrait des registres du Directoire du départ du Gard," 25 Brumaire Year 2 (November 15, 1794), AP Guizot, no. 252.

33. Agreement between Jeanne and Marguerite Guizot, 20 Floréal Year 3 (May 10, 1795); Sale of Paul Guizot's inheritance, 5 Thermidor Year 3 (July 14, 1795), AP Guizot, nos. 252 and 248.

34. AP Guizot, *passim*; État civil de (EC) St-Geniès-de-Malgoirès, AD Gard. 5 Mi 11–38 and 11–39, *passim*.

35. Pierre Almoradin's declaration at the Admiralty of France, February 28, 1778, "Registre [no. 7] pour servir aux declarations qui se font au sujet des Negres" (1777–90), fol. 18, Centre d'accueil et de recherches des Archives nationales, z/1D/139z/1D/139.

36. RP Versailles, par. St-Louis, B 1745 (AD Yvelines online, 11125156, view 24). I am grateful to Philippe Cappe, whose family is collateral to the Almoradins, to have directed me to this document as well as some of the descending Almoradin lineages.

37. Marriage act, September 1, 1760, RP Sceaux, BMS 1757–60 (AD Hauts-de-Seine online, E NUM SCE BMS 12, view 97), fol. 15v-16. This act and other documents concerning him indicate his occupation in the service of Dombes and Eu. See for instance, RP Bû, BMS 1768–92 (AD Eure-et-Loir online, 3E064/4, view 3).

38. Baptisms, October 25, 1761 and September 21, 1762, RP Sceaux, BMS 1761–66 (AD Hauts-de-Seine online, E NUM SCE BMS 13, views 26 and 151) and December 23, 1763, RP Bû, BMS 1742–67 (AD Eure-et-Loir online, 3E064/3, view 277).

39. The Bû parish records indicate a number of such servants, including several Swiss guards.

40. AD Eure-et-Loir online, 3E064/7 (EC Bû, Year 11, 1806), view 173, and 3E064/9 (EC Bû, 1813–1819), view 342.

41. *Laboureurs* means plowmen or peasant capitalists owning a plow and a team of oxen that they provided to others for a fee.

42. He is listed as Eu's *pensionnaire* in the declaration of February 28, 1778, see note 35 herein.

43. *Garde bois* in 1793 (3E064/5, views 5 and 11); *concierge de l'administration* in Years 8 and 9 (1800–1801), when he signs numerous acts in that capacity (AD Eure-et-Loir online, 3E064/6, views 178–203); *commissionnaire de son vivant* in 1816 (AD Eure-et-Loir online, 3E064/9, view 254); *pensionnaire de l'État* and *rentier* in Years 9 and 10 (1801) (AD Eure-et-Loir online, 3E064/6, views 205 and 313).

44. For the French average in the late eighteenth and early nineteenth centuries (50 percent reaching marriageable age), see Marcel Reinhard, André Armangaud, and Jacques Dupâquier, *Histoire générale de la population mondiale* (Paris: Éditions Monchrestien, 1968), 258; "What Length of Life Did our Fourbears Have?," *Population and Society* 380 (June 2002): 1, http://ined.fr/en/publications/pop_soc/bdd/publications/474/, accessed March 20, 2010.

45. Marriages on January 27, 1807, and November 21, 1816, respectively (AD Eure-et-Loir online, 3E064/8, view 8, and 3E064/9, view 254).

46. Marriage on January 24, 1809 (AD Eure-et-Loir online, 3E098/5 [EC Chérisy, Year 9 (1809)], views 358–59). Two of his children were stillborn, two lived less than one day, one less than a week, and the last died in his ninth year. 3E007/10 (EC Anet, 1814–19), view 291, and 3E0071/11 (1820–26), views 77 and 242; 3E064/8 (EC Bû, 1807–1809), views 156–57, and 3E064/8bis (1810–12), view 101; 3E321/6 (EC Rouvres, 1813–15), view 17, and 3E321/7 (1816–25), view 6.

47. *Deffenseur de la patrie,* 22 Nivôse Year 5 (January 11, 1797), AD Eure-et-Loir online, 3E064/5, view 265; *garde champêtre,* 19 Prairial Year 7 (June 7, 1799) and 3 Nivôse Year 12 (December 24, 1802), 3E064/6, view 20 and 3E064/7, view 7.

48. To Elizabeth Midy, sometime before 1797, during his service in the army; to Marguerite Flore Dubreuil on December 2, 1818 (AD Eure-et-Loir online, 3E064/9, view 381).

49. The duc de Penthièvre's daughter was Louise Marie Adélaïde de Bourbon, widow of Philippe-Égalité and mother of the future King Louis-Philippe.

50. *Garde forestier* in 1815–18 (AD Eure-et-Loir online, 3E373/11 [EC Senonches, 1815–20], view 11 and 3E413/3 [EC La Ville-aux-Nonains, an 12 (1822)], view 175); *journalier* in 1824 (3E064/10 [EC Bû 1820–27], view 236); *garde champêtre* at the marriage of two daughters in Houdan, in 1835 and 1838 (AD Yvelines online, 1134389, view 180 and 113490/1, views 42–43).

51. The fourth generation (b. 1882–99) was too young at the end of the century to have been indicated with an occupation in pre-1902 état-civil registers.

52. AD Cher, 3E0268 online (RP Plou, BMS 1731–69, 416), view 215. Much of the information for this case was collected by the novelist Françoise Chandernagor and her father, direct descendents of Charles François and was kindly provided by her in a letter dated January 12, 2008.

53. AD Indre-et-Loire en ligne (RP Saint-Germain, Bourgueil, BMS 1771), view 12.

54. On Bussy, see Alfred Martineau, *Bussy et l'Inde française, 1720–1785* (Paris: Société de l'histoire des colonies françaises and Librairie Ernest Leroux, 1935).

55. Martineau, *Bussy et l'Inde française,* 235.

56. The log of the *Lys* upon which Dumersan came does not indicate Bengale's presence, even though the Black domestic of another passenger is listed (Service historique de la Marine, Lorient, Cie des Indes, roles d'équipages, 1/P/190a, January–June 1752). However, Lorient's logs, while indicating Black passengers, do not always indicate Indian ones.

57. This is the interpretation, to which I subscribe, given to the act by Françoise Chandernagor.

58. Crébuchet, Castelnau estate manager, to Bussy, April 26, 1765, AD Cher, 34/J/257 (Fonds Castelnau), fol. 1v.

59. On October 30, 1780, RP Civray, St-Nicolas, BMS 1780–82, fol. 28-v (AD Vienne online, 9E92/3, views 32–33).

60. *Traiteur à Sivray* [*sic*] on an ex libris, post-1789, of a cook book having belonged to Charles François, and at the marriage of a daughter, on October 26, 1808, EC Civray, M 1808, fols 9v-10 (AD Vienne online 9E92/5/3, view 57); "cabaretier" on his testament, signed August 18, 1821, AD Vienne, E/4/74/266 (Et. Jean Serph, Minutes, August–September 1821, no. 480). It is only on the record of his widow's death, on January 8, 1827 (EC Civray, D 1822–27, 9E92/9/2, view 93) that he is listed as "aubergiste" by his son-in-law, who took over the practice. One would assume that the latter sought to raise the family's status on that occasion.

61. *Tisserand* at his marriage, October 26, 1808; *aubergiste* at his mother-in-law's death, in 1827.

62. AD Vienne online, 9E92/11/3 (EC Civray, M 1846–52), views 10–11.

63. AD Vienne online, 9E92/24/1 (EC Civray, M 1883–87), view 28.

64. July 21, 1813, AD Vienne online, 9E92/8/1 (EC Civray, M 1813–20), views 9–10.

65. November 7, 1834 AD Vienne online, 9E92/11/1 (EC Civray, M 1833–1839), view 38.

66. Françoise Chandernagor's letter, January 12, 2008.

67. November 16, 1814, AD Vienne online, 9E92/8/1 (EC Civray, M 1813–20), views 26–27.

68. AD Vienne online, 9E92/8/1, views 26–27.

69. Françoise Chandernagor's letter, January 12, 2008, and various E.C. records.

70. Françoise Chandernagor's letter, January 12, 2008.

71. *Garde particulier* from 1851 to his death (see AD Vienne, 8 M 3/34, Recensement Civray 1851, and various E.C. records); Mayor of Civray to Prefect of Vienne, September 18, 1861 (photocopy provided by Françoise Chandernagor).

72. "André Chandernagor," *Wikipedia*, https://fr.wikipedia.org/wiki/Andre_Chandernagor, accessed April 1, 2012.

73. Biography of Françoise Chandernagor at http://www.francoisechandernagor.com, accessed May 5, 2012.

74. Pierre H. Boulle and Sue Peabody, *Le droit des noirs en France au temps de l'esclavage, textes choisis et commentés* (Paris: L'Harmattan, 2014), 187–88.

75. On the General's family, see Robert Landru, *À propos d'Alexandre Dumas: les aïeux, le general, le bailli, premiers amis* (Vincennes, n.p., 1977). On the General himself, see Bernard Gainot, *Les officiers de couleur dans les armées de la République et de l'Empire, 1792–1815* (Paris: Karthala, 2007), 139–47, and Tom Reiss's commercially titled but well-researched biography, *Black Count: Glory, Revolution, Betrayal, and the Real Count of Monte Cristo* (New York: Broadway Paperbacks, 2012).

76. There's a substantial literature, to which I do not entirely subscribe, that differentiates the essence of eighteenth century "color prejudice" from that of nineteenth century "scientific racism."

77. Pierre Caron, *Paris pendant la Terreur: Rapports des agents secrets du Ministre de l'intérieur*, 7 vols. (Paris: H. Champion, 1910–78), 3:333.

78. Quote from Françoise Chandernagor's letter, January 12, 2008.

79. *Classes laborieuses, classes dangereuses* (Paris: Plon, 1958; repr. Livre de Poche, 1978).

5

By Land or By Sea

Marins Indigènes and Maritime Economies of Race and Labor

MINAYO NASIALI

Near the end of the First World War, Ibrahim Ishmaa'il "heard of a place called Europe, which was [on] the other side of Djibouti."[1] Ishmaa'il was born near Laas-qorai, an old East African coastal city in what was, at the time, British Somaliland. For much of his youth Ishmaa'il travelled widely on the Red Sea and Indian Ocean, working as a sailor aboard Arab-owned dhows. But in 1919 Ishmaa'il decided to travel to Marseille, where he had heard that "life was easier, wages being higher."[2] From Djibouti, the main port of the French colony La Côte Française des Somalis, Ish-maa'il stowed away aboard a ship "transporting creole soldiers."[3] Once in Marseille he joined a community of sailors from Djibouti, other parts of Africa, and southern Yemen who sought work aboard French cargo and passenger steamships. Although Ishmaa'il was technically part of the British Empire, he nonetheless applied for and somehow received French identification papers. Somali sailors in Marseille had advised him that it was easier to get hired aboard a French ship with French papers. During his years at sea, Ishmaa'il journeyed throughout the French and British empires, calling at diverse ports including Marseille, Algiers, Cardiff, and Aden. He worked mostly as a stoker or trimmer (*chauffeur* or *soutier*) and his job was to shovel coal and stoke the fires in the boiler rooms of the steamships that transported the world's peoples and goods. As a merchant mariner his life was fundamentally shaped by movement. The ships on which he served followed sea routes that crisscrossed imperial borders and left littoral boundaries altogether for open water. Ishmaa'il's labor on board these ships was integral to shaping a system of global circulation and trade that defined the first part of the twentieth century.[4]

But there were also limitations to Ishmaa'il's mobility. His maritime trajectories and those of other colonial sailors were circumscribed by racialized systems of labor.[5] A widespread, and racist, assumption within the European shipping industry was that sailors from colonial Africa and the Red Sea region were best suited to toiling in the stokehold—where temperatures often rose to 140 degrees Fahrenheit—because they could better withstand the heat and hazardous conditions than their white European counterparts.[6] Shipping companies also maintained that sailors of color were not proficient at other forms of shipboard labor, which meant that these mariners competed with each other for a limited number of boiler room jobs.[7] In the case of France's largest shipping company, the Messageries Maritimes, not only did it institute labor practices that limited sailors of color to working in the stokehole, it also ranked their competency as chauffeurs and soutiers in racial terms. For its Red Sea and Indian Ocean routes, the Messageries Maritimes preferred to hire Yemeni sailors out of British-controlled Aden over Somali sailors out of French Djibouti, claiming that "Arab" seafarers were more capable than "Black" ones.

For the Messageries Maritimes, being French was not an important prerequisite for working on company vessels as it frequently hired non-French sailors out of foreign ports and also employed sailors with questionable work papers. By contrast, proving one's Frenchness was important for the French imperial state and for metropolitan sailor unions. In the 1910s French maritime officials partnered with syndicates on the mainland to develop race-based regulations aimed at protecting and privileging the labor of white French sailors. These policies helped to construct labor institutions that privileged Frenchness and whiteness within the Marine Marchande.

Shipping companies and the French state thus constructed two somewhat distinct and often conflicting systems of labor that were both premised on a racialized hierarchy of work. Importantly, colonial sailors developed strategies for circumnavigating these systems. To improve their chances of getting hired aboard ships flying French flags, colonial sailors from diverse provenances claimed to be French. Many did so by participating in alternative economies and trading in fraudulent work papers, often with the tacit support of shipping companies. Some mariners highlighted their wartime service to the *patrie*. Others capitalized on legal loopholes that governed how the French imperial state defined citizenship and subjecthood.

As sailors like Ishmaa'il jumped from port to port, they formed a highly mobile and diverse workforce. They also cultivated robust networks, relying on friends, family, or on local officials to acquire necessary work permits and identification papers. According to Ishmaa'il: "Since it is by his papers that a man is judged and I had lost mine in Djibouti, a Somali friend gave me his own."[8] Depending on the origin of the ship on which they sought work, sailors exchanged one nationality or subject status for another. Counterfeit, borrowed, or illegally obtained documents were fungible commodities that could be traded as part of alternative maritime economies. From the 1920s until just after World War II, Djibouti emerged as a key hub and central marketplace for sailors in search of French papers.

Djibouti was the main port city of La Côte Française des Somalis and it had grown since the late-nineteenth century into an important coaling station for French ships traveling through the Suez Canal, along the East Coast of Africa, and into the Indian Ocean. Its main competitor was British-controlled Aden in what is now southern Yemen.[9] The French and British, along with the Portuguese and Dutch before them, were relative newcomers to these waters as Arab, East African, and Southeast Asian merchants had historically dominated these maritime trade routes.[10] By the end of the 1930s Djibouti was the French colonial capital of a region that had been divided into three distinct imperial domains. The French, the British, and the Italians all laid claim to a section of what they called Somaliland. Importantly, these new territories also created opportunities to transgress colonial boundaries. As a critical port and gateway from the Red Sea to the Indian Ocean, Djibouti was a significant point of departure for sailors from the horn of Africa and from Aden.

While some sailors, like Ishmaa'il, tapped into kinship networks to obtain papers, others looked to local colonial and maritime officials. According to a memo from the French Ministry of Colonies, maritime authorities in Djibouti often issued work permits "to *chauffeurs* and *soutiers* without conducting the most basic of checks to ascertain the nationality of applicants."[11] The same report claimed that many of the sailors embarking from Djibouti "are not even from the French colony, but are British and Italian Somalis" or from Aden.[12] Ishmaa'il, for example, was officially a British colonial subject and had travelled overland across the border to reach Djibouti before stowing away to Marseille.

Authorities from metropolitan France turned a critical eye on the Djibouti Inscription Maritime, the local office where mariners registered as sailors and received their work papers, known as *livrets*. According to officials at the Ministry of Colonies, the Djibouti Inscription maritime was at best "poorly organized, poorly supervised, and negligent."[13] It was widely rumored that the Djibouti office was corrupt and that its employees accepted bribes as a matter of course in exchange for issuing livrets.

The Djibouti Inscription Maritime was part of a decentralized system in which local bureaus around the French empire maintained control over sailor registration rolls. Interestingly, this practice had its roots in the very foundation of the French merchant navy, which was created by Jean-Baptiste Colbert in 1669 as part of a series of reforms intended to empower the absolutist state.[14] Although Colbert was committed to creating strong, centralized institutions, the maritime system he developed depended on regional offices in port cities to register seamen.[15]

In the 1930s authorities from mainland France introduced new reforms they hoped could bring the Djibouti Inscription Maritime to heel. In 1931 a new decree specified that "all *indigènes* hired out of Djibouti on a French boat," regardless of nationality, had to first register with the *commissaire de police*.[16] After submitting to a rigorous examination, if a sailor was determined to be part of the French Empire his work permit would be affixed with "a large tricolor sticker."[17] Almost immediately, however, these red, white, and blue ribbons became another commodity on the black market. It was relatively easy for sailors in search of the right papers to bribe a local official or otherwise illicitly obtain the sticker and place it on their sailor's book.[18]

In 1938 another attempt was made to fix the problem of lax control at the Djibouti office. According to the decree of September 13, "All *marins indigènes* who are French subjects must apply for a new type B *livret* before becoming eligible to be hired onboard a merchant vessel."[19] According to the new order, sailors from the Côte Française des Somalis needed to completely reregister and replace their old livret with a new one. The lengthy process entailed presenting to authorities "a certificate of good moral standing, a residency certificate, proof of a clear police record. . . . and two photographs." [20] While French authorities had hoped this policy change would ameliorate the problem of the thriving illicit market in counterfeit documents, "confusion and irregularity continued to reign" for much of the 1930s at the Djibouti Inscription Maritime.[21]

The start of the Second World War also negatively affected efforts to regularize sailors' identity and work papers. For the duration of the conflict, all efforts to oversee the Djibouti office effectively ceased. After the war merchant mariners, including Somali and Yemeni sailors, continued to produce whatever identification and work permits they had at hand. In the late 1940s some were using livrets issued immediately after the First World War. Many were using permits with the large tricolor sticker prominently displayed. A few had managed to go through the lengthy reregistration process on the eve of the Second World War and had the new "series B" permits. The result was that merchant mariners had a number of tools at the ready to aid in their efforts to secure employment aboard cargo and passenger ships. For shipping companies more interested in hiring sailors than making sure their papers were in order, the widespread confusion and disarray surrounding the regulation of work permits was more a boon than an impediment to doing business.

Colonial sailors and shipping companies shared a common perspective. Both saw French laws governing nationality and subject status as obstacles that could be circumnavigated. The informal economies that sailors created in order to trade in French documents were often done with the tacit support of shipping companies. The industry preferred to maintain a mobile workforce of sailors who could be easily engaged out of any port. If a sailor fell sick, was injured on the job, or deserted, companies wanted to be able to hire a replacement quickly in order to maintain the shipping schedule and the integrity of the supply chain. Companies were thus willing to look the other way if a sailor's papers did not seem perfectly in order. They also routinely worked with headmen in colonial ports. These local intermediaries were charged with rounding up a certain quota of chauffeurs and soutiers to man the stokehole and they were hired as a unit, not as individuals. On ships' logs these sailors were often not listed by name but grouped together by number under the heading "personnel *indigène*."

While the shipping industry wanted an unregulated work force, French metropolitan sailor unions demanded new laws to protect the jobs and pensions of their members, who were overwhelmingly white and from the mainland.[22] In the 1910s France's largest sailor union, the Fédération nationale des syndicats maritimes (FNSM) launched a campaign in favor of industry-wide changes to labor practices. The FNSM claimed that "foreigners," whom it defined as both non-French nationals and French colonial subjects, were taking French jobs because they were willing to work at lower rates of pay than unionized sailors from the metropole. This agitation ultimately resulted in several new laws that limited the number of foreigners allowed to work aboard French merchant vessels. New legislation also required sailors from French colonies to apply for a special livret that identified them as subjects, not citizens. The FNSM hoped that these regulations would make it more difficult for shipping companies to undercut the labor market by hiring sailors out of foreign ports and out of the colonies. These decrees also served the interests of the French imperial state. As scholars have shown, beginning in the nineteenth century France cultivated new methods for surveilling and classifying its population of citizens and subjects.[23] In the 1920s and 1930s French officials on the mainland were especially concerned about policing the identities of colonial sailors. New labor regulations thus attempted to protect white unionized sailors while simultaneously limiting the mobility of colonial mariners. These regulations thus created a hierarchical labor system that privileged whiteness and Frenchness within the merchant navy.

By contrast, shipping companies generated a distinct system of work that downplayed Frenchness but nonetheless understood shipboard labor in terms of hierarchies of race. The Messageries Maritimes, for example, made labor policies based on racist stereotypes. It limited colonial sailors to working in the engine room and claimed that these employees were best suited to the dangerous conditions below deck. It also ranked the work of the engine room crew based on assumptions about their racial difference. In internal memos and in correspondence with French government officials, the Messageries Maritimes asserted that Arab sailors were better than Somali ones. Since the opening of the Suez Canal, the Messageries Maritimes preferred to hire sailors out of British-controlled Aden rather than from French Djibouti.[24] Somali sailors, the company claimed, were "mediocre mariners" and Arab sailors "constitute the personnel of choice."[25] According to a government memo analyzing Messageries Maritimes hiring practices, the company preferred Arabs because they were "white of Semitic origin" while "Somalis are of the Black race."[26]

State authorities, in partnership with French unions, tried to maintain one employment system based on a racialized hierarchy of work, while shipping companies generated another. These competing interests posed two distinct sets of limitations for colonial sailors. From the 1930s through the years immediately following the Second World War, they also created opportunities as both Somali and Yemeni sailors devised strategies for claiming they were authentically French.

In the 1930s, at the height of the Great Depression, the state mandated that the Messageries Maritimes had to hire a certain number of sailors from La Côte Française des Somalis or risk losing lucrative government contracts and subsidies.[27] While French authorities still required the majority of sailors working on French boats to come from the mainland, it stipulated that on sea routes serving the Red Sea and Indian Ocean, companies must hire French colonial subjects before they could engage British ones. The Messageries Maritimes attempted to push back at what it saw to be government encroachment on its business practices. Ultimately, however, company executives capitulated and agreed to hire more sailors out of Djibouti. This further incentivized mariners from both Aden and Djibouti to claim they were French subjects.

Somali seafarers declared they were legitimate residents of Djibouti and therefore more deserving of stokehold jobs. They cited two decrees that stipulated the conditions under which residents of the colony could qualify for subjecthood. A set of policies implemented in 1937 and 1939 specified that to attain subject status one had to have lived in La Côte

Française des Somalis "with one's family and have navigated for at least ten years aboard French ships."[28] Or one had to have lived in the colony for ten years "and established oneself in an honest trade."[29] Based on these decrees, Somali sailors claimed that because they—along with their families—were residents of Djibouti and had worked on French ships as productive members of the empire, they had the right to claim French jobs.

The problem was that, according to these same criteria, many sailors originally from Aden or southern Yemen also qualified for French subjecthood. Although many were technically either foreign nationals or subjects of a foreign empire, Yemeni sailors argued that they had settled in Djibouti and had sailed on French ships for years. As one French official explained: "The Arabs retort, not without reason, that it is true that a few of them are foreigners, but that they have lived for numerous years with their families in Djibouti."[30] In fact, since the government decree that the Messageries Maritimes had to hire sailors out of Djibouti, the company had found ways to dodge those regulations. It began to routinely discharge and hire Yemeni sailors out of Djibouti, instead of Aden. This had resulted in a growing community of mariners who lived in Djibouti but were originally from Aden who could make some claim to residency within the French empire.

In the late 1940s and early 1950s representatives from the Amicale des originaires de la Côte Française des Somalis, which was based in both Marseille and Djibouti, protested that Yemeni sailors were still being hired by the Messageries Maritimes in greater numbers than French Somali sailors.[31] According to a report from the Ministry of Colonies, "this accusation was not without grounds."[32] The report specified that despite state requirements that the Messageries Maritimes hire French colonial subjects, "Arabs, without a doubt, are hired more frequently than Somalis on merchant vessels."[33] Members of the Amicale des originaires de la Côte Française des Somalis remained frustrated that Yemeni sailors who they argued "should be considered subjects of foreign powers" were given preference for French jobs.[34]

In response many Yemeni sailors argued that they not only were residents of Djibouti but had also served aboard French ships during both world wars. Their claim to Frenchness was further buttressed by their service to France. One sailor and vocal local leader in Marseille, Radhi Abdoul Gabar, who French officials labelled the "Chef des Arabes," reportedly gathered data on enemy ships and naval activities and had delivered crucial information to Marseille-based members of the resistance during World War II. Because of these activities Gabar had been at grave risk of being "arrested by the Gestapo."[35] According to French officials many other Arab sailors "had fought in both world wars. They had served France . . . Many of them also gave their lives for France which they considered to be their true *patrie*."[36] In other words, because of their wartime service many Yemeni sailors had acted like Frenchmen. They therefore made the case that they especially deserved French boiler rooms jobs because of their sacrifices and loyalty to France.

Somalis also served in both world wars as sailors and soldiers. During the Great War, Le Battalion Somali, which was comprised of about 1,700 men from the Côte Française des Somalis, took part in numerous offensive attacks and served at Verdun.[37] During World War II Somali sailors also served in the Forces Navales de la France libre. Others were conscripted as part of Vichy's Service Travail Obligatoire and were compelled to work as forced laborers in Nazi Germany. Some ended up in concentration camps.[38]

Therefore both Yemeni and Somali sailors claimed that because they resided in Djibouti and because of their wartime service they deserved to be considered French subjects. According to French officials, many did qualify for French subjecthood even though some, particularly sailors originally from Aden or other parts of southern Yemen, were technically subjects of a foreign empire.

This essay has examined how colonial sailors like Ibrahim Ishmaa'il engaged with and circumvented the economic and imperial regimes that employed and monitored them. These seamen did the hazardous work of shoveling coal and stoking fires in the engine rooms of the steamships that transported the world's peoples and goods during the first half of the twentieth century. While shipping companies relied on colonial sailors to power their fleets, they also characterized their labor in racialized terms and sought to keep it unregulated. By contrast, French government officials, in partnership with metropolitan sailor unions, attempted to regulate colonial seafarers by policing their status as colonial subjects. Shipping companies and the French imperial state thus created two competing systems of work that were both premised on racialized and hierarchical understandings of mariners and their labor.

Colonial sailors devised strategies to circumnavigate these systems. Some cultivated alternative economies, others highlighted their wartime service to France and loyalty to the patrie. Some capitalized on changing residency requirements to claim their right to French subjecthood. Each of these examples illustrates how sailors of color understood subjecthood not as an essential category but as a thing that could be traded and exchanged. These examples also illustrate how membership in the French empire was one of many identities harnessed by Black sailors. For example, although Ibrahim Ishmaa'il was from British Somaliland, his very mobility demonstrates how sailors from the horn of Africa and Red Sea region harnessed multiple and shifting identities to navigate across colonial boundaries. Significantly, Ishmaa'il's experiences underscore how notions of race are necessarily constructed and forged in relation to other categories including understandings of maritime labor, nationality, and imperial space.

NOTES

1. Richard Pankhurst (translator of Ibrahim Ishmaa'il's autobiography), "An Early Somali Autobiography," *Africa: Rivista trimestrale di studi e documentazione dell'Istituo italiano per l'Africa et l'Oriente* 32, no. 3 (September 1977): 369.

2. Pankhurst, "An Early Somali Autobiography," 369.

3. Pankhurst, "An Early Somali Autobiography," 368.

4. Most scholarship on maritime labor and capitalism focuses on the early modern period. See for example Markus Rediker, *Between the Devil and the Deep Blue Sea: Merchant Seamen, Pirates, and the Anglo-American Maritime World, 1700–1750* (Cambridge, UK: Cambridge University Press, 1987); Peter Linebaugh and Markus Rediker, *The Many-Headed Hydra: Sailors, Slaves, Commoners, and the Hidden History of the Revolutionary Atlantic* (Boston: Beacon, 2013); Alain Cabantous, *La mer et les hommes: Pêcheurs et matelots dunkerquois de Louis XIV à la Révolution* (Dunkerque, France: Westhoek, 1980); Alain Cabantous and Gilbert Buti, *Etre marin: En Europe occidentale (1550–1850)* (Rennes, France: Presses universitaires de Rennes, 2016); W. Jeffrey Bolster, *Black Jacks: African Ameri-*

can Seamen in the Age of Sail (Cambridge MA: Harvard University Press, 1998). Several studies of global trade and colonial sailors during the age of steam do exist but focus mainly on the British empire: Gopalan Balachandran, *Globalizing Labour?: Indian Seafarers and World Shipping, c. 1870–1945* (Oxford, UK: Oxford University Press, 2012); Mohammad Siddique Seddon, *The Last of the Lascars: Yemeni Muslims in Britain 1836–2012* (Markfield, UK: Kube, 2014). For a twentieth-century history of the European merchant marines with particular focus on the elite networks of agents and executives who headed the industry, see Michael B. Miller, *Europe and the Maritime World: A Twentieth Century History* (Cambridge, UK: Cambridge University Press, 2012).

5. For analysis of racialized systems of labor and hierarchical forms of work, see Laura Tabili, "'Keeping the Natives under Control': Race Segregation and the Domestic Dimensions of Empire (1920–1939)" *International and Working-Class History* 4 (Fall 1993): 64–78; Laura Tabili, *We Ask for British Justice: Workers and Racial Difference in Late Imperial Britain* (Ithaca NY: Cornell University Press, 1994).

6. On racist stereotypes about colonial sailors, see Balachandran, *Globalizing Labour?*. For descriptions of conditions in the stokehold, see Alston Kennerly, "Stoking the Boilers: Firemen and Trimmers in British Merchant Ships, 1850–1950," *International Journal of Maritime History* 20, no. 1 (June 2008): 191–220; David Simpson et al, "Firemen, Trimmers and Stokers," http://www .barrymerchantseamen.org.uk/articles/bmsfiretrim.html, accessed March 5, 2020.

7. For a discussion of colonial sailors and technical expertise, see Minayo Nasiali, "An Inconvenient Expertise: French Colonial Sailors and Technological Knowledge in the Union Française," *French Politics, Culture, & Society* 37, no. 1 (Spring 2019): 117–38. For scholarship examining the categories of expertise, gender, class, and race, see Anne Game and Rosemary Pringle, *Gender at Work* (North Sydney, Australia: Allen and Unwen, 1938); Harry Braveman, *Labor and Monopoly Capital: The Degradation of Work in the Twentieth Century* (New York: Monthly Review, 1974); Laura Ann Twagira, "Robot Farmers and Cosmopolitan Workers: Technological Masculinity and Agricultural Development in the French Soudan (Mali), 1945–68," *Gender & History* 26, no. 3 (November 2014): 459–77; Robyn D'Avignon, "Making 'Artisanal' Miners: Nature, Knowledge and Subterranean History in Senegal" (Ph.D. diss., University of Michigan, 2016).

8. Pankhurst, "An Early Somali Autobiography," 371.

9. Edward A. Alpers, "The Somali Community at Aden in the Nineteenth Century," *Northeast African Studies* 8, nos. 2–3 (1986): 143–49.

10. For scholarship on Red Sea and Indian Ocean maritime communities and commerce, see Janet J. Ewald, "Crossers of the Sea: Slaves, Freedmen, and other Migrants in the Northwestern Indian Ocean, c. 1750–1914," *American Historical Review* 105, no. 1 (February 2000): 69–91; Sanjay Subrahmanyam, *Empires*

between *Islam and Christianity, 1500–1800* (Albany: State University of New York Press, 2019); Jonathan Miran, *Red Sea Citizens: Cosmopolitan Society and Cultural Change in Massawa* (Bloomington: Indiana University Press, 2009); K. N. Chaudhuri, *Trade and Civilisation in the Indian Ocean: History from the Rise of Islam to 1750* (Cambridge UK: Cambridge University Press, 1985); K. McPherson, *The Indian Ocean: A History of People and the Sea* (Oxford, UK: Oxford University Press, 1993).

11. Enquête sur la Condition des navigateurs originaires des territoires d'outre-mer résidant à Marseille, Rapport no. 2, Ministre des colonies, April 30, 1946, Archives Nationale d'Outre-mer (ANOM) IAFFPOL 3708, 7.

12. Enquête sur la Condition des navigateurs originaires, 5.

13. Enquête sur la Condition des navigateurs originaires, 6.

14. For scholarship on the French maritime communities and the Marine Marchande, see Alain Cabantous, *Dix mille marins face à l'Océan: Les populations maritimes de Dunkerque au Havre aux XVIIe et XVIIIe siècles (vers 1650–1794): étude sociale* (Paris: Editions Publisud, 1991); John Barzman, "Travail et travailleurs maritimes XVIIIe–XXe siècle," *Revue d'histoire maritime* 18 (2014/1); Michel Vergé-Franceschi and Eric Rieth, *La France maritime au temps de Louis XIV* (Paris: du Layer, 2001); Marie-Françoise Berneron-Couvenhes, Bernard Cassagnou, Jean-Pierre Poussou, and Michel Vergé-Franceschi, *La marine marchande française de 1850 à 2000* (Paris: Presses de l'Université Paris-Sorbonne, 2006); Bernard Cassagnou, *Les Grandes Mutationes de la Marine marchande francaise (1945–1995)*, *vols. 1–2* (Paris: Comité pour l'histoire économique et financière de la France, 2002).

15. Indeed the pension system Colbert instituted for the Marine Marchande served as an important precursor that helped lay the foundation for the modern welfare state. Even today, records for merchant mariners are not located in the National Archives at Pierefitte, which contains the records of the Marine Marchande, but mostly in departmental repositories around France.

16. Enquête sur la Condition des navigateurs originaires, 7–8.

17. Enquête sur la Condition des navigateurs originaires, 7–8.

18. Enquête sur la Condition des navigateurs originaires, 7–8.

19. Enquête sur la Condition des navigateurs originaires, 7–8.

20. Enquête sur la Condition des navigateurs originaires, 7–8.

21. Enquête sur la Condition des navigateurs originaires, 8.

22. For scholarship on French maritime syndicalism, see Ronan Viaud, *Le Syndicalisme maritime française: Les organisations, les hommes, les luttes (1890–1950)* (Rennes, France: Presses Universitaires de Rennes, 2005); John Barzman, *Dockers, métallos, ménagères: mouvements sociaux et cultures militantes au Havre 1912–1923* (Rouen, France: Presses Universitaires de Rouen et du Havre, 1997).

23. For studies of governmentality and French methods for classifying citizens and subjects, see Clifford Rosenberg, *Policing Paris: The Origins of Modern Immigra-*

tion Control between the Wars (Ithaca NY: Cornell University Press, 2006); Mary Dewhurst Lewis, *The Boundaries of the Republic: Migrant Rights and the Limits of Universalism in France, 1918–1940* (Stanford CA: Stanford University Press, 2007); Jacques Donzelot, *The Policing of Families* (New York: Pantheon, 1979).

24. Laleh Khalili, *Sinews of War and Trade: Shipping and Capitalism in the Arabian Peninsula* (London: Verso, 2020), 229.

25. Enquête sur la Condition des navigateurs originaires, 6.

26. Enquête sur la Condition des navigateurs originaires, 2, 6.

27. Note au sujet des embarquements de marins indigènes à bord des navires des Messageries Maritimes, August 6, 1937, ANOM SLOTFOM 3, 41.

28. Enquête sur la Condition des navigateurs originaires, 5.

29. Enquête sur la Condition des navigateurs originaires, 5.

30. Enquête sur la Condition des navigateurs originaires, 4.

31. Lettre de l'Amicale des originaires de la Cote Francaise des Somalis à Monsieur le préfet des Bouches du Rhone, February 6, 1953, 1 AFFPOL 3708 Archives d'Outre-Mer. See also Un lettre du Ministre de la France d'Outre-Mer à Monsieur le Chef du Service des Affaires Sociales, objet: Demande de secours de l'Amicale des originaires de La Côte Française des Somalis, July 2, 1952, ANOM 1AFFPOL 3708; Un lettre du Ministre de la France d'Outre-Mer à Monsieur le Gouverneur de la Côte Française des Somalis, objet: L'association Amicale des Originaires de la Côte Française des Somalis, September 24, 1952, ANOM 1AFFPOL 3708; Amicale des originaires de La Côte Française des Somalis, Remaniement des statuts, 1952, ANOM 1 AFFPOL 3408.

32. Enquête sur la Condition des navigateurs originaires, 4–5.

33. Enquête sur la Condition des navigateurs originaires, 5–6.

34. Enquête sur la Condition des navigateurs originaires, 4. See also Renseignement des Originaires de la Cote Francaise des Somalis, SLOTFOM, May 7, 1958, ANOM 1AFFPOL 3708.

35. Enquête sur la Condition des navigateurs originaires, 4–5.

36. Enquête sur la Condition des navigateurs originaires, 4–5.

37. Philippe Oberlé, *Afars et Somalis: Le dossier de Djibouti* (Paris: Editions Présence Africaine, 1971), 104.

38. Enquête sur la Condition des navigateurs originaires, 4, 9.

6

"A Woman Like Any Other"

The Intimacy of Dislocation in Early Twentieth-Century Paris and Rufisque

JENNIFER ANNE BOITTIN

After World War I Roberte Horth made her way from French Guiana to Paris via ship to prepare the prestigious *agrégation* exam in philosophy. The move inspired the twenty-seven-year-old Horthe to write a very perceptive short story titled "Une histoire sans importance/A thing of no importance."[1] In it she explored the disarticulation that Black women felt when their independent, intelligent existences were confronted with the external eroticization of their bodies, a dislocation they felt was accentuated both by their skin color and by their relative isolation as women of color, who were a minority among minorities in the French metropole. In this diasporic space Horth and other Black women felt torn. She reacted by publishing her short story in 1932 in *La Revue du monde noir/The Review of the Black World*, a bilingual literary, cultural, and political journal that helped to generate the Négritude movement, a political and cultural statement of race consciousness most associated with Aimé Césaire, Léon-Gontran Damas, and Léopold Sédar Senghor. "A thing of no importance" tells the story of a young woman named Léa, whose path in many ways mirrors Horth's own.

Roberte Horth concludes her brief almost anthropological exploration of Léa, a character who was also a student in Paris, with this powerful summation: "One might excuse 'narrow minded people, dead souls, shut up in their little worlds' for considering [Léa] as only a fetish, but that the best of them while opening wide the doors of their spiritual treasure should guard closely those of their hearts; that they should flatter and cajole her in their drawing-rooms and not dare to accept her into the intimacy of their homes like any other young woman . . . , that passed understanding. In this country, [Léa] will never be a woman like any other, with a right to a woman's happiness."[2]

Like Horth in her short story, this chapter explores some of the ways Black migrant women in the French empire wrote about sex (or the lack thereof) and its links to love, intimacy, and comfort. There is surprising continuity in how autonomous and cosmopolitan women negotiated sexuality and its ties to race consciousness and mobility in two urban spaces that tethered the French empire to the Black Atlantic: Paris, France, and Rufisque, Senegal. Women who moved through diasporic channels displayed an extraordinary independence of mind and body. But they were also forever on display.[3] I will not be discussing the already very well-known images in the shadows of which Black women labored, their most famous renditions captured by the extraordinary performances of race and sexuality created by the American singer, dancer, actress, and businesswoman Josephine Baker.[4] Instead, I ask: how did African women and women of African descent speak of their own sexuality? How did they write of pleasure and in so doing challenge racial and gendered hierarchies? How, finally, did women such as Léa and her creator, Horth, react when other people and popular culture constructed them as sexual beings?[5] Women countered with their own definitions of intimacy, often by challenging or overturning presumed norms regarding proper behavior and by establishing connections with other women whose experiences were similar. For if Horth's short story is about race-fueled objectification, it is also one woman's attempt to address what it means for a body to be eroticized publicly and also ignored as part of a deeper and more complete intimacy. Lea was sexualized in public but felt alienated from the more complete intimacy of private pleasures, leading her to conclude that she cannot be a "woman like any other." In short, via Lea, Horth explored how mobility, for example the act of traveling and of moving socioculturally, could inspire women to critique supposedly fixed categories, such as that of "woman," as they related to sex, race, and intimacy.[6]

The intimacy of sex as it relates to race is difficult to trace.[7] As Matt Houlbrook puts it: "How much do you know about the sex lives of your family or closest friends? . . . Turn to the past, and such silences grow more deafening."[8] When turning to the past we also face the non-negligible issue of how to avoid imposing categories and labels, such as homosexual, that have both lost and gained in fluidity or meaning over time, especially when historical actors did not choose explicitly to identify themselves in any particular way.[9] Michelle Wright and Antje Schumann remind us that Black sexuality is generally "framed by two extremes, a hypermasculinity that is always Black and a hyperfemininity that is always white," leaving the far more prevalent in-betweens, including the questioning of "woman" articulated by Horth, to be more difficult to trace.[10] In turning to the French empire's past, sex can be found to pierce the silences during moments of mobility. These instances provoked some women to write of race in relation to sex. Mobility within the French empire thus acted as a mirror of sorts and as a provocation inviting women to self-reflect upon their own desires and to contest the manner in which others sexed them. This self-reflection is present not only in autobiography-infused fiction written and published in Paris but also in archival dossiers filled with letters women wrote to and from Rufisque. Although they feature very different types of writing, both illuminate how movement through the French empire helped women think through components of their sexual identities. Among other things, the archetypes of the supposed hypermasculinity of the majority male Black migrants of Paris and the supposed hyperfemininity of the bourgeois white ideals of womanhood taught to Black students in Rufisque provoked some women to challenge their experiences and expectations of intimacy. Instead of these extremes, they saw an interlocking system of material and sentimental attachments that went hand-in-hand with sex.

Intimacy, here, serves as a term that moves us past sex and domesticity as they relate to power structures.[11] Intimacy often serves as a more sophisticated synonym for sex, which is certainly part of what Horth meant when she claimed that she would never be "a woman like any other" and lamented that she could not seem to find heartfelt companionship with a partner. Yet sex is too often studied, especially when it comes to people originally from the Global South, as all about power and thus separate from the emotional and communal ties that allow people to feel they belong in a particular space or time.[12] Largely absent from such studies of sex is a broader sense of community. After all, when Black women expressed angst at the idea that they might never have the "right to a woman's happiness," they were sharing that emotion with an audience. Letters preserved in archives were intended for a private audience and published texts for a broad public. In both cases, this audience included other Black women who heard in such expressions of or yearnings for sexuality an opportunity: intimacy, if not always with the partners they sought then at the very least with a supportive, race-conscious network of women, could help to foster belonging. Here, then, the term intimacy signals how independently mobile women created ties when they talked about sex and race and thus in part overcame the isolation that migratory travels might otherwise foster. The first part of this chapter explores the work women did to belong in Paris via their literary musings, and the second part turns to archivally preserved oral expressions of what historian Todd Shepard has termed "sex talk." This sex talk created a sense of community among a group of young women from around West Africa who gathered at a school in Rufisque.

Transatlantic Mobility and Desire in Paris

There was a tension for travelers such as Léa and the author of the short story, Horth, and in particular for those who sought to establish a more permanent and embedded contact with other cultures, not only between race and gender but also between independence and sex. In *Black Skin, White Masks* Frantz Fanon famously considered how the "main preoccupation" of Antillean men of color "on setting foot in France was to sleep with a white woman. Barely off the ship in Le Havre, they head for the bordellos. Once they have achieved this ritual of initiation into 'authentic' manhood, they take the train to Paris."[13] While Fanon offers a somewhat conventional analysis of a positively framed male virility, he also raises the important question of how mobility within the Empire provoked and defined men's desires. After all, these men's end goal was not having sex with a white woman in the brothel but reaching the city of Paris.

Intraimperial movement also helped to shape intersections between gender and sexuality for Black migrant women who, like men, wrestled with movement and desire. Even in mainland France where interracial sex was never illegal and did not provoke the extreme violence of lynching, administrators paid close attention to white women who slept and loved across the color line, actions that occasionally caused interracial skirmishes.[14] Administrators also watched Black women who were recruited as performers during the Colonial Exposition in Paris in 1931. Observers assumed a woman from Madagascar who entered a room with a partner and then closed the door behind them was in the business of sex rather than pursuing independent, unpaid, and perhaps even pleasurable sex.[15] This assumption regarding material gain was common not only for white administrators but also for Black men who watched how and with whom women had sex or formed affective ties. While sometimes they construed the Black woman as victim, in other venues she was an agent, just not a particularly likable one. For example, one pamphlet circulating in interwar Paris noted of colonization in Africa that "each night the European 'civilizers' also organize drinking bouts and orgies, kidnapping young *négresses* and seducing married women."[16] The text simultaneously references rape and seduction, with the word "seducing" implying some degree of complicity on the part of African women. In a similar vein, in the novel *Banjo* the American Harlem Renaissance writer Claude McKay's character Ray, based in Marseille, summarizes the Black woman in harsh terms: "She is cast in a passive role and she worships the active success of man and rewards it with her body," adding, "If she is not inhibited by race feeling she'll give herself to the white man because he stands for power and property. Property controls sex."[17] Ray contends in his Marxist and masculinist analysis that women of color are universally subject to a gendered power dynamic in which they succumb to masculinity in its most domineering construction. Black women travelers were perceived as unable to control their desires when offered material gain and thus reduced to eroticism by both European culture and media and Black men. In one of Léopold Sédar Senghor's more famous poems, "Femme noire," written in France between 1934 and 1937, he used the sensuality of nude African women's bodies to convey his ideas about universalism. Lines such as "Firm-fleshed ripe fruit, sombre raptures of black wine, mouth making lyrical my mouth" focus the reader's attention on the corporeal rather than the intellectual dimensions of the Black woman in these early cogitations of a key Négritude writer.[18]

Some women confronted the images and interpretations of their sexuality that media, popular culture, white administrators, and Black men all constructed by turning to a literary format that among other things had the capacity to shield them even as they spoke of potentially delicate questions. In a different vein from Horth, in 1924 the Guadeloupean writer Suzanne Lacascade, who was living in Paris when her novel was published, considered the influence of mobility on sex and race in *Claire-Solange: âme africaine* (*Claire-Solange: African Soul*). Lacascade tells the story of a *métis* woman from the Caribbean who accompanies her white French father to Paris. In some ways the novel is a conventional love story: while in Paris Claire-Solange meets her aunt-in-law's white godson, Jacques Danzel, but Claire-Solange is so busy dreaming of returning to her beloved Caribbean that she does not see his potential as a marital partner until it is almost too late. She comes to understand the nature of her feelings for him only after he enlists voluntarily at the beginning of World War I. The story is, as others have argued, an early example of Négritude thinking that predates Césaire, Damas, and Senghor and that is made all the more mysterious by how little we know about its author.[19] The novel's traditional storyline nonetheless bends past (and present) notions of gender and sexuality. Claire-Solange is a woman who takes control of her own path when she accepts that desire (and thus sex) is an essential dimension of love and that Blackness is an essential dimension of her French identity.

Claire-Solange receives a warm welcome in Paris from her father's white family, yet she refuses, out of respect for her Black mother, to attenuate her bold race consciousness while in their presence. She takes pride in the term *"mulâtresse française"* (French mulatto), claiming it publicly even after she is mistaken for Spanish rather than Black.[20] When her aunt challenges Claire-Solange's self-description as *nègre*, she points to her features, including "my frizzy hair," "the angle of my face," and "the supple hips," concluding that "to repudiate my African origin I would have to live beneath a veil."[21] When her father, who is very proud of his daughter's race consciousness, suggests in an attempt to smooth over family relations that she "allow your fighting instincts to rest, in France color matters so little," she reminds him that "my ancestors have been fighting for the cause of color for over a century."[22] Claire-Solange declares pride in her complex heritage, explaining to her aunt: "My passion? . . . To defend, glorify, the black race" for "I am African," a heritage she claims on the basis of slavery.[23]

Although she references slavery, she is not overtly anticolonial, instead arguing that colonial life has the potential to lead white administrators to promote universalism and a common humanity. It is through this lens of universalism that we can start to understand how a character so filled with pride and race consciousness allows her passion for the white man Jacques Danzel to blossom. When Jacques is described throughout the novel, it is not following the traditionally celebrated elements of masculinity. One of Claire-Solange's Guadeloupean relatives explains that "this young man so taken with women's hearsay, this male gossip . . . can never be admirable or deserving of pity," the two qualities that might cause an African woman to fall in love with him.[24] The war changes everything, however, allowing Claire-Solange to see Jacques as truly masculine for the first time when the supposedly effeminate man immediately enlists: "I understood my man's worth only the day of general mobilization."[25] Shortly thereafter she starts to desire him, in particular after witnessing a kiss between two anonymous wartime lovers, a kiss so intimate and passionate that it leaves Claire-Solange feeling cold because it reminds her of the unbearable distance of the man she so desires. Yet when Jacques returns from the war mutilated, he refuses to believe she truly loves him, reading her newfound sympathy as pity rather than desire.

To convince Danzel that she does not pity him, Claire-Solange returns to her race consciousness and her African roots, the very ones that early in the novel made Jacques seem like an impossible partner. She explains that what he dismisses as mere pity, "I give it to you, dear, replete with warm sun, perfumed, burning with passion." What he calls her pity for him, she explains quite differently: "My pity . . . It's a need, a passionate hope for . . . that which you will give me, right? It's a prodigious craving that you, you alone, can quench." Her final declaration of love is also a declaration of sexual self-awareness, one made possible by her time spent in Paris, far from the Caribbean she so loves. She hopes it will convince him that she wants him as a lover and that his virility is intact even though he is maimed and white. Danzel tries to respond with a joke until he realizes that, very simply, "she was offering every bit of herself, lost in her immense and marvelous love, the unique love of an African woman."[26] Indeed, if there are early elements of Négritude in this novel, it is in part because an Antillean woman repeatedly references her African identity. This bold sign of support for Black internationalism was rarely articulated by Antilleans in the interwar years.[27] But Claire-Solange also comes to the realization during the war that both metropolitan and colonial France must work together, leading her to imply that universalism lies in a sort of transcolonial Frenchness. She previously recognized this quality in her white father and she now recognizes it in soldiers from around the Empire, including the colonial soldiers who fought for France and her own Jacques, with whom she can be Antillean, African, and French.[28]

Lacascade thus wrote of a sexual awakening rendered clear in love but defined by her characters' mobility throughout the empire and finally to its capital of Paris. Still, especially because Lacascade was not alone among Black women in using such imagery, it is worth considering why the sensual references in this novel that prefigure Claire-Solange's self-understanding of her desire for Danzel draw upon other Black women's bodies, those of the very women with whom she feels a sense of community, with whom she chats, laughs, and cries. For example, Claire-Solange's aunt Emilienne is a "bromeliad, that thorny exotic plant. The stiff, upright leaves hide the heart. At its flowering, a passerby will discover nothing unless he leans over and looks in, then the blooming can be seen, intimate, and the base of the most tender leaves, on contact, color themselves a virginal rouge."[29] This description could easily be of a vulva, and in other passages women bathing are described in comparably sensual terms. Perhaps more importantly, the character actively seeks out the neighborhood that stretches from Invalides to Montrouge and Porte de Versailles in Paris knowing that she will find other Antillean women and feeling that she can belong there. Lacascade and Horth came closer than many in their community to discussing sex openly. The Martinican sisters Jane and Paulette Nardal, the women today most directly associated with the Négritude movement, only touched upon the question. Jane opened her 1928 article "Pantins exotiques" ("Exotic Puppets") with what was by her standards a relatively explicit reference to Black women's sexuality: "flexible grace has . . . become a sort of sexual poetry, innate in us."[30] Jane Nardal's discussion of sensuality remains largely based in literature and the question of how eroticized images of Black women might affect their control of their own bodies, since they had become "destined to serve as amusement, or to the artistic or sensual pleasure of the white person." Her sister Paulette Nardal also sought to take such sensuous imagery back from both popular culture and men when she incorporated Black women into some of her dynamic descriptions of cultural life in Paris. In "The new *bal nègre* of la Glacière," for example, she describes couples dancing the *biguine*, an Antillean dance. A lone woman who does not seem to have found a man worthy of accompanying her draws Paulette's eye: "she threw herself alone into the dance, arms raised, hips swaying in a sort of rhythmic gallop."[31] Another woman, she writes, "has just entered, rouge-brown complexion, that one senses must be as soft to the touch as silk." The men, however, are merely described as "a lot of Antilleans, Guyanese, Africans and even Abyssinians" who are absent the moving sensations and passion she sees in women.

Black francophone women discussed obliquely not just how their migration placed them on display or kept them from enjoying the pleasures of sex, but also how they were precluded from domesticity more generally. In this approach they identified a matter that scholars are increasingly arguing limits our approaches to studies of sex in the Global South. Emotion and connectivity are just as critical as money and power, but like Claude McKay we tend to focus more on the latter. We know little about Paulette Nardal's personal life (whether she dated, and if she did, whom) and she did not explicitly discuss intimacy in her work in the way that Horth did, even if she did not shy away from sensual imagery. We do know that she celebrated Horth's piece on Léa in her 1932 article titled "Awakening of Race Consciousness." Nardal wrote that "coloured women living alone in the metropolis, until the Colonial Exposition, have certainly been less favoured than coloured men—who are content with a certain easy success. Long before the latter, they have felt the need for a racial solidarity that would not be merely material."[32] In opposition to McKay's Marxist perspective on sex, Nardal replaces materialism with intimacy. She specifically recognized that how one woman in the Black diaspora, Horth, spoke of sex and isolation could be repurposed as the impetus for a powerful unity defined by race and gender: a female-specific race consciousness. The isolation migrant women of the Black diaspora felt was partly a reflection of their objectification and partly a reflection of their domestic lives, which were often those of single women who felt they did not have their male counterparts' "easy success." They turned to other women for their gendered racial consciousness and to create a sense of community. Their discussions of sexual liaisons were discrete, perhaps in part because the blurring between independent single woman and prostitute was such a slippery one throughout the French empire.[33] Descriptions of other Black women's bodies and desires in literature and journalism may also have been a discrete way of thinking through their own. And while they may appear to have simply reflected the portrayals of Black women generated by the men around them, we should not dismiss how generating their own depictions of Black female sensuality gave them control and, given the chronology of these texts, may even have inspired a poem such as Senghor's. Most importantly, we should not dismiss how Horth's illustration of frustration via her character's diasporic longing for intimacy directly inspired Nardal to identify the critical need for community building among Black women and to label that need "race consciousness."

Mobility and Sex in French West Africa

Of course, Black women's migrations were not just transatlantic but also transcontinental in the case of West African women who attended the French school in Senegal known as the École normale de jeunes filles de Rufisque. This institution was supposed to train them to be the first generation of African teachers within the secular French primary school system.[34] The very fact of traveling weeks or in some cases over a month with other young women from their home colony all the way to Senegal generated a certain intimacy among students, one that was reinforced by talk or experiences of sex. The European-generated stereotypes that existed regarding Black women in the metropole pursued them in the colonies as well. Power politics were even more complex overseas, where white men routinely assumed Black women could become their concubines and more rarely their wives and where, if Black women's sexual skills were lauded, sexual assault by the colonizers was a non-negligible threat.[35] Yet even, perhaps especially, in such spaces we must differentiate between the racial and gendered hierarchies colonizers sought to impose and how Black women spoke about their own sexualities as well as how these thoughts in turn impelled them while on the move to create an intimacy that was conscious of race and gender.

When they moved from elsewhere in West Africa to Senegal these Black women overturned several stereotypes. Antillean women traveling to Paris thought about race as part of their isolation in an overwhelmingly white country and within an overwhelmingly masculine Black community in which the complex hierarchies of race that governed Antillean society as a result of centuries of slavery and colonization continued to divide. African women traveling through French West Africa (hereafter AOF) thought about race in other ways. First they considered the differences among various African ethnicities, usually called "races" both in French reports and by Africans themselves. Second, especially when they arrived in the coastal urban centers of Senegal, which had the highest concentrations of white women, to attend schools that aimed to make them more socioculturally French, in the upper-class metropolitan sense, they confronted constructions of whiteness and descriptions of what made a white, French woman. They also spent time with actual white women. That experience in turn led them to think about their own identities within a global construction of race that went beyond West Africa. They recognized race as a feature of colonization that centered skin color as an even more salient element of distinction among persons than geographic origin, language, culture, religion, nation, or class.[36] Mobility thus gave these students the opportunity to consider how white women overseas took on some libidinous stereotypes usually associated with Black women, such as their sexual availability even when married and their inability to control sexual appetites that were supposedly made more voracious in warmer climates, while also leading them to interrogate what made any woman.[37] The very act of chatting about white women's sexuality led to laughter and hence created a bond within classrooms and dormitories that could not be assumed among women whose religions, languages, and cultures did not always easily coexist.[38]

While they laughed as they chatted about white women's sexual adventures, African women also discussed their own sexuality in relation to race, even in a place where race and gender were carefully hierarchized and where scholars have noted that the intimate was extraordinarily political and bodies were sites for encounters and exchanges of power, culture, and knowledge.[39] Thus, like in Paris, mobility appears to have reinforced a sense of intimacy among students that led to a feeling of belonging made possible by a facet of "sex talk," a term encompassing everyday allusions to sex that surface informally. Such talk routinely surfaced in the words and reports of African women who attended the École normale.[40] They were mostly younger than the Antillean women living in Paris. Still, theirs also offers an example of how the invitation to travel from across the unwieldy federation of the AOF to a boarding school in Rufisque revealed thoughts on sex either directly, when they discussed pregnancies and lovers, or indirectly, when superiors questioned their morality. While much of such talk—including informal banter in the dormitory rooms, during breaks between classes, or on lengthy bus rides to and from Rufisque—was unrecorded, some of it has been preserved in writing.

Students were certainly aware of the tiring physical nature of their travels across the AOF, which they had to undertake twice a year around the summer break, and the profound feeling of dislocation that accompanied such travels. Marguerite Thompson, for example, wrote in a letter to the school's director, Germaine Le Goff, that students who left Rufisque, on the coast of Senegal next to Dakar, on July 17, 1941, only arrived in Lomé, a city in their home colony of Togo, on August 16, 1941. Whereas sometimes housing, usually in the form of dorm rooms of some sort, awaited them during their travels, often they were left to their own devices: "In Bobo our fate was not enviable. At first we had no money. And everyday life was so expensive," Thompson wrote in reference to how World War II had caused high food costs.[41] The bulk of their trip took place via train, bus, and truck, but the trip's length was mostly shaped by waiting for the next available bus or truck to turn up at various stopping points along the way. Of the same trip, Frida Lawson wrote back to her director that as they waited for days on end in towns along the way students would "behave very badly," something she deemed "a disgrace!"[42] In fact the young women would claim that they were meeting various and inevitably young male relatives who appeared to have homed in on the arrival of the students' buses during trips to or from their home colonies. The students would then disappear with these men for several hours. To put a stop to this practice, Lawson insisted that all so-called relatives first had to be presented to the entire group of students, who would determine whether the proposed solo excursion was respectable or not. That question of respectability was front and center because as civil servants these women needed to avoid pregnancy and generally maintain a reputation that would allow them to secure a position as a teacher once their studies were complete. Lawson was aware, in part because Le Goff herself emphasized this fact, of the imperative that all of the students meet a higher standard of respectability even than white women. Similar gauges of respectability, defined by heterosexual, European, upper-class moral and bodily norms, have often been used to limit the opportunities available to women of color.[43]

Yet knowing that a higher standard of respectability was expected of them, and even knowing that pregnancy meant their immediate dismissal from school, did not stop young women from having sex, nor did it keep those with less stringent definitions of respectability from sex talk, which in turn served to create intimacy. The details of a case involving a woman whom we shall call Gabriella were revealed during a disciplinary hearing, the participants of which concluded toward the end of their report that: "above all, this student's morality is a deplorable example and a danger for her female companions, over whom Gabriella appears to have acquired influence. . . . [She] maintains clandestine relations with young men, using to this end illicit and unexpected methods."[44] On one hand we have an example of a young woman who managed, much like the young women traveling to and from Rufisque, to find creative ways to pursue physical intimacy with not one but several young men, a series of acts that caused her teachers to label her immoral. More bothersome, however, was the sway that she held over other students. She regaled them with stories of her exploits, and by sharing her techniques for subverting authority and in laughing and joking with fellow students, Gabriella created an intimacy that was dangerous because it undermined French educational officials' push to ensure their schools were viewed as vectors for reason and respectability. Indeed, anytime Le Goff, the school's director, noted overt expressions of sexuality, she intervened as quickly as possible to put an end to both the intimacy between the students and their lovers and the intimacy these encounters generated among students. When another student wrote to her pen pal in France of how "the most languorous tangoes unfolded in bed, between two sheets" at the École normale, the letter was censored and the epistolary connection terminated.[45] In this case the letter did not specify the sexes of the partners in these tangos, thus leaving open the possibility that only women may have been dancing under the covers. When "a gunner of Barguy who for several days had been pursuing one of our older *métisses* with his love" finally succeeded in "penetrating" the school, a word choice that tends more toward the single than the double entendre, Le Goff again quickly intervened to end both the acts and the talk of sex.[46] Students also learned of one another's pregnancies, dismissals from school because of pregnancy, and occasionally of sexual assaults. Thus these young women's physical mobility led not only to an education that culminated in the status of French civil servant, meaning essentially a guaranteed job until retirement, but also led to an intimacy that grounded them while they were far from their homes. As they came into a race consciousness shaped by the knowledge of whiteness they gained while in Senegal, they also came into a gendered consciousness. Both forms of consciousness functioned together in discussions of sex that in turn became intimacy not only with the people with whom they had or hoped to have sex but also with the fellow students with whom they discussed their desires. That complicity was strengthened by the lighthearted conversations students had, which relayed information regarding all that surrounds sex. This talk also included discussions of "shame" that some were told to feel about such acts. That shame was intended to control women's respectability, and fellow students were among the regulators of sex and respectability. Frida Lawson, for example, appeared to feel more intimacy with her school's director, who she contacted with gossip about other students' deviations from respectable behavior, than with many of her fellow students. In contrast, when reacting to students such as Gabriella and those who slipped away to find their lovers as they traveled to and from Senegal or snuck their lovers into their dormitory rooms in Rufisque, other students came together. They discussed the pleasure of sex acts and confronted the complicated potential ramifications—such as pregnancy, sexual assault, and pleasure—these sex acts had for one's job, social standing, and body, and thus for one's future mobility.

Conclusion

As they moved about the AOF, Black women thus revealed their self-awareness of stereotypes regarding Black versus white sexualities in the French empire. They expressed sensuality in both literature and informal oral conversation, and in so doing created lasting ties, anchored in race consciousness, with other independently mobile women. That intimacy created a sense of belonging, and as a result, thoughts on sex became one way to create and sustain a community in Paris or Rufisque. The archival documents from West Africa are both more and less direct than the comparatively controlled, published literary musings of Antillean women in Paris. Still, women used both genres to link sociocultural agility back to the idea that their travels generated a sense of displacement that both forced them to confront the proper behavior expected of a woman and allowed them to circumvent it. After taking a ship, train, truck, or bus from one point of the French empire to another, women wrote or spoke their intimacies, including their self-reflections on the manners in which the meanings and repercussions of their gender, race, and sexuality shifted in different spaces and places. They actively did the nuanced work of interpreting their sexual self-definitions as they travelled, spoke, and wrote.

For migrant women traveling to Paris and Rufisque, a similar tension existed between sex and its social and administrative oversight. Discussions of how their independence tied into their domestic, sexual, or matrimonial habits were delicate, with administrators in France and West Africa often enunciating their beliefs that women of any race who were not properly monitored would end up prostitutes, or pregnant, or both. This same line of thinking meant that administrators and fellow male migrants labeled independently traveling women either prostitutes or very loose women if they were not discreet about their desires.[47] Yet if we move past such attempts to use potential positions of dominance to regulate sexuality, we see clearly that there was power in the ways that women used discussions of sex to foster intimacy. Their experiences were not "a thing of no importance," but a critical asset that they used to create a community. Administrative presumptions regarding proper behavior were reinforced by assumptions not only white men but also Black men made regarding their female compatriots' tendency to bow to market pressures rather than independent desires. Such suppositions shaped the coded ways in which Antillean and African women on the move chose to reveal, or not, their sexual awakenings, adventures, and identities as Black, colonial, intellectual women. Yet for all the subtleties of their musings, these women nonetheless provoked administrators, migrant men, and perhaps most importantly other migrant women to listen to how women defined and interpreted their own desires. Migrant women, in other words, skirted a wavering line, alternately constructed as sexual creatures by the men and women around them and resisting their categorization as women of easy virtue(s) even if in the end they might have preferred, much like Léa, to be both independent and sexual women. Black women counteracted this trite duality by repositioning themselves within the racial and sexual hierarchies of empire. In particular, women used their location within urban transatlantic spaces and their physical mobility across the French empire to recreate race consciousness and social mobility as a gendered experience—one that in the end had surprisingly little to do with the men about, for, and with whom all this sex was supposed to be. Indeed, many of these women seemed most interested in speaking for themselves and directly to an audience of women about mobility as generative of intimacy, the key to understanding how no woman could ever be quite "like any other" yet could nonetheless generate a sense of belonging with many others.

NOTES

1. Note that *La Revue du monde noire*, in which Horth's article was published, was a bilingual review. I have mostly kept the original translations while recognizing that they are imperfect. However, for the title of my article I have offered my own translation of the original French. The review's editors translated the French more literally as: "a woman like the others."
2. Roberte Horth, "Une histoire sans importance," *La revue du monde noire* 2 (1931): 50.

3. Yaël Simpson Fletcher, "Unsettling Settlers: Colonial migrants and racialised sexuality in interwar Marseilles," in *Gender, Sexuality and Colonial Modernities*, ed. Antoinette Burton (New York: Routledge, 1999).

4. Bennetta Jules-Rosette, *Josephine Baker in Art and Life: The Icon and the Image* (Urbana: University of Illinois Press, 2007); T. Denean Sharpley-Whiting, *Black Venus: Sexualized Savages, Primal Fears, and Primitive Narratives in French* (Durham NC: Duke University Press, 1999).

5. For more on such constructions of sexuality and respectability see Jacqueline Couti, "Am I My Sister's Keeper? The Politics of Propriety and the Fight for Equality in the Works of French Antillean Women Writers, 1920s-40s," in *Black French Women and the Struggle for Equality*, ed. Silyane Larcher and Félix Germain (Lincoln: University of Nebraska Press, 2018); Jacqueline Couti, "La Doudou contre-attaque: Féminisme noir, sexualisation et doudouisme en question dans l'entre-deux-guerres," *Comment s'en sortir* 1 (2015): 111–39.

6. On mobility studies see Stephen Greenblatt, ed., *Cultural Mobility: A Manifesto* (Cambridge, UK: Cambridge University Press, 2010); Stephanie Ponsavady, "Moteurs de mécontentement et de désir: Automobiles et routes en Indochine Coloniale (1898–1939)" (Ph.D. diss., New York University, 2012).

7. Anjali Arondekar, "Without a Trace: Sexuality and the Colonial Archive," *Journal of the History of Sexuality* 14, no. 1–2 (2005): 10–27.

8. Matt Houlbrook, "Sexing the History of Sexuality," *History Workshop Journal* 60, no. 1 (2005): 216–17.

9. David M. Halperin, "How to do the History of Male Homosexuality," in *How to do the History of Homosexuality*, ed. David M. Halperin (Chicago: University of Chicago Press, 2002).

10. Michelle M. Wright and Antje Schuhmann, "Blackness and Sexualities: Introduction," in *Blackness and Sexualities*, ed. Michelle Wright and Antje Schuhmann (Berlin: Lit Verlag, 2007), 9.

11. A few examples of excellent work on sex, domesticity and power include Julia Ann Clancy-Smith and Frances Gouda, *Domesticating the Empire: Race, Gender, and Family Life in French and Dutch Colonialism* (Charlottesville: University Press of Virginia, 1998); Ann Laura Stoler, *Carnal Knowledge and Imperial Power: Race and the Intimate in Colonial Rule* (Berkeley: Universiy of California Press, 2002).

12. A number of scholars have started to critique the excessive association of sex and power to the detriment of the study of sex and emotion. See Jennifer Cole and Lynn M. Thomas, *Love in Africa* (Chicago: University of Chicago Press, 2009); Rachel Jean-Baptiste, *Conjugal Rights: Marriage, Sexuality, and Urban Life in Colonial Libreville, Gabon* (Athens: Ohio University Press, 2014).

13. Frantz Fanon, *Black Skin, White Masks*, trans. Richard Philcox (New York: Grove, 2008), 54.

14. On violence, race and sex see for example Tyler Edward Stovall, "Love, Labor, and Race: Colonial Men and White Women in France during the Great War," in

French Civilization and Its Discontents: Nationalism, Colonialism, Race, ed. Tyler
Edward Stovall and Georges Van Den Abbeele (Lanham MD: Lexington, 2003).

15. Jennifer Anne Boittin, "'Among Them Complicit'? Life and Politics in France's
Black Communities, 1919–1939" in Africans in Europe in the Long Twentieth Century, ed. Eve Rosenhaft and Robbie Aitken (Liverpool, UK: Liverpool University Press, 2012), 62.

16. Comité Syndical International des Ouvriers Nègres, Sous le joug de l'impérialisme: Les orgies impérialistes en Afrique, SLOTFOM (Service de liaison des originaires des territoires français d'outre-mer) 3/47, Archives Nationales d'Outre-Mer, Aix-en-Provence, France.

17. Claude McKay, Banjo (London: X Press, 2000), 178.

18. Léopold Sédar Senghor, "Black Woman" in Selected Poems, trans. John Reed and Clive Wake (New York: Atheneum, 1964), 6.

19. Valerie Orlando, "The Politics of Race and Patriarchy in 'Claire-Solange, âme africaine' by Suzanne Lacascade," Studies in Twentieth and Twenty-First Century Literature 29, no. 1 (2005): 118–34; Jennifer M. Wilks, Race, Gender & Comparative Black Modernism: Suzanne Lacascade, Marita Bonner, Suzanne Césaire, Dorothy West (Baton Rouge: Louisiana State University Press, 2008).

20. Suzanne Lacascade, Claire-Solange, âme africaine (Paris: Eugène Figuière, 1924), 89.

21. Lacascade, Claire-Solange, âme africaine, 36. This last comment could be a reference to Claire de Duras's 1823 novella Ourika.

22. Lacascade, Claire-Solange, âme africaine, 37.

23. Lacascade, Claire-Solange, âme africaine, 66.

24. Lacascade, Claire-Solange, âme africaine, 80.

25. Lacascade, Claire-Solange, âme africaine, 173.

26. Lacascade, Claire-Solange, âme africaine, 220.

27. Jennifer Anne Boittin, Colonial Metropolis: The Urban Grounds of Anti-Imperialism and Feminism in Interwar Paris (Lincoln: University of Nebraska Press, 2010), Chapter 3.

28. Ruth Ginio, The French Army and its African Soldiers (Lincoln: University of Nebraska Press, 2017); Sarah J. Zimmerman, Militarizing Marriage: West African Soldiers' Conjugal Traditions in Modern French Empire (Athens: Ohio University Press, 2020).

29. Lacascade, Claire-Solange, âme africaine, 8, 186.

30. Jane Nardal, "Pantins exotiques," La Dépêche Africaine 1, no. 8 (October 15, 1928): 2.

31. Paulette Nardal, "Le nouveau bal nègre de la Glacière," La Dépêche Africaine 2, no. 14 (May 30, 1928): 3.

32. Paulette Nardal, "Eveil de la conscience de race" La Revue du monde noir 6 (1932): 29.

33. Elisa Camiscioli, "Trafficking Histories: Women's Migration and Sexual Labor in the Early Twentieth Century," Deportate, esuli, profughe: Rivista telematica di studi sulla memoria femminile 40 (2019); Christina Elizabeth Firpo, Black Market

Business: Selling Sex in Northern Vietnam, 1920–1945 (Ithaca NY: Cornell University Press, 2020); Stoler, *Carnal Knowledge*; Christelle Taraud, *La prostitution coloniale: Algérie, Tunisie, Maroc (1830–1962)* (Paris: Payot, 2003). Note that while some of the women discussed went on to marry, others (such as Horth) died at a young age, and others never openly mentioned in the documents I have read thus far having any partners whatsoever.

34. For more on the École normale de jeunes filles de Rufisque, see Pascale Barthélémy, "'Nanan du plaisir' Germaine Le Goff (1891–1986), première directrice de l'École normale de jeunes filles de l'AOF," in *"Mama Africa": Hommage à Catherine Coquery-Vidrovitch*, ed. Chantal Chanson-Jabeur and Odile Goerg (Paris: L'Harmattan, 2005); Pascale Barthélémy, *Africaines et diplômées à l'époque coloniale (1918–1957)* (Rennes, France: Presses Universitaires de Rennes, 2010).

35. Jean-Baptiste, *Conjugal Rights*, 4.

36. On the color line and constructions of race see W. E. B. Du Bois, for example, originally published in 1903, W. E. B. Du Bois, *The Souls of Black Folk*, ed. with an introduction and notes by Brent Hayes Edwards (Oxford: Oxford University Press, 2007). See also Carina E. Ray, *Crossing the Color Line: Race, Sex, and the Contested Politics of Colonialism in Ghana* (Athens: Ohio University Press, 2015); Tyler Edward Stovall, *White Freedom: The Racial History of an Idea* (Princeton NJ: Princeton University Press, 2021).

37. Jennifer Anne Boittin, "'Are You Trying to Play a White Woman?' La Mère Patrie and the Female Body in French West Africa," *Signs: Journal of Women in Culture and Society* 40, no. 4 (2015): 841–64. See also Alice Conklin, "Redefining 'Frenchness': Citizenship, Race Regeneration, and Imperial Motherhood in France and West Africa, 1914–40," in *Domesticating the Empire: Race, Gender, and Family Life in French and Dutch Colonialism*, ed. Julia Ann Clancy-Smith and Frances Gouda (Charlottesville: University Press of Virginia, 1998).

38. This is particularly salient in a series of informal chats compiled by the school's director: "La femme blanche jugée par la femme noire [The white woman judged by the Black woman]," Germaine Le Goff and students, O/212 (31), 1939, Archives Nationales du Sénégal (ANS), Dakar, Senegal.

39. Tony Ballantyne and Antoinette Burton, "Introduction: Bodies, Empires, and World Histories," in *Bodies in Contact: Rethinking Colonial Encounters in World History*, ed. Tony Ballantyne and Antoinette Burton (Durham NC: Duke University Press, 2005).

40. Todd Shepard, "'Something Notably Erotic': Politics, 'Arab Men,' and Sexual Revolution in Post-Decolonization France, 1962–1974," *Journal of Modern History* 84, no. 1 (2012): 80–115.

41. Letter from Marguerite Thompson to Germaine Le Goff, August 23, 1941, O/119 (31), ANS.

42. Frida Lawson to le Goff, Lomé, August 28, 1941, O/119 (31), ANS.

43. Brittney C. Cooper, *Beyond Respectability: The Intellectual Thought of Race Women* (Urbana: University of Illinois Press, 2017); Frances E. White, *Dark Continent of Our Bodies: Black Feminism and the Politics of Respectability* (Philadelphia: Temple University Press, 2001).

44. Conseil de discipline, Rufisque, May 7, 1947, O/119 (31), ANS. Name changed. Note: I have changed some names in this section. None of the documents I consulted were subject to *dérogation*, but topics of rumor, pregnancy, and sexual assault warrant this measure.

45. Letter to Mlle Huyghé, Faculté de Médecine à Lille, February 13, 1947, O/119 (31), ANS. Name changed.

46. Le Goff to Directeur de l'Institution Publique, Rufisque, February 16, 1944, O/119 (31), ANS.

47. Officials in West Africa routinely assumed that women traveling alone were in the business of sex. See for example Governor General of AOF to the Minister of the Colonies, 6 P.J., in response to communications dated 15 January and 28 March 1939, 200MI3076_21G148, Archives Nationales, Pierrefitte-sur-Seine, France.

7

BUMIDOM 1963–82

Organizing Overseas Migrations to the Metropole, Actions and Contradictions

SYLVAIN PATTIEU

TRANSLATED BY TYLER STOVALL

In 1962 Great Britain established the Commonwealth Immigrant Act, which limited the rights of entry of people from the Commonwealth. In the years that followed, especially in 1968, other similar laws followed. Henceforth a voucher or work permit became necessary. Of 165,000 applications for vouchers in the year after the promulgation of the law, only 45,000 were granted. The number of people from the Caribbean who immigrated to Britain fell from 66,000 to 6,000. In France that same year the BUMIDOM (Bureau des migrations d'Outre-mer, or Overseas Migration Office) was created with the goal of organizing and increasing the migratory flow from the Caribbean and Réunion. The population of Caribbean origin in the metropole had already risen to 100,000 and the goal was to increase it.

At the base of these contrasting decisions were two riots: the first occurring in 1958 in Nottingham, England, in a neighborhood with a strong concentration of Caribbean immigrants, and the second in Fort-de-France in Martinique the same year. The responses to these socially explosive situations were different: France wanted to diffuse the latent social crisis in the overseas departments (DOM) by promoting immigration to the metropole, whereas Britain, worried by race riots in its territory, decided to put a brake on immigration. I do not wish to push the comparison further, since the size and scope of the Commonwealth countries differs vastly from those of the French DOM. Nonetheless, one can use this comparison to underline the original character of the BUMIDOM as an institution. For France it was a question of the unprecedented (to my knowledge) organization of a specific process of migration: by its length, its management, and the means deployed to make it happen. In this sense, the politics of the BUMIDOM can be summed up as shown in chart 1, which appeared on the cover of its 1971 report. This report summed up its activities with an ascending curve of the number of migrants, a vision above all quantitative of migration as a function of the goals established by the government and the relevant ministries.

The context of the creation of the institution was that of the Trentes Glorieuses, the postwar years of prosperity when the metropole experienced full employment and high wages but the DOM remained incomparably more impoverished. There was of course a certain convergence, albeit one that remains to be demonstrated, between the interests of the government in diffusing the social crisis and of employers in recruiting labor in the context of the working-class insubordination after the events of May 1968, as well as the desire of the immigrants themselves to escape their extremely degraded social situation by profiting from the opportunities offered in the metropole. As the prefect Jean-Emile Vié explained when he became president of the BUMIDOM as part of his function as secretary-general of the DOM, the creation of the BUMIDOM responded to urgent policy needs: "It is possible to call on people to assume their responsibilities, to encourage birth control. Having done that, one can influence the future but not the present. One can develop agriculture, encourage industrialization, explore the creation of secondary and tertiary employment. The results, however, will only be significant long-term. Only migration has immediate effects."[1]

In one decade, however, the economic climate declined and the activity of BUMIDOM found itself affected by the timeline of the downturn. Thus, the following graph shows the net decline of the number of migrants starting near the end of the 1970s. Adopting the categories of Alejandro Portes as outlined by Audrey Célestine, the socioeconomic trajectories of the migrants were shaped by the context of their destinations, in other words both by the structures and the conditions of their reception.

The economic decline was not the only contradiction faced by BUMIDOM. First, its goal was to bring French citizens to the metropole. Citizenship was a quality the bureau frequently emphasized with claims such as,

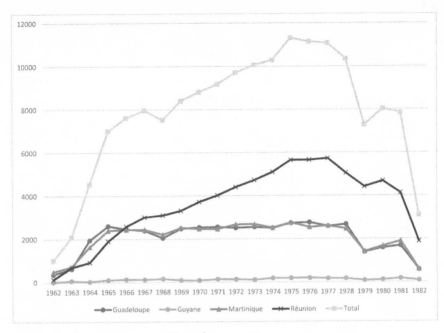

Chart I. Total migrations. Created by author.

"Migration is uniquely dictated by the spirit of national solidarity,"[2] and "it must be admitted that the migrants from the DOM onto the metropolitan labor market *must be counted* among French citizens."[3] Migrants from the DOM are compared to Bretons, Corsicans, Savoyards, people from the Alps, Auvergnats, and Basques, for whom "solutions analogous to those used for the Caribbean immigrants" were adopted.[4] However, it is very true that specific policies were applied to them, requiring a "considerable financial and social effort" that was "fundamentally different from that done for other migrations" and justified by the "particular" isolation of the islands, but with the goal of "avoiding the creation of a specialized social service that would tend to reinforce their particularism and contradict the desired goal."[5] Between recognition and denial of the particularity of the concerned populations, BUMIDOM walked a razor's edge.

The second contradiction was that BUMIDOM faced lively challenges in the overseas departments and thus was obliged to pursue a relative and frequently criticized discretion. Finally, the policies of the BUMIDOM did not prevent the persistence of spontaneous migrations, which were just as large as the official migrations, during its existence. The eventual responsibilities of the BUMIDOM to the spontaneous migrants prompted a number of internal discussions.

In this essay I plan to explore the activities of the BUMIDOM concerning the different aspects of migration that it directed: selecting the migrants locally, receiving them in the metropole, training them both before and after their arrival, placing them (in other words finding them a job), and finally getting them to stay in France, since both an implicit and explicit objective was to make their migration permanent. My approach will follow these different stages in order to understand better the originality of this organized migration.

Selecting the Migrants

The local BUMIDOM branches were charged with selecting candidates for migration. For the BUMIDOM, "A well conducted or correctly organized migration should to a significant degree be concerned with young workers entering the job market and to orient them, to the extent possible, toward professional job training in the metropole."[6] This approach thus privileged bringing the most dynamic elements to the metropole. Several qualities were considered in choosing candidates and looking at individual resumés. The potential migrant was subjected to a social investigation performed by BUMIDOM local agents. He was submitted to a medical visit and to psychotechnical tests. The goal was to establish "a diverse migration ranging from the skilled to the semi-skilled worker."[7] The information contained in the dossiers resulting from the inquiry show that very often the migrants were young (if one excludes some of those coming to the metropole for the purposes of family reunification), from very poor backgrounds, and with a low level of schooling. For example, let us take the case of Rose A., born in 1951. Originally from Saint-Pierre de la Reunion, she was the second of six children, left school in seventh grade, and lived with her family in "a wooden house with a sheet metal roof divided into four rooms," without water or electricity.[8] Or take the case of Thérèse T., born in 1947, who hailed from Saint-Georges Basse-Terre in Guadeloupe. Having a sixth-grade education and a deceased father, she lived with her mother and two other members of her family in a one-room wooden house with electricity.[9] The information asked for by the dossiers included the morality of the candidates, their religion, and elements concerning their physical appearance: "Good presentation. Simplicity. Sincerity. A fairly pleasant face."[10] One candidate left "a generally good impression. An elegant and very pretty young woman . . . clearly robust, strong."[11] Another was described as being in "Good physical constitution, serious, moderately expressive."[12] For the many underage candidates, parental authorizations were requested, as well as specific agreements concerning the eventual agreement of the parents to permit their child to attend Catholic Mass regularly. For those women with a child, the family had to furnish a certificate guaranteeing they would take charge of him during the absence of his mother.

While refusing the "unskilled street sweepers" who had come to symbolize the "cut-rate" immigration from which it wanted to distinguish itself, BUMIDOM frequently expressed its hope to recruit migrants as widely as possible. In particular it challenged medical visits and excessively strict psychotechnical tests that slowed down the review of the migration dossiers and eliminated many candidates. For example, in Martinique in 1965, 50 percent of the nineteen-year-old candidates were eliminated by the tests.[13] The BUMIDOM was interested in these "unfit candidates" because "these youths, uneducated and unemployed, were an element of social discord and weighed heavily on the departmental economies." BUMIDOM's interest in these failed candidates led it to develop a style of training that will be analyzed in detail below. BUMIDOM even considered, without any political means to make it happen, reducing public assistance locally, especially at the municipal level, in order to persuade these "voluntary idlers" and other "searchers for haphazard work."[14]

Family reunification was also one of the criteria for choosing immigrants and grew more and more important as migration became more permanent. This kind of immigration was seen as a "mark of the stability of the migrants,"[15] and as a means for fighting against the "overpopulation" of the islands.[16] The documents requested in these cases, such as dossiers from the civil registry (*état-civil*) and prenuptial certificates for fiancés, emphasized the need to establish family relations. This migration especially tended to concern young people such as spouses or children,

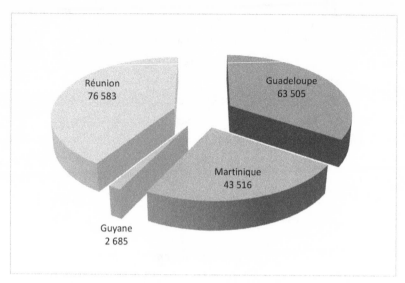

Chart 2. Total distribution of migrations through BUMIDOM. Created by author.

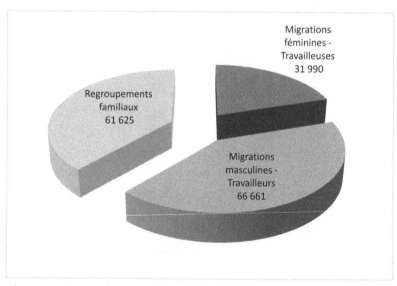

Chart 3. Gender distribution of migrations. Created by author.

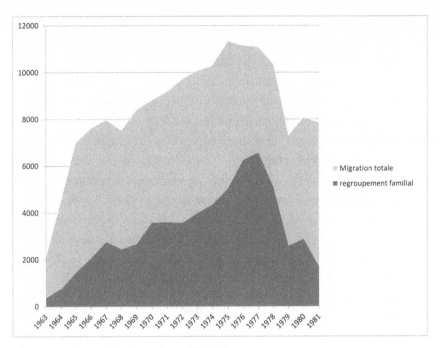

Chart 4. Family reunifications. Created by author.

but also included older family members. For example, in March 1972 Guy M. requested to bring his mother, born in 1911, from Martinique to the metropole after having already organized the migration of one brother and three sisters.[17]

Finally, certain immigrant selections were organized directly by companies themselves. In these cases BUMIDOM still required an investigation, but it was minimal. This was especially true of the automobile industry, in particular Renault in La Réunion during the 1960s or Chrysler at the beginning of the 1970s. BUMIDOM viewed such actions very favorably, and while it organized immigration in general it left the selection of the candidates as well as their placement, training, and housing to the companies.

Training and Placement

The Predominance of Industry

BUMIDOM's placement functions were essential because jobs were one of the main motivations for migration. Until 1975, when ANPE (Agence nationale pour l'emploi, or National Employment Agency) took over this prerogative, BUMIDOM took responsibility for direct placements. These became more difficult with the economic downturn of the 1970s. Almost one third of migrants came to the metropole as a result of direct placements, as the graph below illustrates. There is no accurate data on their composition, but one can imagine that some of them concerned placements in the public sector. Some companies recruited directly, establishing their own local offices: Renault, the SNCF (Societe national des chemins de fer, or French National Railway Society), of which BUMIDOM complained that the worst jobs involving the maintenance of the tracks were reserved for immigrants, Peugeot, Michelin, Chrysler, and SIMCA (Societe industrielle de mecanique et carosserie automobile, or Mechanical and Automotive Body Manufacturing Company). In 1971 Chrysler created a local recruiting office in La Réunion, where the selected candidates passed through the training center at la Sakay. Peugeot left it to BUMIDOM to take care of the specific formalities of immigration but provided for the housing of migrants it employed.

For the large factories, the context of working-class unrest during the 1970s played a major role, and the decision to recruit outside the metropole had the goal of providing a more docile labor supply. Michelin stopped recruiting migrants through BUMIDOM when a worker from Martinique and one from Guadeloupe stood for election on the CGT (Confederation generale du travail, or National Federation of Labor) list. The company then decided to recruit Portuguese workers, provoking the ire of the BUMIDOM.

A not inconsiderable proportion of the immigrants were sent to training programs. If one adds to their number those workers trained before migration, one sees that this aspect constituted one of the principal activities of the BUMIDOM. One leitmotif of BUMIDOM was the idea of migration as upward social mobility. This ceaselessly repeated idea enabled BUMIDOM to respond to the criticisms from the overseas departments themselves. Many different types of training programs were thus established: in the centers for professional education for adults (FPA), among interns in the metropole, and also in specific centers for basic training, some of them in the overseas departments themselves, like the one in la Sakay (Babetville) in Madagascar, or those in the metropole at Crouy-sur-Ourcq (1965),

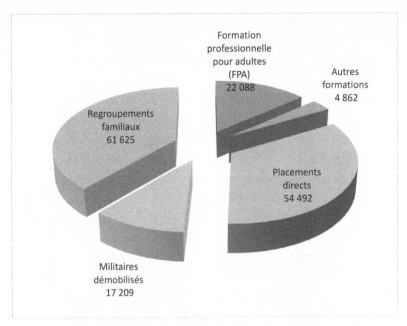

Chart 5. Evolution of the principal types of migrations, 1962–81. Created by author.

Simandres (1968), Marseilles (1969), or Cassan (1978). Large numbers of immigrants passed through these centers, including 1,500 out of a total of 7,900 in 1979. Between 1962 and 1981 over 22,000 immigrants passed through the FPA. In addition to that number we must add 4,800 who took other training programs, as well as without a doubt a proportion of the migrants placed directly in jobs, some of whom had gone through centers of basic training. In the context of the profile of those migrants selected, this is a key question. This training had a double dimension: training not only for a profession but also for life in the metropole, something that differentiated immigrants from the DOM from immigrants from the metropolitan provinces.

The majority of the training programs proposed by the BUMIDOM were in the FPA, especially for industry as we see in the diagram below. The two principal sectors for training for men were the metals industry and construction, a fact that nuances the image of migrants from the DOM as primarily lower-level public sector employees. The reports from the BUMIDOM nonetheless evoke, especially with regard to the construction industry, "overheated careers," professions deemed too difficult "for Creoles who can't deal with a rigorous climate." These psychotechnical selections pitilessly oriented the immigrants toward the unqualified and undervalued industrial sectors.[18]

For women, however, industry did not account for the majority of employment: service jobs, such as those as house servants and cleaning ladies, and public sector work (notably a strong proportion of health caregivers) provided them with numerous employment markets. During the 1970s the number of working women increased notably because of the resistance of many to work as domestics. But the end of the 1970s was marked by an economic downturn and the diversity of job opportunities declined. The number of female semiskilled workers decreased and the recruitment of hospital workers also became more difficult. The Office of Public Assistance estimated that it had enough workers from the DOM, some 12 percent of its personnel (more in the lower ranks), and reproached these workers for "excessive susceptibility" and the fact that they gave "the impression of working in slow motion."

The BUMIDOM Centers

The immigrants trained in the FPS were mixed in with the adult population in the metropole. BUMIDOM also established its own training centers specifically dedicated to the immigrants from the DOM.

The Simandes center in the Lyon region was reserved for men and dedicated to industry. For the migrants it was a question of "going from work overseas to a job in a metropolitan factory." The first two weeks of the six weeks of training courses were broken down into adaptation to metropolitan life, everyday life, psychomotor training, or "the individual's attitude to the machine, increase of physical and psychic resistance," "finesse of touch, precision of gestures, hand safety, rapidity of movements, independence of the two hands." This was followed by four weeks of initiation into professional life in order to "place immigrants in the actual ambiance of factory work" and teach them to respect the cadences of work and safety rules. The teachers came from the Berliet or Brandt companies. Of the four weeks, three took place inside the actual factory under the authority of the supervisors: "their factory work covers the cost of the instruction by the companies." These contacts for semiskilled jobs with the companies of the Lyons region often resulted in disappointment after the initial training session. Not everyone in the program ended up with a job. But for the BUMIDOM, "what counts, after all, is the fact that our immigrants should not be false workers or marginal employees. We have noted, with the factory inspectors, that during the first two weeks in the factory many of the interns experience discouragement and indifference to their jobs." These difficulties, attributed to a variety of complexes or to unrealized professional aspirations, diminished in the third and fourth weeks, "when the intern no longer feels marginal to the other workers, when he identifies with the team, with the workshop, with the factory." Six hundred interns went through this center every year during the 1970s, but the local factories were generally disinterested, much to the frustration of the BUMIDOM.

The basic training centers focused on enabling the migration of candidates judged too inadequate, whose living conditions were too different from those in the metropole, or who had failed the psychotechnical tests. The main ones were Crouy-sur-Ourcq, for women, and la Sakay, in Madagascar, for natives of Réunion. The need was particularly great in Réunion and the BUMIDOM ended up "sorting out and retraining an average of four hundred unfit workers per year." This program ended up dealing with 72 percent of those rejected from the selection process in Réunion.[19] As many as 40 percent of the interns were illiterate during the 1960s.[20] Of the immigrants from Réunion admitted to the FPA centers in the metropole, 60 percent went through the Sakay center. There they went through a kind of "manual refinement" and "remedial basic education." The objective of this program was also adaptation to metropolitan life. The intention was to cut off the interns from their native milieu, to teach them how to read, and to house them in a dormitory that would "give the intern a sense of collective life and give him missing ideas like discipline, regular attendance, and a sense of schedules." Sports, including judo, football, basketball, were required in order to "remedy certain physical inadequacies." The interns gained four to five kilograms. They worked in carpentry, masonry, and metalworking in particular. Some also learned how to operate farm machinery. For female interns, the Trinity sisters directed an apprenticeship in domestic arts. The interns had a full daily program: one hour of gymnastics, three and a half hours of remedial scholarship, as well as applied arts. The women's program was divided between embroidery, French, calculus, history-geography, civic instruction, work with farm animals, domestic economy, cooking, housework, needlework, and darning. At the end of the 1960s five hundred interns went through this center every year, for a total of 6,200. It closed in June 1977 after political changes in Madagascar and a resultant hostility to the French. The centers in Marseilles and Cassan took up the slack, with at least initially similar functions.

The other emblematic center of basic education and BUMIDOM activities was Crouy-sur-Ourcq, which became a destination for young girls. Here the emphasis was on know-how and social skills. BUMIDOM gave the girls a *trousseau* (a coat or a suit, a skirt, a cardigan vest, a sweater or a blouse, two American shirts, and three pairs of underwear) and the young women stayed at the center between fifteen and forty-five days. The goal of the training program was "to adapt them to the food and the lifestyle of the metropole" and to teach them how to use household machinery (as seen in the attached photos). The principal goal was to train domestics, and bourgeois families came to recruit them directly (such as in the case of the Debré family). By the 1970s this program had largely lost its appeal, losing out to nursing assistants or nurses in general. There were also training programs for office workers or typists. To the chagrin of the BUMIDOM there was a lot of resistance to household work. Many migrant women chose to abandon the internship, leave the center, or look for a job unrelated to their training.

Starting in the late 1970s the sociocultural dimension became as important as professional training in these centers. Therefore the Marseilles center, initially devoted to welcoming primarily immigrants from Réunion, began to accept immigrants from the FPA who hadn't found work. Starting in 1979 training tended to focus on social education and pedagogy, with a classic curriculum (calculus, French, professional training) proposed to recent immigrants, and labor in work sites for those already well established in the metropole. A program of various activities, not just training, was established, with athletic, cultural, or local interest activities. At the same time, the Cassan center, not opened until 1978, brought together its interns for fourteen weeks in a center for young workers conceived of as a sociocultural space, with lectures on apartheid, the Socialist party, guitar and photography courses, and a film club.

The Social Dimension of BUMIDOM

The social action of BUMIDOM arose out of a double preoccupation: to handle the criticisms from the overseas departments and to avoid provoking challenges to immigration in the metropole. This therefore meant dealing with the problems of the migrants in order to avoid being held responsible for them. BUMIDOM welcomed and received the immigrants, organizing transfers from Orly or the train stations. In 1970 it organized 840 bus trips from the airport. The same year BUMIDOM provided for the clothing of 1,320 immigrants, proposed 800 monetary subsidies, and 2,000 subsidies for equipment. By organizing the reception of the immigrants BUMIDOM thus tried to disperse them throughout the country. It had ten regional offices with two staff employees each.

Housing was the biggest problem. This was a recurring problem in the history of the BUMIDOM, and it was never completely resolved. BUMIDOM was aware that this was a problem for the French in general, but it was especially grave for the many migrants who could not count on family or local support to deal with it. The question of racial prejudice also appeared at least implicitly: in 1966 BUMIDOM recognized that "rare are the housing agencies that want to include the migrants in their clientele. Even rarer are those landlords willing to house them." Migrants from the overseas departments were frequently obliged to put up with housing conditions of the worst quality. The migrants had a bad reputation for having "too generous a sense of hospitality," resulting in "overcrowding," "noise, too many people in the apartments, property destruction, and, finally, many unpaid rents." The BUMIDOM was torn between defending the migrants and a clumsy emphasis on certain problems. In 1971 a letter from BUMIDOM responding to an article by a journalist in *Le Monde* took up these accusations: "It has been sometimes contended that the residents damage the rooms they have been given. For example, government-regulated rooms in a one-star hotel—therefore equipped with undeniable levels of amenities—experienced 120,000 francs worth of damages in a few months (broken sinks and showers, central heating and water pipes twisted and torn out, doors pushed in, furnishings destroyed, stairways broken, railings torn out, etc . . .)." In-house visits organized by BUMIDOM in 1974 came to much less harsh conclusions: the majority of homes inhabited by migrants that they visited were in good condition.

In 1976 eleven thousand migrants arrived in France but BUMIDOM had only 759 housing units and 604 beds at its disposal. BUMIDOM granted 425 migrants financial aid in the form of loans and helped 932 migrants find housing without financial help. A reported 4,292 migrants found temporary housing in shelters, hotels, or through BUMIDOM quotas. Housing was especially a problem in the Paris area. It was easier in the provinces to negotiate with large companies for housing as well as job placement. The HLM (Habitations a loyers moderes, or housing at moderate rent) showed little interest in BUMIDOM's proposal that they reserve a number of housing units in exchange for financial support, preferring the more considerable subsidies offered by employers. The immigrants themselves refused to live too far from the center of Paris or to share a SONACOTRA (Societe nationale de construction de logements pour les travailleurs, or National Society for Working Class Housing) residence with North African workers in Lyons.

As far as social support was concerned, BUMIDOM's activity was limited by the small number of employees in this service: only eight total in the 1970s, dividing their time between visits to hospitals and maternity wards, in-home visits, visits to employers, investigations of residences, searches for housing, and writing up administrative dossiers (for family subsidies or Social Security). Even if the personnel of the central social services office only worked with the immigrants in the Paris area, their task was already overwhelming.

One last function of the social action of the BUMIDOM was organizing vacation trips at low cost thanks to agreements with Air France. Such trips were seen as indispensable for the psychological well-being of the immigrants, the maintenance of ties with the homeland being seen as necessary. Twenty thousand people benefitted from these trips starting in 1976, and the number of vacationers was higher than the number of immigrants starting in 1972. For BUMIDOM this was also proof of the success of migration, since almost all of the vacationers returned to the metropole.

In general, much of the social action of BUMIDOM seems to have been delegated to ad hoc associations, autonomous from BUMIDOM but dependent on it financially, like AMITAG (Amicale des travailleurs antillais et guyannais de metropole, Association of Caribbean Workers in Metropolitan France), CASODOM (Comite d'action sociale en faveur des originaires des departments d'outre-mer, or Social Action Committee for Natives of Overseas Departments), or CNARM (Comite national d'accueil et d'action pour les reunionnais en metropole, or National Committee for Natives of Reunion in Metropolitan France). BUMIDOM therefore delegated a part of its social policy to organizations over which it only exercised partial control, encouraging them to develop residences, means of professional advancement like night courses, and cultural activities.

Conclusion

From the beginning the policies of the BUMIDOM were violently challenged both in the overseas departments and in the metropole during the 1970s, notably by the actions of the UGTRF (Union generale des travailleurs Reunionnais en France, or General Union of Workers from Reunion in France) against the local offices or residences associated with it. In spite of the criticisms, in spite of the limitations, with its decline the policies implemented by the BUMIDOM seem interesting in more than one respect. Certainly, they cannot be separated from the disastrous local socioeconomic situation. But they represent nonetheless one of the rare examples of such an organized migration, one that desired and encouraged family reunification. They took place in the context of a political perspective that was clearly assimilationist, though one that was not without its ambiguities since it was based in certain assumptions about social, cultural, and ethnic specificity. Over the long term this specific emphasis shifted more and more from the social to the socio-cultural, seeming to anticipate the policies of the ANT (Agence nationale pour l'insertion et la protection des travailleurs d'outre-mer, or National Agency for the Integration and Protection of Overseas Workers), the organization which replaced the BUMIDOM in 1982 with a goal less of organizing migration and more of using a variety of policies to help those from the overseas departments adjust to life in the metropole.

The history of the BUMIDOM thus lies at the intersection of several histories: that of immigration, but also those of labor, of the working classes, of women, and of Black populations in France. In order to pursue it further one must work on different levels: national, regional, with both local organizations and centers of reception and training. It should lead the researcher to consider multiple perspectives, those of the metropolitan authorities but also instances of local politics, and finally, those of the migrants themselves. This is thus a privileged terrain for a social history that intersects with economic and political history.

NOTES

1. Archives Nationales (AN), 1982 0104/1, Compte-rendu du Conseil d'administration du BUMIDOM, October 11, 1971, declaration de Jean-Emile Vié.
2. AN, 1982 0104/1, Compte-rendu du Conseil d'administration du BUMIDOM, February 22, 1972, declaration de Jean-Emile Vié.
3. AN, 1982 0104/1, Compte-rendu du Conseil d'administration du BUMIDOM, February 22, 1972, declaration de M. Servat.
4. AN, 1982 0104/1, Compte-rendu du Conseil d'administration du BUMIDOM, October 11, 1971, declaration de M. Servat.
5. AN, 1982 0104/1, Compte-rendu du Conseil d'administration du BUMIDOM, June 16, 1971, intervention de M. Bros, administrateur-délégué du BUMIDOM.
6. AN, 1982 0104/3, Rapport du December 20, 1966.
7. AN, 1982 0104/1, Compte-rendu du Conseil d'administration du BUMIDOM, June 30, 1970, intervention de M. Bros, administrateur-délégué du BUMIDOM.
8. AN, 1994 0429/146, enquête sociale du March 15, 1971, dossier 58413.
9. AN, 1994 0429/146, enquête sociale du April 10, 1967, dossier 58158.
10. AN, 1994 0429/146, dossier 58007.
11. AN, 1994 0429/146, dossier 58353.
12. AN, 1994 0429/146, dossier 58363/364.
13. AN, 1982 0104/3, Rapport no. 1 du December 20, 1966.
14. AN, 1982 0104/3, Rapport d'activités du BUMIDOM au December 31, 1969.
15. AN, 1982 0104/3, Rapport no. 4 du December 20, 1966.
16. AN, 1982 0104/3, Compte-rendu d'activités au December 31, 1967.
17. AN, 1994 0429/146, dossier 58363/364.
18. AN, 1982 0104/3, Rapport d'activités du BUMIDOM au December 31, 1970.
19. AN, 1982 0104/3, Rapport d'activités du BUMIDOM au December 31, 1967.
20. AN, 1982 0104/3, Rapport d'activités du BUMIDOM au December 31, 1970.

PART 3

The Politics of Race in France Today

8

Contemporary French
Caribbean Politics

AUDREY CÉLESTINE

TRANSLATED BY TYLER STOVALL

Migrants from overseas France and their descendants have had privileged interlocutors among the public authorities since the 1960s. Whether it was BUMIDOM (Bureau pour le développement des migrations dans les départements d'outre-mer), which could represent them to certain state agencies,[1] ANT (Agence nationale pour l'insertion et la promotion des travailleurs d'outre-mer), which served as an interlocutor with Overseas France associations,[2] or the DGOM (Délégation nationale à l'outre-mer) of Paris City Hall, they offered (and sometimes continue to offer) migrants from overseas France access to political leaders.[3] The establishment of the Interministerial Delegation for the Equality of Opportunity of Overseas French (DIECFOM) in 2007 after the election of Nicolas Sarkozy represented the culmination of an old pattern.[4] The creation of this organization in effect marked the culmination of a process that tended to underscore the "specific" condition of migrants from overseas France in the hexagon. This justified the assumption of authority by the associations' leaders and the specific arrangements made by the public authorities.

In the case of the DIECFOM, it dealt in particular with the specificity of discrimination experienced by French citizens of overseas origin. This article will examine more closely the process that paradoxically led to the distinct treatment of this population in a context that was officially hostile to the recognition of ethnic and racial identities. During the last decade, several organizational mobilizations have reinforced this tendency and can in part take credit for the birth of an agency dedicated to equality of opportunity for this population. Established to respond to the specific situation of discrimination against migrants from the French overseas territories, it took place in a broader context marked by assigning important roles to the world of associations as representatives of that population while at the same time refusing to acknowledge race or ethnicity directly.

The Fashioning of a Specific Group

Since the beginning of the 1960s the French government has established institutions to deal with people from overseas France living in the hexagon. First there was BUMIDOM, which was in charge of the recruitment, transport, training, and placement of migrants from Martinique, Guadeloupe, Réunion, and French Guiana. Created in 1962, this organization relied on the associations with which it signed agreements for the reception and support of the first generation of migrants. At the same time a network of national committees to welcome migrants from the Caribbean and Réunion arose. These initiatives contributed to the development of a specific approach to the overseas populations. In their relations with the HLM (Habitations à loyer modéré, or public housing estates) and other agencies or administrations of civil law, one can observe the difficulties involved in treating this particular population group objectively. Leïla Wuhl thus shows how this category of Caribbean migrants in France made no sense for the representatives of BUMIDOM, linking the regular rejection of the files they sent to the HLM offices to the agency's difficulties in treating this population of migrants objectively.[5] These difficulties have been attributed to the agency's small budget.[6] Yet according to Wuhl they can also be read as a form of hesitation as to how to treat this population of migrants, many of whom had been in the metropole for a long time.[7] BUMIDOM's actions thus gave rise to the idea of "French of Overseas Origin" without essentially giving this concept a stable and objective meaning, especially concerning its interactions with other state agencies.

With the victory of the Left in the 1981 elections, the organized migration policy was officially suppressed.[8] After that point priority was given, among other things, to the creation of the ANT in order to deal with the difficulties of integration encountered by these populations.[9] The new tasks of the agency and the ideas guiding their implementation also aligned its actions with the idea of treating the "French of overseas origin" as a specific group.[10] The ANT intervened in social action policies concerning housing, professional education, and the funding of cultural activities.

Starting in 1977 an extramunicipal commission of coordination, "Antilles-Guyane," was established, and the following year it was transformed into the Municipal Center for the Reception and Information for the French of overseas origin, the CMAI-Dom-Tom.[11] This center, which still exists, was intended to welcome the migrants from the DOM (Départements d'outre-mer, or overseas departments) and see to their daily needs. Over time the Center gradually took the leaders of the migrant associations in hand, notably by increasing correspondence between them and by establishing subsidies. The mission of the CMAI was made explicit starting with its reorganization in 1988: it was supposed to encourage relations between the DOM population and the organizations of civil society in the fields of employment, education, housing, and social assistance.

The actions of the BUMIDOM, then part of the overseas Ministry, as well as ANT and the Paris City Hall thus contributed to the emergence of the identification of the "French of overseas origin" as an objectivized category, notably by the attribution of small fees or subsidies to "overseas" associations. Migrant associations sometimes implemented the activities of these agencies: this was the case of CASODOM (Comité d'action sociale en faveur des originaires des départements d'outre-mer en Métropole), which in the context of agreements made with the BUMIDOM, ANT, and more recently LADOM (l'Agence de l'outre-mer pour la mobilité) since the end of the 1950s pursued a mission of receiving and monitoring newly arrived migrants primarily from the Caribbean.

The links forged by these associations from the beginnings of organized migration and maintained over the years with the ANT and the overseas Ministry made them privileged interlocutors, indeed the legitimate representatives of the overseas populations to the public authorities. In 1983 and 1987 sessions devoted to the situation of the "French of overseas origin" in the hexagon were organized, and during the 2009 overseas Estates-General organized in the aftermath of social movements primarily in Martinique and Guadeloupe, a large part of the members in different workshops belonged to "overseas" associations.[12]

The beginning of the twenty-first century saw the emergence of national collective mobilizations bringing together people from the Caribbean that seemed to modify the collective forms of action sponsored by the associations. In effect the Collectif DOM, formed in 2003 to protest against significant increases in the cost of air travel to the Caribbean, engaged in protests against the traditional state agencies while at the same time bypassing the overseas Ministry, a privileged interlocutor of overseas associations, to question the elected representatives of the overseas territories and the members of Parliament (and not just those from overseas districts) directly.[13] The leader of the association took this step deliberately in an attempt to take action on a national scale and go beyond the traditional "overseas" networks.

This activism also arose from several new perspectives and directions, including not only legal expertise on issues affecting the overseas territories and their inhabitants but also a desire to represent both the populations living in the hexagon as well as those living overseas. The first challenge of this activism was "territorial continuity," defined as a principle of public service in which the objective was to reinforce the cohesion between different territories of one state in order to compensate for the handicaps linked to their remoteness from each other due to isolation or difficulty of access. Since 2004 the question of discrimination lay at the heart of the association's demands, moving from mobilization around the technical question of airline pricing to one of discrimination against a particular population: French people of overseas origin.

On the Interests of the Associational Form

We have seen that the public authorities developed special links with the world of overseas associations in the metropole. Coupled with an "apolitical" discourse, or rather a "transpartisan" approach to questions concerning overseas France, the associational form allowed the directors of the Collectif DOM in particular to foreground the neutral character of their activism. The promotion of an apolitical image was both characteristic of the discourse about the world of associations and is contradicted by several scholarly works.[14] Vincent Geisser shows how at the end of the 1980s and the beginning of the 1990s the antiracist association France Plus played the apolitical card in order to limit the effects of governmental disfavor; it was a question of survival in the political system.[15] In the case of the Collectif DOM the apolitical stance that it highlighted at the start of its activism served to construct a specific view of overseas problems that went beyond partisan struggles. This was equally the argument that permitted people to pretend to "not play the game of institutions" while at the same time supporting certain politicians not on the basis of their partisan affiliations but because they were "friends of overseas peoples," such as was the case for Nicolas Sarkozy starting at the end of 2005.

The discourse concerning the specific nature of the problems encountered by people from the Caribbean and overseas existed also in the Center-Right UMP Party (Union pour un mouvement populaire), leading to the creation of a position of "national secretary for the overseas presence in the metropole" occupied by Marie-Dominique Aeschlimann, a Guadeloupean city councilor in the Paris suburb of Asnières-sur-Seine. This tendency was reinforced when during the presidential campaigns of 2007 and 2012 candidates held meetings in Paris oriented toward French people of overseas origin.[16] There were people at the heart of the different candidates' campaign organizations in charge of outreach to the population of overseas origin in the metropole.

One example is Patrick Karam who worked with Sarkozy's 2007 campaign. After having resigned from the presidency of the Collectif DOM, he announced he would become the leader of a coalition of organizations called "France Overseas with Sarko." In spite of the organization's apolitical discourse, the announcement of Patrick Karam's support for the candidacy of Sarkozy did not surprise the majority of people working in the Collectif DOM or those who had quit it in 2006. There had been frequent contacts during the protest movement, culminating in Sarkozy's request for aid from the collective to support Aimé Césaire. In parallel fashion, Marie-Domenique Aeschlimann, supported by Michel Diefenbacher, frequently evoked "the specific situation of the DOM" all the while supporting the actions of the collective.[17] This was notably the case during a demonstration organized on May 4, 2007, between the first and second rounds of the presidential election.

On this occasion Marie-Domenique Aeschlimann gave a speech that largely underscored the themes and challenges around which the association mobilized, with a leitmotif of the specificity of the problems of the overseas peoples. She discussed discrimination against the overseas French population in the metropole notably concerning housing, labor, and the ability to obtain bank loans. Aeschlimann also outlined the specific problems of overseas France—distance, isolation, and the fact of being "physically different"—parallel to the relationship with their French citizenship: "We have been French longer than Corsica or Savoy." The theme of visibility was also addressed since the overseas French population was described as "invisible in all aspects of life." She denounced in particular the effective absence of political officials or of overseas candidates in electoral lists. "Participation" or investment in political life must thus respond to this invisibility. Aeschlimann portrayed the French citizens from overseas as having "more than a million individuals according to INSEE, more than three million according to *other sources*" that were not specified during her speech.

During a meeting organized by Patrick Karam at the Le Meridien hotel in support of Nicolas Sarkozy that attracted more than three thousand people, one could see at Sarkozy's side the vice president of the association, Frédéric Bulver.

The presence of several activists of the Collective on the platform of the UMP was important not just for UMP members like Jean-Claude Beaujour but also for members on the left of the political chessboard, confirming the transpartisan strategy of the association. This convergence concerned both the individuals involved and the themes and the vocabulary used by the association. Thus Sarkozy's speech reiterated to a significant degree the overall themes and perspectives of the association, especially the idea of "specific kinds of discrimination against the overseas French" before explicitly thanking Patrick Karam for organizing the meeting.

The Socialist Party was not idle. Candidate Ségolène Royal also organized a meeting devoted specifically to the overseas French population, mobilizing parliamentary deputies from both the hexagon and overseas, primarily from the Caribbean and French Guiana. This meeting also provided the candidate an opportunity to show her support on May 23, a date pushed forward by several groups for the commemoration of the abolition of slavery in France. Several candidates who had attended the meeting at Le Méridien with Sarkozy one month earlier attended this meeting as well.

The DIECFOM: An Institutionalization of the Mobilization

The development of collective actions led by associations like the Collectif DOM favored an alignment with political movements. As we have seen, the development of the theme of "specific discriminations" was symbolized by the creation of an Interministerial Delegation of French of Overseas Origin (DIECFOM).

Created by the decree 2007–1062 after the election of Nicolas Sarkozy, the delegation endorsed both the specific character of issues relating to the overseas French population and the leading role of the Collectif DOM, and Patrick Karam in particular, at the head of the delegation. As Samia Badat, the chief of the cabinet, explained to me, "It is not me that says it, it is him: this is a job for Patrick Karam, by Patrick Karam."[18] The delegation was thus established around the personality of Karam and the objectives and concerns of the Collectif DOM. In a study of the creation of the Haute Autorité de Lutte contre les Discriminations et pour l'Égalité (HALDE), Vincent-Arnaud Chappe explores the long deliberative process that led to the establishment of such an organization.[19] He shows in effect that extensive consultations took place with political and association actors in order to found the HALDE on the most consensual basis possible. DIECFOM's ambitions were much more limited, since it only dealt with overseas populations and it did very little to publicize its efforts. One can nevertheless note that no consultative process took place before its establishment that corresponded to the new president's resumption of proposals from an important association, the Collectif DOM.

The establishment of the delegation also allowed a redistribution of roles with the establishment in 2007 of an Overseas Secretary of State in charge of overseas France and an "overseas community" whose management was formalized by DIECFOM. This reflected both the culmination of the mobilizations of the year 2000 and the hardening of a tendency already present at the beginnings of mass Caribbean migration to the metropole: the existence of privileged access routes to power for the overseas groups and associations, especially those from the Caribbean. It was, however, the theme of "rupture" that was privileged by Karam, DIECFOM being presented as an original project signifying a new era for the overseas French population in the metropole.

The existence of the delegation was attributed to the "strong personality" of the former president of the Collectif DOM, and his powers were presented as coming directly from the Élysée Palace. As Badat explained:

> At the level of hierarchy, DIECFOM answered to the Prime minister, like all interministerial delegations; at a functional level, it answered to the minister of the Interior, which is why it was decided to locate it here rather than in the Place Beauvau [site of the Ministry of the Interior]. In the rue Oudinot one is closer to the files, that is also symbolic. But in actual fact it answers to the Élysée Palace, it is there that Patrick Karam receives his directives. In fact, Patrick Karam also plays a role in what happens there (in the Overseas ministry): it is not a question of legal legitimacy but rather of intervention based on charismatic legitimacy.[20]

The power allocated to the delegation came also from the lesser authority of the Overseas Secretariat of State, whose power declined during the same period. DIECFOM nonetheless only had a limited staff (eight people "including the chauffeur"), but it "reflected overseas France" since the staff was exclusively composed of people of overseas origin. The head of the cabinet came from Réunion, the communications officer from Martinique, and Patrick Karam was Guadeloupean. The delegation did not have its own budget but could "dip into the budgets of the other ministries" depending on the reasons for its expenses. In theory the DIECFOM could draw upon the budget of the ministry of culture to finance cultural projects and other initiatives. Today the DIECFOM is considered one of the three Overseas entities (along with the cabinet of the Overseas Minister and the Overseas General Delegation), and its operating expenses are supposed to come from the budget of the Overseas ministry. Members of DIECFOM played a role in commissions charged with distributing subsidies from the Overseas Secretariat of State, and doubtlessly there they could exercise influence. In supporting certain causes, DIECFOM was able to influence the number of subsidies granted to overseas associations, and Karam was even portrayed by an administrator of the rue Oudinot as the man who really "had his hand on subsidies." The official mission of DIECFOM was nonetheless to participate in the struggle against discrimination experienced by the French from overseas. Several dossiers corresponding to the Collectif DOM's action items were started at the same time, the demand for recognition of the status of overseas students and questions of housing discrimination in particular. From the beginning Karam expressed his desire to reinforce the role of the associations in the representation of the population of overseas origin.[21]

The establishment of this delegation did not proceed without conflicts with Christian Estrosi, the first Overseas Secretary of State under the Sarkozy presidency, who saw some of his authority nibbled away. The delegation in effect competed with the Overseas Secretariat of State, which had for years developed relationships with overseas French people living in the hexagon, as we have seen. These relationships seemed in fact to be one of the important prerogatives of the ministry of (or Secretariat of State of) Overseas France.[22] With the nomination of Yves Jégo in March 2008 the lines of authority seemed more clearly established: the secretary of state was in charge of France overseas, while Karam took charge of the overseas French population in the hexagon.

Karam presented the question of the "structuring" of the associative milieu as a priority. He considered the associations to be permanent tools for organizing the community not only culturally but also in social and political affairs. "To strengthen the associative milieu" was for Karam a means of pursuing the "nonproblematic" trajectory of the Antilleans since that had supposedly limited their participation in the 2005 riots.[23] One structured the community by creating a variety of councils that brought together association leaders around themes like culture, social affairs, and sport. As Badat told me, "We are in constant contact with the associations: we have established a consultative council of the associations which meets once a month and over which Patrick Karam presides one time out of every five. . . . We have also created 'Overseas Commissions' and in particular a 'Who's Who,' the Overseas Club to promote and count the entire overseas elite, associative, intellectual, cultural, and economic."[24]

The creation of representative institutions overseas thus constituted a response to an elitist logic already at play in the discourse of the Collectif DOM. DIECFOM wanted to present the image of a successful, organized, and polished community corresponding to a population "without problems." This perspective was the result of a successful marriage between a socio-political context open to diversity and equality of opportunity as systems that did not hinder the promotion of minority elites and the mobilization of an association that had an interest in the struggle against discrimination was limited to those problems encountered by elites. The promotion of diversity in France was marked by certain rhetorical specificities and the absence of specific antidiscrimination policies, the signing of "charters" being generally favored.[25] DIECFOM's struggles against discrimination equally emphasized the establishment of charters with no enforcement powers but the signing of which was marked by solemnity and included the presence of ministers or secretaries of state concerned with the issues raised by the charter. Thus in September 2008 the signature of a "Charter against discriminatory housing practices encountered by French of overseas origin" took place. This charter had no legal value but served to display the goodwill of a number of landlords, HALDE, DIECFOM, and the ministry of housing to put an end to discriminatory practices against overseas French people, especially concerning the refusal of security deposits drawn on overseas banks.

After a decree on March 31, 2011, Patrick Karam was replaced by Claudy Siar, of Guadelopean origin, the founder of the radio station Tropiques FM and a producer of radio musicals. Upon his arrival, Claudy Siar outlined three objectives for the delegation: "The creation and coordination of actions in favor of the equality of opportunity of the overseas French population in political, economic, social and cultural domains; The promotion of measures destined to end discrimination, especially in education, employment, health, and access to social positions of responsibility; The monitoring and enforcement of measures decided on in the Overseas Estates General."

With the arrival of Claudy Siar the approach to equality of opportunity and to a lesser extent that of discrimination became less and less legalistic. Vincent Arnaud-Chappe has shown how the establishment of the HALDE contributed to orienting the work of the HALDE and the struggle against discrimination to the question of the effectiveness of the law. The case of DIECFOM did not reveal the judicialization of the issue of discrimination against French citizens of overseas origin. Rather, it privileged the promotion of a positive image and a better "understanding" of the group by social and economic leaders.

The delegation continued to exist in 2012 after the victory of François Hollande. This survival corresponded to a reinforcement of the idea that overseas French people in the metropole had specific concerns.[26] The continued existence of this body established by Sarkozy constituted an important campaign promise to prolong the process of integration of French people of overseas origin as a specific entity in French political life. It also reinforced the idea that the concerns of this population were transpartisan—an important argument for the associations.

Nonetheless, one could observe an important change. The new interministerial delegate did not come from the associative or cultural world of the Caribbean and Guyana. She was an economic development professional, a veteran of questions of local development. Her discreet personality and her professional trajectory seemed to break with those of her predecessors. One of her priorities was to promote "overseas audacity," an idea that went together with publicizing the little-appreciated qualities of French people of overseas origin.[27] Concretely, the delegate traveled across France to meet innovators and support the realization of their projects. Her action was less linked to the associations of the Paris area and more anchored in the places where the populations of overseas origin actually lived. It also reflected an important voluntarism. One can nonetheless note that it relied more on a strategy of promoting the population rather than a use of the law in the struggle for equality of opportunity. The objective of structuring the associations was pursued since the delegate used the creation of CREFOM (Conseil Répresentatif des Français d'outre-mer) to affirm that it would be a privileged interlocutor.

Conflict Resolution and Institutionalization

Vincent Arnaud-Chappe has shown how the activists who established the HALDE tended to orient its work and the struggle against discrimination in

general toward the question of the effectiveness of the law.[28] He has analyzed how it resolved conflicts over the issue of discrimination by shifting
it from a political and social to a juridical question. The case of DIECFOM
did not involve the legalization of issues of discrimination against French
of overseas origin. Rather, it favored the promotion of a positive image
and a better understanding of the group by economic and social leaders.
From the first decree nominating an interministerial DIECFOM delegate,
it became clear that it was not only a matter of applying the law or ren-
dering it effective but also of inscribing the actions of the delegation in
the public policies concerning the overseas French population.[29] If the
distinct dynamic of legalization analyzed by Chappe held sway over questions of discrimination, DIECFOM also explored other forms of conflict
resolution. In effect, presenting the question of equality of opportunity
for the overseas French population as an issue beyond political divisions
and the existence of DIECFOM was a no-brainer for both the Left and the
Right and strongly contributed to dissipating the eventual political conflicts around specific cases.

The emergence of the issue of "specific discriminations" could appear
relatively problematic from a political point of view because it reduced
the possibility of alliances with other populations victimized by discrimination, of joint struggles en masse. The insistence on the best possible
understanding of the populations of overseas origin did not envisage
discrimination from an individual point of view, but rather as an aspect
of collective fear, which could bring about a veritable historicization
of the treatment of these populations. This was the perspective, at the
moment of the founding of the HALDE, of certain actors who advocated
a comprehensive and not simply juridical approach to the question of
discrimination with the idea that it was also necessary to adopt a socio-
logical perspective to understand it. This approach was more attentive
to the cumulative dimensions of discrimination that, if they did not take
the form of criminal behaviors that could be qualified as discriminatory,
nonetheless took the form of objective and durable inequalities that certain actors linked to systemic forms of discrimination.[30] The treatment of
specific discriminations also ran counter to the dominant approach in the
struggle against discrimination. One could observe, in effect, precisely by

the use of the law, a tendency to erase the hierarchy of criteria promoting discrimination in favor of an egalitarian treatment of all types of bigotry. With DIECFOM, acts of discrimination against peoples from overseas were considered as being of a particular nature.

Finally, the promotion of the achievements of people of overseas origin tended to risk privileging exceptional achievements and highlighting model trajectories. This produced tension between the achievements of an individual or group on the one hand and the lack of opportunities for this group on the other hand, which should illustrate discriminatory situations. The resolution of this tension constituted one of the challenges for DIECFOM.

Conclusion

The establishment of the DIECFOM in 2007 constituted the culmination of the assumption of responsibility for the French population of overseas origin by the public powers. In effect, since the beginnings of the policy of organized migration with the BUMIDOM there were instances of special relations with this population contributing to giving it special access to public authorities. The associationist milieu, considered the legitimate representative of French people of overseas origin, thus built and maintained strong and privileged links with a certain number of state institutions or agencies: BUMIDOM, then ANT and LADOM, the CMAI Dom-Tom, and the General Overseas Delegation of the Paris City Hall, among others.

The terms of the establishment of the DIECFOM in 2007 following the election of Nicolas Sarkozy followed this movement and was reinforced by the slogans of the mass movements of the first decade of the twenty-first century, in particular those of the Collectif DOM. The delegation's work for equality of opportunity for the overseas French population thus had the political effect of sharply limiting the possibilities of alliances with other groups. Contrary to other instances that could have been at the forefront of the struggle against discrimination, the action of the delegation did not just address the question of the effectiveness of the law but was equally oriented toward the promotion of activities undertaken by the overseas French population and the better understanding of them by society as a whole. If such a perspective could facilitate the understanding of the issue of discrimination from a more comprehensive perspective, it could equally contribute to reinforcing the tension between the discrimination experienced by and the demonstrated competence of a group. In other words, seeking to understand a population better and present it under the most favorable light did not constitute—far from it—a guarantee against discrimination.

The reinforcement of a movement tending to make associations the representatives of overseas populations also risked enabling association officials to assume the position of leaders in institutionalized relationships with the public authorities for several decades. Finally, the existence of such relationships between the state and a very heterogeneous population lumped together with the term "overseas French" also throws light on the contorted way that France approached the management of ethnic and racial minority populations.

NOTES

1. Leïla Wuhl-Ebguy, *Migrants de l'intérieur: Les Antillais de métropole entre integration et mobilisations collectives* (Thèse de doctorat, Science Politique, Université Paris-Dauphine, December 2006).

2. The Agence nationale pour l'insertion et la promotion des travailleurs d'outre-mer (ANT) is a national agency for the incorporation and promotion of workers from the French Overseas Territories.

3. The Délégation nationale à l'outre-mer (DGOM) is an office that provides services to municipal workers from the French overseas territories.

4. For current information about the Interministerial Delegation for the Equality of Opportunity of Overseas French (DIECFOM), see http://www.ultramarins.gouv.fr.

5. Wuhl-Ebguy, *Migrants de l'intérieur*, 80.

6. BUMIDOM, *Compte-rendu d'activité*, November 30, 1964.

7. Wuhl-Ebguy, *Migrants de l'intérieur*, 85.

8. Fred Constant, "La politique française de l'immigration antillaise 1946–1987," *Revue Européene des Migrations Internationales* 3 (1987): 9–31.

9. As Fred Constant emphasized, the establishment of l'ANT responded to a triple assessment: the need to aid integration rather than to encourage migration, the impossibility to direct large numbers of return trips to territories of origin, and the necessity to assure favorable migration conditions.

10. Audrey Celestine, "Originaires d'Outre-Mer," *La Vie des idées* (May 28, 2012), http://www.laviedesidees.fr/Originaires-d-outre-mer.html.

11. Wuhl-Ebguy, *Migrants de l'intérieur*, 113.

12. In 1983 the Overseas Ministry organized the National Assises of Overseas French. In 1987 Paris City Hall organized the Estates General of Associations of French of Overseas Origin.

13. The essentials concerning the Caribbean associative milieu have been brought together in my book, Audrey Celestine, *La fabrique des identités. L'encadrement politique des minorités caribéennes à Paris et New York* (Paris: Karthala, 2018).

14. Martine Barthelemy, *Associations : un nouvel âge de la participation* (Paris: Presses de Sciences Po, 2000).

15. Vincent Geisser, *Ethnicité républicaine* (Paris: Presses de Sciences Po, 1997), 178.

16. Audrey Celestine and Aurélie Roger, "'L'outre-mer' à la croisée du local et du national. Construction, évolution et appropriations d'une catégorie sur trois terrains ultramarines," *Terrains et Travaux* 24, no. 1 (2014): 124–42.

17. Enarque (a graduate of France's prestigious National School of Administration), Michel Diefenbacher spent a large part of his career in the DOM and became prefect in 1992. Since 2005 he has been national secretary of the UMP for overseas France.

18. Interview with Samia Badat, chief of the cabinet of Patrick Karam in DIECFOM, September 2008.

19. Vincent-Arnaud Chappe, "Le cadrage juridique, une ressource politique? La creation de la HALDE comme solution au problème de l'effectivité des norms anti-discriminatoires," *Politix* 2, no. 94 (2011): 107–30.

20. Badat, interview.

21. The CREFOM (Representative Council of the French from Overseas) was finally established in January 2014 under the aegis of Overseas minister Victorin Lurel and with Patrick Karam as president.

22. The interviews with the members of the cabinet of the Overseas minister give this implication. Relations with the "representatives" of what was called at the time the "fifth DOM" were an essential aspect of the minister's role.

23. François-Xavier Guillerm, "3 questions à Patrick Karam. Créer une vraie offre associative," *France-Antilles*, April 3, 2008, http://www.fxgpariscaraibe.com/article-18418340.html.

24. Badat, interview.

25. Laure Bereni, "Faire de la diversité une richesse pour l'entreprise. La transformation d'une contrainte juridique en catégorie managériale," *Raisons Politiques* 35 (2009): 87–106.

26. This element was particularly visible during the 2012 election. See Audrey Celestine and Aurélie Roger, "Un enjeu mineur en campagne: l' 'Outre-Mer' dans l'élection présidentielle de 2012," in *Le lobbying electoral: Groupes en campagne présidentielle*, ed. Julie Gervais, J. and Guillaume Courty (Villeneuve-d'Ascq, France: Presses Universitaires du Septentrion, 2016).

27. The retranscriptions of remarks and debates during the colloquium organized in the Senate, "L'audace ultramarine en metropole" are available on the website http://www.senat.fr/evenement/colloque/outre_mer/audace_ultramarine_en _hexagone.html.

28. Chappe, "Le cadrage juridique, une ressource politique?"

29. Decree number 2007–1062 of July 5, 2007, instituting an interministerial delegate indicated in effect that "he will work in close liaison with the independent administrative authorities and the public establishments intervening in public policy in order to assure the equal opportunity of the overseas French." https://www.legifrance.gouv.fr/loda/id/LEGITEXT000006056554/2007-07-06/.

30. Chappe, "Le cadrage juridique, une ressource politique?."

9

Racially Imprinted Bodies

The Black Feminine Press in Contemporary France

SARAH FILA-BAKABADIO

In November 2014 the latest performance from the South African artist Brett Bailey, *Exhibit B*, was presented at the Théâtre Gérard Philippe in Saint Denis, in the outskirts of Paris. *Exhibit B* displays Black characters ranging from an enchained slave carrying an iron muzzle hiding most his face to the powerless figure of the African migrant locked in immigration detention camps. Each character appeared as an archetype of a subjugated Blackness placed in a global and timeless human zoo. This work had already aroused heated controversies in Edinburgh, London, and Berlin about a white man's representation of Black people and their history. Though the artist explained he intended to deconstruct racial clichés about Black people and Africa, his *tableaux vivants* also revived stereotypes about Black people. But while a shocking reenactment does not systematically raise consciousness or open itself to self-critique, Bailey's insistence on historically engaged art confronted two important aspects of contemporary debates about Blackness in France.

One is the context his piece was presented in. For more than a decade, debates have arisen about the political, social, and media representation of Black populations in Europe. These populations have organized in networks of associations like ISD (Initiative Schwarze Menschen in Deutschland) in Germany, BEMA (Black and Ethnic Minorities Association) and BARAC (Black Activists Against Rising Cuts) in England, and the CRAN (Representative Council of Black Associations) in France. All deal with minorities' political, social, and economic status; criticize the absence of race in national founding myths; and address discrimination at national and continental levels. Bailey's installation was presented at the same time that matters of visibility and othering were flowing throughout Western Europe. Second, beyond the deleterious critics of the artist's racial positionality, one question was barely addressed: What is the Black body? How can it be considered per se not as a "scene of display" of stereotypes and counterimages but as a site of Black experiences?[1]

This chapter explores this large question by discussing the representations of the Black body developed in the Black feminine press that has emerged in France in the early 2000s. The point is to explore Black corporeity by observing the evolution of the Black feminine press in France since 1972. From the African-based and male-dominated *Amina*, first dedicated to African women in France, to the transatlantic perspective of *Miss Ebène*, which links together American, African, and Caribbean models, the Black feminine press has developed visual counterdiscourses that tie together beauty and Blackness. The feminine press may appear as a futile object that with its emphasis on beauty cannot be considered seriously in the scientific and political arenas, but, as one knows, studying Blackness inevitably puts the body under focus. Centuries of exogenous and endogenous representations of Blackness have opposed to define its meaning to the world. Today, the Black feminine press contributes to this long-lasting discussion by proposing images that define what being Black in contemporary France means.

The Surface of the Black Body

> I am aware of my skin surface, my *epidermal encasement* through my body image and particularly when I am "seen." Saying that I have a body is thus a way of saying that I can be as an object that I try to be seen as a subject, that another can be my master so that shame and shamelessness express the dialectic of plurality of consciousness and have a metaphysical significance.
> —Frantz Fanon, *Black Skin, White Masks* [2]

Frantz Fanon wrote these lines in 1952 to describe how being Black meant being "locked into [one's] body," the surface of which determined one's political and social identity.[3] Experiencing the Black body implies knowing that its surface is used to define its interiority. Fanon detailed the feeling of estrangement from a space that his mind could not shape but in which his existence to the world relied on someone else's gaze. "I am my body while I am also *not* my body," he explained.[4]

The articulation between the overexposure and overcoding of Blackness that Fanon denounced shaped Black corporeality. In France as in other Western countries, Blackness was invented through the naturalization of bodies fragmented into pieces (skin, skull, face, morphology) later interpreted as signs of otherness if not othering. The Black body was created, represented, and described as a visual negative of whiteness the definition of which lied in the denial of the self and its apparent and yet artificial absence of (Western) history.[5] The body mediates race. But as Colette Guillaumin and Didier Fassin have noted, thinking of the Black body as a racial signifier is not self-evident.[6] Indeed, physical features have become historically and socially meaningful because of racialization processes that leveled human beings into categories.

In January 1924 on the cover of the first issue of *La presse coloniale illustrée* were sketched portraits of two men painted by the Belgium explorer Henri Cayon. Under the title "France and its countries" (*"La France et ses pays"*) and amidst the forest, two faces appeared. In the background a French soldier looked at the reader with clear eyes and a determined gaze. He wore a helmet marked with the acronym of the French Republic, RF. At the bottom of the image, a colonized African man wearing headscarf and cowry jewelry smiled blissfully and looked afar to an unknown future. The two faces were here used as signifiers of civilization and savagery that justified French colonization. Their features, facial expressions, and postures were the subtexts to the colonial discourse. Images opened to the visualization of the other who was no longer imagined but seen. Sketches and photographs fixed bodies in a series of clichés that generated a coding of the Black body—if not a visual grammar—replicated in various newspapers that fleshed out a collective and yet political imaginary. *Le journal colonial, Le courrier colonial illustré, La Gazette coloniale, Le bulletin colonial,* and *La presse coloniale illustrée* regularly offered images of the colonized that confirmed archetypes of social, cultural, and historical inferiority scripted on the body. Visualizing the other turned into a "revelation" of some "truth" as photography was largely used to portray bare-chested girls, naked soldiers, and aging chiefs that added to the representation of the primitive. Photography was used to "demonstrate" Africans' and Black people's "*état de nature*." Naked and motionless bodies illustrated the accounts from discoverers and colonial officials. They embodied African "types" that both carried a "Black phenotype" and represented the diversity of African peoples: the Agni or the Senoufo types from the Ivory Coast.[7] Ethnic, cultural, and political classifications merged into these types exposed by photography. Even more than the many engravings of slaves in the fields or etchings of the colonized, photography opened to a large circulation of images back and forth from the metropole to the colonies. Postcards, boxes, figurines, and statuettes allowed the stereotypes of the Black body to enter French people's daily lives.

Europeans' and French people's racialized gazes not only shaped representations of the Black body but the Black body itself. It was turned into an essentialized space the existence of which stemmed from "external form, substance, [and] the physiological . . . processes" and even temperament.[8] Europeans' gaze developed Blackness out of physicality as "the whole set of visible and tangible expressions." It naturalized the Black body and reduced it to a set of "morphological and physiological characteristics that are intrinsic to it."[9] The body was a sign of a lack of interiority that then meant the absence of civilization. Physicality initiated and contained Blackness both by coding its presence to the world and by limiting Black people's agency to physical traits.[10] While France celebrated its universalist model, explorers, scientists, and artists constructed Kantian representations of the Black body.[11] In this officially color-blind nation, their gaze determined the commonalities of a race—the "Black race"—and inextinguishable "embodied natural differences" that distanced it from whiteness.[12] It disjoined Frenchness and Blackness and turned the Black body into a "surface[s] of inscription" that shaped out a double lens: the photographer's and the viewer's.[13] Images then confirmed their intention to capture this "irreducible exteriority" named Blackness.[14]

Visibility and the History of the Black Presence

Since the early 2000s visual archives on the Black presence in France have flowered in bookstores, the internet, and the media. Along with academic works, numerous essays, monographs, biographies, public debates, exhibitions, and festivals, images have contributed to renew and expand debates about "the Black question" in France.[15] Many of these publications visualize the Black presence. From *Être noir au XVIIIe siècle* to *Noir blanc rouge: Trente-cinq Noirs oubliés de l'histoire de France*, visuality doubles the texts: images are illustrations that represent the trajectories of Black men and women who, since the fifteenth century, intertwined Frenchness and Blackness.[16] Paintings of Toussaint L'Ouverture or photographs of the 1956 Congress of Black Writers and Artists confirm how intricately connected France has become with Blackness. Images are collected, compiled, and somehow accumulated in visual monographs like Pascal Blanchard et al.'s *Black France*.[19] In more than one hundred engravings, paintings, and photographs, *Black France* assesses that France has always been a multiracial country. Like in other publications, most images tend to refer to prominent political and cultural figures like Aimé Césaire. Though countering the tropes of the color-blind myth with images of Blackness surely is relevant, these publications do not question what it means. Rather, the body is "viewed as a text that can be 'read' as a symbol or signifier of the social world it inhabits."[18] Photographs are like historical snapshots used to represent the temporality a long Black French history and not of Caribbean or African histories. The Black body then materializes the "complex relations of domination and subordination linked to the inscription of history as it pertains to Black people" in France "and the global oppressed."[19] It becomes a trace that tells the readers about the existence of Blackness in France through the forms of discrimination it generated. Yet, unlike scholarly productions, they emphasize visibility. Black bodies are displayed, not analyzed. They are archetypes of Blackness—the slave body, the colonized one or a postcolonial self—readers might not be aware of. They are (re)interpreted out of clichés and not analyzed per se. But images of Black bodies are known. As the exhibition *Le Modèle Noir* showed,[20] we are familiar with the *Portrait d'une négresse* from Marie-Guillemine Benoist (1800) or *Etude de nègre* by Théodore Chassériau (1836).[21] They represented archetypes but not people. They anonymized Madeleine, a servant, and Joseph, the professional Dominican model for the Paris École des Beaux-Arts, behind the category "Black." The visibility of Black bodies exists but turning them into sites of agency and resistance is what people ask for today. Black populations seek images that valorize Blackness and reflect the abundance of African, African American, Caribbean, or Reunionese multiplicities built for more than a century through migrations in and out of the metropole and transatlantic encounters.

Two further points are not addressed in these illustrative images but are recurrent questions in popular productions such as the Black feminine press. One is visual conformity if not mimicry in the images selected. Indeed, most of the exceptional characters mentioned in these visual histories were painted by white artists who for the most part imagined them as typical examples of an estranged race. The paintings of the now famous Chevalier de St George are quite telling. He was usually presented as a noble man (seated, wearing a white wig, floppy necktie, gloves, and a foil). The outfit, the hairdo, the posture, and the setting referred to a *gentilhomme* aesthetic that concealed the Black body. Only the skin color and sometimes the facial features were associated with Blackness. But such images cannot only be read as the symbol of some Black agents achieving top-ranking positions in eighteenth-century France. They should also be considered through the violence of normalizing processes that sought to transform the Black body into a derivative of a white one. These paintings as much as photographs reproduced assigned representations that, at times, challenged stereotypes of "uncivilized" Black bodies but most emphasized the trajectories of exceptions to their "race."[22] Images were composed in-between mimesis and self-affirmation. A visual history of Black French people should develop, as Anne Lafont offers, a critical analysis that does not equal visibility to power but discusses the articulation between images, racial biopolitics, othering, and agency.[23]

Amina, Beauty, and Imprinted Bodies

In a bookstore in downtown Paris the cover of a poster-size magazine strikes my eyes. A close-up portrait of a Black woman appears. Motionless and expressionless, she seems lost in her thoughts, not paying attention to the photographer. Her body and hair are covered with a dark Black paint that contrasts with her dazzling red lipstick and the whiteness of her retina.[24] This October 2014 issue of *L'insensé*, an art magazine, is entitled "Africa." Though the contents show a genuine interest in the works of African contemporary artists, the cover reinstates the skin color and facial features as symbols of a close or distant link to Africa. The viewer's gaze travels throughout the image, from the skin to the kinky hair and the thick lips, and recomposes the visual lexicon of Blackness formed out of slave and colonial histories. In between art, haute couture, and fashion, *L'insensé*, like the fashion magazine *FashizBlack*, represents a new type of publications that celebrate the singularity of a Black form of beauty and yet continue to promote images that seal the Black body in a racial definition.[25] This bias partly originates in the history of the Black female press in France.

In 1972 Michel de Breteuil, a French entrepreneur, became the president of the publishing company his father Charles de Breteuil created in Dakar in 1933: the SAPEF (*Société africaine de publicité et d'édition fusionnée*). In the emerging economy of this former French colony, de Breteuil held that francophone West African women did not have a magazine they could identify with. He entered a field long occupied by the iconic *Awa: la revue de la femme noire*.[26] Along with four sports and news magazines, de Breteuil founded *Amina*, which would stand as the reference publication for Francophone African women for the next thirty years. As its first editor in chief, he hired freelance journalists throughout West Africa who filled the magazine with articles on social issues (health care, economy, and childcare, among others), portraits of prominent African women (athletes, local activists, or artists like Angélique Kidjo) and the emblematic photoromances.[27] Countless articles on braidings, fashion, and makeup appeared along with ones on serious matters like sexual mutilations, forced marriages, or poverty. The covers usually showed role models women are to identify with: local entrepreneurs, professional models like the 2000 Miss France, Sonia Rolland, or "first ladies."[28] In-between the local and the transnational, *Amina* developed as the magazine for "modern" African women juggling family and work.[29]

However, in the 1970s and 1980s de Breteuil and his overwhelmingly masculine staff proposed a rather paternalistic and Eurocentric perspective on African women. In his monthly editorial, Simon Kiba, the publication's editor in chief from 1975 to 1983, praised chastity before marriage and "reassured" single women (they would find a husband), while numerous articles on embroidering and fertility appeared throughout the five hundred issues of the magazine. Though it emphasized modernity, *Amina* represented women as mothers whose main role was to maintain the unity of the household. In 1983 Aissatou Diallo, *Amina*'s former staff secretary, became the first female editor in chief. But the paternalist tone of the journal remained, pulling away younger generations.[30] Similarly, while it celebrated the beauty of African and Black women, *Amina* long proposed a white, masculine, and Western representation of beauty. In the early 1980s as the publication expanded in the Caribbean and in Europe, it needed more financial resources. Most international advertisers refused to enter this niche market, leaving space for smaller Francophone and African American companies.[31] Ads for creams, make up, hair pomades from Mizani, Activilong, Palmer's, or Fashion Fair filled the pages of the magazine and gradually shaped the Black beauty market in France. Companies like the historic hair care company Dark & Lovely developed this French African market as an extension of the African American one. They used the same commercial practices. They advertised the same products up to five times in each issue of *Amina* for at least a year and invented models the customers should identify with. Month after month, readers were confronted with American ideals introduced by catchy slogans ("right from the United States," "African American," and so on).

A point of contention lies in the dual representation of beauty both *Amina* and these advertisers proposed. On the one hand, articles celebrated the beauty of African and Caribbean women and singled out the specifics of their beauty practices (braiding and weaves, for instance). From braiding to jewelry and natural cosmetics, journalists focused on positive images of the Black body. Singers, athletes, and community activists appeared with limited makeup and natural hair, trying to enhance who they were without aesthetic transformation. On the other hand, most ads promoted bleaching creams and hair relaxers. While some products like Skin Success, Métissage, or Skin Fair claimed they could help readers to soothe skin problems that Black populations regularly experience like dark spots. Others like Clearmovate and Belle Dam clearly associated beauty with a fair (if not white) skin. Bel Dam specialized in bleaching skin products.

Throughout the 1980s each of its ads played on words Bel Dam and "belle dame" ("beautiful lady") constantly suggesting that only a light-colored person could be beautiful. In the 1980s Tanda, another leading skincare company, suggested that "when [living] in Northern countries," Black women should look like local people. Racial mixing then appeared as a white-derived model of beauty customers should try to achieve. Consequently, most models presented were racially mixed people. This message became even more ambivalent when *Amina* addressed Caribbean populations. A 1987 ad for the brand Miss Antilles showed a young woman with a dazzling smile and painted blue eyes presented relaxing creams and oils. Her naturally straight hair represented what buyers could supposedly achieve thanks to the relaxers and softening creams Miss Antilles offered. But that body was unreal: her eyes were painted with the same blue as the product packaging, her skin was artificially tanned, and her hair tinted dark Black. Yet the message is quite clear: having long hair and fair skin makes you beautiful and desirable. In the pages of *Amina*, Black women were regularly encouraged to use strange products that any Black population now knows to use in order to look like this woman: egg shampoos, placenta relaxers, mink oil lotions, or cholesterol balms that promise to turn kinky hair curly. On one out five pages of the magazine, readers were constantly reminded that natural was not beautiful except if mixed or white. Dark skin or kinky hair were signs of past subjugated bodies whose features defined their absence to the world. Blackness then had to be transformed to be beautiful. The ads for bleaching creams gradually disappeared from *Amina* by the 1990s as debates about the dangerous effects of hydroquinone on consumers' health grew. However, today the magazine still emphasizes Black women's need to transform themselves. It offers photoshopped images that still turn beauty into an unreal and unreachable assemblage.

Another point is controversial. *Amina* is not a political magazine though it has witnessed the changes and ruptures that the continent went through over the last fifty years. But the magazine seems to escape temporality and historicity. Though it was founded in Leopold Sedar Senghor's Senegal and experienced Africa's tremendous and usually turbulent evolution, it has never discussed how politics impacts African and Black women. The long-term impact of colonial imagery on the representation of Black bodies and Black women, the visual rhetoric of independent and communist-oriented regimes, and African women's self-representations in contemporary Africa slip away from the pages of *Amina*. Similarly, the publication barely addresses the representations of the Black bodies in contemporary France that it creates.[32] One could argue that a feminine magazine does not need to address historical, social, and political issues. But beauty is not disconnected from the context it is produced in. It is historical, socially, and politically situated. Yet at times, *Amina* took a stand. In 1975 it reproduced three full-length speeches from the North Korean dictator Kim Jung-Il and regularly praises first ladies whose wealth and social statuses originated in the oppression of their people.[33]

Amina lacks a decolonial vision that would reflect upon racial prejudice and the impact of biopolitics on its representation of Black forms of beauty. In the early 2010s, as a new Black feminine press emerged in France, *Amina* developed a web magazine. It includes articles on international artists like Beyoncé and Rihanna as well as recently renowned artists like the Oscar-winning Kenyan actress Lupita Nyong'o or the Nigerian writer Chimamanda Ngozi Adichie. It also celebrates the achievements of Black French figures like the journalists Audrey Pulvar and Kareen Guiock or the activist Rokhaya Diallo. The web magazine refers to a global Black world in which women share the same concerns about career, family, and beauty and admire the same celebrities. However, the magazine has not changed. It still focuses on the African continent, at times referring to Black people in France. The coexistence of the webzine and the magazine shows the uncertain posture of a publishing group that developed as the reference for African women in France but not yet for Black French ones.

Visual Commitment and Intersected Blackness

Amina's lack of mobility has distanced younger generations of Black people whose lives, identities and cultures are shaped in between France and Africa, the metropole and the overseas territories, and the United States. These mostly French-born people refuse to conceal Blackness behind the myth of a color-blind nation. They criticize the universalist myth and the Republican imagery that stigmatizes them as immigrants' descendants or as "the second generation." They equally refuse to be confined to a state of appearance as the "visible minorities" at times represented in the media by journalists such as Audrey Pulvar and Harry Roselmack or public figures like Omar Sy. They seek images that reflect their multilayered ascriptions, postcolonial histories, and transnational sense of belonging to a "Black condition." To them, images—including beauty ones—not only reflect a connection to a family homeland but are tools to empower themselves in present-day France.

Aside from *Amina* and white-based mainstream publications like *Elle*, *Marie Claire*, or *Femme Actuelle* that barely represent Black people, since 2001 this new readership can look at *Miss Ebène*, a magazine founded by two French-African male entrepreneurs, Almamy Lô and Achille Tobbo.[34] In the first issue of what would become a leading publication, Tobbo stressed the need to provide Black populations in France with positive images that would counter those of subjugated Black bodies.[35] *Miss Ebène* refers to global Blackness not to local beauty practices defined as Congolese or Malian. It proposes international archetypes of Black beauty derived from the American media and film industries. In its pages, ads alternate with articles on Alicia Keys's latest hairdos or Kerry Washington's fashion style. They are from international Black beauty trademarks like Black Up, Black Opal, and Dark & Lovely, which now compete with global beauty groups like L'Oréal or Lancôme to rule over the booming Black beauty market.[36] In *Miss Ebène*, Black models replace white ones to sell the newest Maybelline lipstick or foundation.[37] Images reverse color codes from white to Black but the message is unchanged: being beautiful means transforming oneself. Foundation, lipstick, and fake lashes are necessary to be beautiful. But beyond this emphasis on sophistication common to all beauty magazines, *Miss Ebène*, like *Black Beauty*, presents Black bodies that piece together signs of Blackness and whiteness (skin color or hair texture). The body is a composite space that displays physical features associated with each race. It should visually represent the readers' multiple cultures and identities. Afro wigs are paired with blue or green color contact lenses, Brazilian weaves with Indian laces, dark skin with "African buttocks." Physical features are mixed not fused. Each piece is easily recognizable as a reference to Blackness or whiteness. The body is a creation that does not challenge discriminatory images of Blackness. It reverses their meaning to defend a Black form of beauty that follows a dominant aesthetic later adapted to Black populations.

The leading African American beauty magazines *Essence* and *Ebony* have inspired *Miss Ébène*'s visual rhetoric of beauty. Most covers and articles deal with the lives and images of American and African American singers, actors, or models such as Rihanna, Beyoncé, Gabrielle Union, or Halle Berry. Some celebrities, like Jordin Sparks, a singer from the TV show *American Idol*, or Eva Marcille, the 2006 winner of the *America's Next Top Model*, are barely known to most French readers. Yet they frequently appear in the magazine. Black French readers are confronted with models shaped by the American music, cinema, and beauty industries. If Aïssa Maïga, Sonia Rolland, and Noémie Lenoir appear alongside Omar Sy, they only represent a limited part of each issue published to this point. The founders explain that African American artists appeal to the readers that they are familiar with. But these photoshopped images standardize Blackness. Bodies are homogenized. The same makeup techniques (eyebrows, fake lashes, foundation) shape the curves of faces to look alike whatever one's features are. From the wavy lace style to the supposedly authentic nappy style, the body is shaped and imagined to fit into the ideal that diversity should represent the specifics of a Black form of beauty.[38] Moreover, most model figures are again, like Rihanna or the actress Zoé Saldana, of mixed origin. They naturally combine some of the features defined as beautiful.

Miss Ebène classifies the Black body following global beauty styles proposed and/or imposed on Black populations by a beauty market first developed in the United States for the African American population. Throughout the twentieth and twenty-first centuries, cosmetic companies like Naomi Sims or Fashion Fair developed the niche created in the 1900s by Madame C. J. Walker. They generated beauty practices (hair grooming, products made of cocoa, shea, or any resource recalling Africa, among others) which invented Black beauty.[39] Coupled with a discourse on modernity and racial uplift, they turned clichés from the skinny, fair-complexioned Jezebel incarnated by actresses like Lena Horne or Dorothy Dandridge to the hefty Mammy into symbols of Black multiplicities.

Black phenotypes were developed to define how distant they were from white aesthetic standards. *Miss Ebène* reproduces these body types while also arguing that capturing images of the Black body is a tool for social, political, and cultural recognition of Black populations in France. Yet it never questions the meaning of race nor the classifications it generates. Many Black female magazines like *Black Beauty* follow the same line. They address teenagers and young women born and/or raised in France that are interested in fashion and encouraged to shape self-representation out of visuals of African American stars. Unlike *Amina*, these magazines are not for immigrant women keeping ties with their homelands but for Black populations living in Western countries.

From 2003 to 2015 seven new magazines have appeared in newsstands challenging *Miss Ebène*'s new monopoly. *Brune, Culture femme*, and *Première Dame* replicate *Amina*'s concept and deal with women's daily lives. Family, health care, politics, and money are their guidelines. These publications appeal to readers in their thirties up to those in their fifties. Unlike *Miss Ebène*, they connect Black populations in France to homelands whether in the Caribbean or in Africa. For their founders, the point is to represent the readers' transnational cultures. Like *Amina*, the focus is on a Francophone arena, sometimes clearly eluding any identification to African American stars. The Black body appears in articles celebrating the achievements of artists, social activists, designers, and even members of African presidential families.[40] References to local matters (mother/daughter relationships, couple issues, cooking, and more) increase the impression of proximity. The same goes for beauty pages. They have a simple and quite traditional focus ("twenty pages for the best look," "weaves and wigs," "the top nail polish of the season," and so on). Beauty seems accessible though sophisticated.

From *Miss Ebène* to *Brune* and *Black Beauty*, the Black feminine press emphasizes visibility as a form of political, social, and economic positionality for Black populations in France. But, as in the past, the images they print continue to shape the Black body. From wig fashions to the increasing nappy trend, the natural body never appears. It is molded by hair lotions, sprays, makeup, and powders that define its color, shape, and sometimes texture. Images continue to represent codified Black bodies whose existence to the world requires their transformation. Such a visibility, though necessary, relies on the construction of the Black body that cannot apparently escape construction.

Imperfect Bodies

In his book *Critique de la raison nègre* (2013), Achille Mbembé proposes a timeline of the concept of "Black" and defines two moments. One spans from the eighteenth to the nineteenth centuries, a time when race was constructed in Western societies as an inevitable prism to justify domination. The second moment, which actually intertwines part of the first one, is a time of "recognition": Black people capture and reverse of discriminatory rhetoric and celebrate the "negro" as a positive categorization on which they built political and artistic forms of identification as did the authors of the Harlem Renaissance and the Négritude movement. The Black feminine press in France prolongs this moment. It still struggles against persisting stereotypes that actualize the Kantian metaphor of the Black body as the symbol of ugliness. It proposes body types that should counter past images. Yet it does not deconstruct Blackness in a critical perspective that would challenge aesthetic norms that still use whiteness as its standard. Nor does it tackle the readers' internalization of racist imageries that systematically deem the Black body a dissenting and even subversive body. Black corporeality is affirmed and defended as the ground for a legitimate racialized sense of aesthetic. Its role in categorizing Black people is not questioned. Rather, it invents a Black form of beauty that now codes the Black body as a site of resistance to discriminatory representations. The surface of the body and its phenotype are reinterpreted as signs of social and political subjectivity. A pending question is to what extent these racialized representations of Blackness can actually contribute to defining a "unifying [visual] framework" that could help "building up [an] identity across ethnic and cultural difference between the difference communities" and represent the experiences of Black populations in France.[41]

NOTES

1. See Rosemary A. Joyce, "Archaeology of the Body," *Annual Review of Anthropology* 34 (2005): 139–58.

2. Frantz Fanon, *Black Skin, White Masks*, quoted in Charles Johnson, "A Phenomenology of the Black Body," in *The Male Body: Features, Destinies, Exposures*, ed. Laurence Goldstein (Ann Arbor: University of Michigan Press, 1994), 127.

3. George Yancy, "Whiteness and the Return of the Black Body," *Journal of Speculative Philosophy* 19, no. 4 (2005): 219.

4. Fanon quoted in Johnson, "A Phenomenology of the Black Body," 124.

5. See Achille Mbembé, *Critique de la raison nègre* (Paris: La Découverte, 2013), 25–64.

6. Colette Guillaumin, *Racism, Sexism, Power and Ideology* (London, Routledge, 1995); Didier Fassin, "Racialization: How to do Races with Bodies," in *A Companion to the Anthropology of the Body and Embodiment*, ed. Frances E. Mascia-Lees (London: Blackwell), 420.

7. The word "type" appears in the supplement to the *Le Courrier colonial* entitled: "populations et forêts de la Côte d'Ivoire," December 25, 1930.

8. Philippe Descola, *Beyond nature and culture* 2nd ed., Chicago: University of Chicago Press, 2013), 116. On race and temperament, see Elsa Dorlin, *La matrice de la race* (Paris: La Découverte, 2003).

9. Elsa Dorlin, *La matrice de la race* (Paris: La Découverte), 2003.

10. Many studies have explored Black people's representations in Western countries and more particularly in France. Some refer to the Black body as a symbol of time periods when it embodied another (human) specimen displayed in medical practices or as in human zoos. Others emphasize its commodification into types (the slave body, the *indigene* or colonized body) the existence of which was determined by their economic role. Gilles Boestch, ed., *Corps normalisé, corps stigmatisé, corps racialisé* (Bruxelles: De Boeck Université, 2007); Didier Fassin and Dominique Memmi, eds., *Le gouverment des corps* (Paris: École des Hauters Études en Sciences Sociales, 2004). See also Joan Anim-Addo and Scafe Suzanne, *I am Black/White/Yellow: An Introduction to the Black Body in Europe* (London: Mango, 2007).

11. Along with Edmund Burke, Immanuel Kant described the Black body as a dark space generating disgust and sometimes horror among Europeans. See Immanuel Kant, *Observations on the Feeling of the Beautiful and the Sublime* (Berkley: University of California Press, 2003), 97–116.

12. Deborah Poole, *Vision, Race, and Modernity: A Visual Economy of the Andean Image World* (Princeton NJ: Princeton University Press, 1997), 14–15.

13. Rosemary A. Joyce, "Archaeology of the Body," 140.

14. Michele Wallace, *Constructing the Black Masculine: Identity and Ideality in African American Men's Literature and Culture, 1775–1995* (Durham NC: Duke University Press, 2002), 46.

15. See Claude Ribbe, *Alexandre Dumas, le dragon de la reine* (Paris: Édition du Rocher, 2002); Benoît Hopquin, *Ces noirs qui ont fait la France: du chevalier de St George à Aimé Césaire* (Paris: Calman-Lévy, 2009). For academic references, see Miriam Cottias, *La Question noire: Histoire d'une construction coloniale* (Paris:

Bayard, 2007). On the expansion of studies on Black populations in France, see Sarah Fila-Bakabadio, "The Imbricated Registers of Black Studies in France," in *Black Studies in Europe*, ed. Nicole Grégoire, Sarah Fila-Bakabadio, and Jacinthe Mazzochetti (Evanston IL: Northwestern University Press, forthcoming).

16. Erick Noël, *Être noir en France au XVIIIe siècle* (Paris: Tallandier, 2006); Valéry Rouben, *Noir blanc rouge: Trente-cinq Noirs oubliés de l'histoire de France* (Paris, Vuibert, 2014). Most of these essays are published by leading publishing houses like Calman-Lévy, La Découverte, Vuibert, or Plon. In most essays, images are not analyzed but illustrate the authors' point.

17. Pascal Blanchard et al., *La France noire* (Paris, La Découverte, 2011).

18. Erica Reischer and Kathryn S. Koo, "The Body Beautiful: Symbolism and Agency in the Social World," *Annual Review of Anthropology* 33 (2004): 300.

19. Alexander Weheliye, "The Grooves of Temporality," *Public Culture* 17, no. 2 (2005): 322.

20. *Le Modèle noir: de Géricaut à Matisse*, Musée d'Orsay, Paris, March–September 2019.

21. Théodore Chassériau, *Etude de nègre*, 1836, oil painting,

22. Akiko Shimizu, *Lying Bodies: Survival and Subversion in the Field of Vision* (New York: Peter Lang, 2008).

23. Anne Lafont, *L'art et la race. L'Africain (tout) contre l'oeil des Lumières* (Paris: Les presses du réel, 2018).

24. Such images also recall the Blackface stereotype created in the United States in the nineteenth century. White actors playing in racist minstrel shows painted their faces in black and wore red lipstick to caricature Black physical features.

25. Uli Linke, *German Bodies: Race and Representation After Hitler* (London: Routledge, 2002), 38.

26. *Awa* (1969–73) was a pan-African magazine founded by the Senegalese journalist and feminist activist Annette Mbaye D'Erneville.

27. Each issue ended with ten to fifteen pages of photoromance that the readers eagerly kept up with.

28. A number of special issues were dedicated to several African first ladies without considering the political regimes they lived in.

29. Emphasis in original.

30. Diallo however proposed articles on the "emancipation of African women." Nathalie de Breteuil, the founder's daughter and a journalist at *Amina* since 1994, is the current editor in chief of *Amina*.

31. Two exceptions were Revlon and Helena Rubinstein, which advertised the same products in *Amina* as in any other female magazine.

32. In 2019 tensions were aroused about Aeschylus's *Les Suppliantes* (*The Suppliants*) at Paris Sorbonne University's annual theater festival. Students from Sorbonne University, the *Ligue de défense noire africaine* [The Black African Defense

League] (LDNA) and the CRAN protested against Philippe Brunet's setting: the bodies of white actors were painted in Black and some wore Black masks.

33. These documents were presented as firsthand accounts without any introduction or comment.

34. In 2012 and 2013 *Femme Actuelle* proposed two special issues on Black beauty. Though all copies were sold out, *Femme Actuelle* stopped the publication and did not integrate any reference to Blackness in its weekly issues.

35. *Miss Ebène* 1 (2001): 1.

36. In 2000 L'Oréal acquired the group Softsheen-Carson, which had developed cosmetics for Black populations for almost fifty years. Dark & Lovely was its leading trademark.

37. In this booming market, new French cosmetic companies like Colorii or Inoya also take their share and use this press to reach customers.

38. The nappy hair fashion is growing worldwide as a "natural hairstyle." The "natural" has become a commercial incentive supported by international trademarks like Dark & Lovely that have now captured this emergent market. They propose specific hair products such as Dark and Lovely's "Au Naturale" line used to do "Bantu knots" (sectioned twisted curls).

39. Madame C. J. Walker, an African American self-taught entrepreneur, developed cosmetics for Black women. From facial creams to straightening balms, she laid the bases of what a beautiful Black woman should look like and linked beauty to the transformation of Black physical features.

40. It also carried *Amina*'s heritage of interviewing female family members of African presidents such as Malika Bongo Odimba, the eldest daughter of the current president of Gabon.

41. Stuart Hall, "New Ethnicities," in *Stuart Hall: Critical Dialogues in Cultural Studies*, ed. Kuan Hsing Chen et al. (London: Routledge, 1996), 422.

10

France in *Noir* and Black

Stereotypes and the Politics of the Recognition of Black Populations

FRANCK F. EKUÉ

TRANSLATED BY TYLER STOVALL

France has memory problems
She knows Malcolm X, but not Frantz Fanon nor the FLN
She knows the Blacks but not *les Noirs*
—Rocé (rapper), "Problème de mémoire"

The naming of a social group illustrates the power relations of a given society and represents an important political aspect of struggles for recognition.[1] In the United States the descendants of slaves went from the derogatory designation of "n—" to the euphemisms of "colored" and "Negro" during Reconstruction.[2] They later favored "Black" and "African American" as a result of struggles for recognition.[3] Although they have a different relationship to questions of race, the Black populations linked to the colonial history of France have experienced a similar semantic evolution. The term *"Noir"* replaced the label "Nègre" (Negro in English) in the aftermath of the independence of France's African colonies.[4] However, the strongly pejorative associations of the word Noir in modern societies saw its hegemony disputed by the anglophone expression Black, which explicitly referred to the Anglo-Saxon sociocultural space, in particular that of the United States.[5]

How can one make sense of this recourse to an anglicist expression about a race designation by a nation normally so hostile to such Anglo-Saxon influences, one that moreover rejects all racial discourses?[6] The appearance of the Black anglicism in the French vocabulary seems to confront and to contrast with the more conventional term Noir. Doesn't this balancing act of terms reveal the difficulty of considering, without recourse to an outside perspective, these populations as part of the national community?

The analysis and deconstruction of the term Black addresses its political meaning for the Black populations of France. This genealogy of the racial designation Black, which analyzes the power relations that give rise to this new ethnonym, will be completed by a diachronic analysis that is interested specifically in the context of the emergence, the evolution, and the future of American Blackness.[7] Its circulation is only possible with the support of institutions that guarantee its transmission. Among these mediating institutions one finds in particular those of the entertainment industry, a major source of popular culture.

The use of the word Black echoes historically the relationship between French society and the Black populations in its territory. This essay will follow a chronology beginning at the start of the twentieth century with a Black presence in France originating from the colonies on the one hand and the United States on the other. We will see the creation of an ambivalent discourse about Blacks as others. This exploration will mobilize the scholarship that traces the presence of Black Americans in the French imaginary. I will then show how the racial representations conveyed in the production of Black American culture achieved a worldwide presence as models of hegemonic racial representations. This analysis will rely on songs associated with the slogan "Black Power." Finally, I will consider the use of the anglicism Black in social discourse in France and its ideological implications during its appearance from the years 1980 to 1998.

A Blackness with Two Faces

Colonial discourse was a powerful source of racial alterity. With the support of the media (scientific, iconographic, and performance), it was able to display racial differentiation in a way that shaped the white gaze on non-European populations. It described these people as "savage[s] . . . underscoring the idea of a stagnant sub-humanity . . . caught between humanity and bestiality" and served as a justification for colonial conquests and the civilizing mission of France.[8]

Assimilated by the French into their view of Africans, the Black Americans who landed in France at the beginning of the twentieth century were intuitively viewed through this lens.[9] Nonetheless, even when seen as animalistic, these Blacks were not the object of racist distrust. This was due above all to their American nationality, which made them a part of the civilized world (in contrast to the Blacks from the colonies). Small in number and playing specific limited roles (including as soldiers, musicians, and novelists), Black Americans thus did not pose a direct threat to French society in contrast to the colonial subjects that French workers accused of taking their jobs during World War I.[10]

Far from being seen as a problem, Blacks from America seemed rather to be part of the solution to France's troubles. This perception arose in part from their participation as soldiers in the Great War (a popularity they shared with other colonial soldiers). More subtly, however, I would argue that their favorable reception in France was facilitated by the specific institutional framework of their stay there. The structure of segregation that excluded Black Americans from the mainstream of their own society led them to develop their own institutions (such as sports leagues and musical groups) through which they created what I like to call a racial professionalism as a tactic.[11] This form of resistance had been developed for the days of slavery, and it consists of performing a racial identity in sync with the expectations of the white gaze.[12]

This conception of identity racialized as a market performance and negotiable in an exchange relationship took on a new dimension in French society. In a time of national doubt after the crushing defeat of the French Army by Prussia, the performances of boxers like Jack Johnson, for example, offered an example of bestial and combative manliness calculated to stimulate the fighting spirit of the French.[13] Similarly the Black American performance troupe La Revue Nègre, which Josephine Baker danced for, used its artistic *savoir faire* to highlight colonial fantasmagoria.[14] Unlike the "Negro villages" that aimed at excluding Blacks from humanity (in the context of colonial conquest), the scenes portrayed by Black Americans displayed a cheerful, childlike imagery suitable to a benevolent and paternalistic gaze (justifying France's civilizing mission). It was therefore as "suppliers of racial and commercial services" that personalities like Jack Johnson, jazz musicians, or Josephine Baker were so warmly welcomed and generously paid to nourish a new French passion for a Black primitivism that could make one forget the horrors of progress.[15]

This Black American presence, however, did not just serve to promote the colonial order. It "served [equally] as perfect vehicle for promoting" the French myth of a color-blind nation.[16] Their presence attested to the moral superiority of the French nation in contrast to the United States. This myth enabled the national discourse to respond to the loss of confidence and to the conflicts linked respectively to the capitulation of the French army to Prussia leading to the fall of the Second Empire in 1870 and to the Dreyfus Affair.[17] In contrast to the racial segregation which kept the Blacks of America from feeling at home in their own country, the Republic could pride itself on being a hospitable refuge for these pariahs.[18] And even if this welcome was above all ideological, taking place in the context of a national renaissance, it offered Black Americans opportunities for not only financial ease and sexual liberty but also the possibility to define themselves outside of the degrading prism of racist stigmas.[19] Here one sees all the ambiguity of the French discourse about race, which served colonial and nationalist rhetoric while at the same time offering Black Americans the ability to reconstruct their own racial subjectivity. Some expatriates like James Baldwin or Claude McKay were fully conscious of the ambiguity of French racial discourse.[20] Others, in contrast, ignored it, enchanted by the appeal of a recognition that allowed them to reconstruct themselves racially.[21]

The rationality of this double reading (negative and positive) of Blackness in French society must be understood in its context. Although located on the periphery, colonial populations were subject to the yoke of French sovereignty. From this perspective the center (of the Empire) posed as the universal norm to which the colonies had to adjust.[22] In contrast, Black Americans were outside the nation but at the heart of modernity (because they bore the seal of the United States).[23] Their recognition on French territory demonstrated the power relations between two nations that were certainly equal but competed about the respective value of their modernity.[24] From its dual and contradictory relationship with Blackness (American and colonial), France established its modernity both from on high (in opposition to the United States) and from below (in conflict with the so-called primitive races) with the Black body as the unifying thread.

The Black American presence illustrates Stuart Hall's analysis of race as a "floating signifier."[25] Hall uses this expression to underline the idea that race is above all a discourse serving to make sense of things that then become racial symbols. Its social and historical dimension, "subject to the constant process of redefinition and appropriation," gives race its "floating" character.[26] This twice-dyed presence, which was first mobilized by colonial propaganda, contrasts with its evolution after the Second World War. The Black American migration of this period was more intellectual (with authors like Richard Wright and those that formed the Harlem Renaissance).[27] Race, or rather Black American racialness, became the floating signifier both of the struggle against imperialism and its avatar, racism, and of the growing wave of anti-imperialism. Although only a few of them lived in France, Black Americans had a significant influence on national discourse thanks to their literary and artistic productions. When the struggle for recognition emerged during the 1950s, popular culture along with commercialization presented a new discourse about race to the world.

A Global "Floating Signifier"

Starting in the 1950s in the United States, Black popular culture became a privileged site of struggle against the infamous norms that justified racial segregation.[28] This commitment consisted of pressuring the media and other image makers to give positive images of Blacks.[29] For instance, a music label like Motown developed a new politics of representation detached from all negative stereotypes (such as lust and obscenity) in order to adjust to the aesthetic standards set by the white and puritan class.[30]

Not all Blacks agreed to this vision, with many seeing it as a sellout to the violence of "White power." The rise of a Black nationalism that rejected any integrationist orientation underscored this point. In this regard James Brown sang in 1969: "Don't give me integration/Give me true communication."[31] This echoed the sharper political line of Black Power. Under the influence of Stokely Carmichael and Charles Hamilton, this message aimed at making Black American communities understand "the need to assert their own definitions, to reclaim their history, their culture; to create their own sense of community and togetherness."[32] This approach offered Blacks the ability to become masters of their own destiny ("Black Empowerment") and to internalize a positive image of themselves by rejecting the racist stereotypes offered by White America.[33] During the 1960s James Brown was one of the successful artists who put this discourse to music. His stage performances revealed a new model of urban Black masculinity that was very popular in the ghettos and promoted self-esteem through triumphant sexuality ("I'm a sex machine," he sang in 1970), sartorial excellence, and a desire for financial autonomy. This individualist affirmation went together with a collective desire for Black emancipation. The political contribution of James Brown led to the creation and redefinition of new norms of Black identity. Many considered him an "icon of Black pride."[34] The most powerful example of this was the way he helped popularize the use of the term "Black" in American society with his song "Say It Loud—I'm Black and I'm Proud." The use of this term (in contrast to Negro) marked the rise of a political consciousness that militantly defied white domination.[35] In taking up a term that had been unpopular but recasting it as a symbol of pride and strength, he made Blacks think of themselves in new ways, going so far as to render the official term Negro obsolete.[36] The new use of the term Black became the object of reinterpretations, notably by Black women who drew from a clearly masculine discourse of Blackness their own ideas about Black liberation. Artists like Nina Simone and Aretha Franklin performed songs like "Young, Gifted, and Black" (sung by both women and used by Franklin as the title of her twenty-fifth album) and "Respect."

Although taking many different forms, the pop music of Motown and the soul music of Black Power created, spread, and ultimately banalized a completely new repertoire of representations of Blackness. The advantage of music in comparison to traditional channels of political ideology (such as speeches and books) lay in its direct and laconic form, which could reach an audience beyond those traditionally engaged with such ideas (like political activists). The Revered Al Sharpton affirmed in an homage to Brown after his death in 2006 that "there were many in the movement who wanted to raise the consciousness of Black America from

Negro to Black. James Brown did it with one song. He could reach the masses much quicker than a lot of leaders."[37] His influence "made people all over the world, whites in America, Asians, like *Black music* and identify with it. He had them actually singing '*I'm Black and I'm Proud,*' people that weren't even remotely Black, didn't know what the chant meant to be Black in America."[38]

Black Power ideology marked a major turning point in racial discourse that extended to the world of sport as shown by the political stance of Muhammad Ali as well as the Black Power salute given by Tommie Smith and John Carlos during the 1968 Olympics in Mexico City. Hip hop culture, which became an international sensation starting in the 1990s, is its direct heir. However, "the music industry is a powerful motor for the distribution of these language practices," and as Sharpton noted, the term became more and more prosaic.[39] Its popularity among those little concerned with "what it meant to be Black in America" deprived the expression of its political and subversive value, instead turning it into a myth, a "depoliticized slogan" stripped of the historicity that gave it its complexity, something that went without saying.[40] This mythologization of the term Black coincided with its emergence as a political discourse critical of the social order (white, capitalist, patriarchal).[41] It arose from the work of the beauty, music, movie, and later sports industries that drew inspiration from this rhetoric, taking care to empty it of its subversive meanings in order to serve their commercial interests and cover their products with a stylized racial significance.[42] In the context of the ever faster circulation of products, and the transformation of industries oriented toward the production of brand names, the commercial mythologization of the "Black is Beautiful" movement superseded its political character.[43] This shift made itself felt not only in the United States but throughout the world as soon as this depoliticized discourse was adopted by mass market economic sectors (beauty, cinema, music, sports, and so on) that were ready to conquer new markets.

The American culture industry is the leading producer and exporter of Blackness as a representation of identity, constantly renewing it in all domains, including politics, the military, economics, sports, and the arts.

In France the reterritorialization of the term Black by the intermediary of the economic sector propagated a new, transnational aesthetic of race that, in an unprecedented manner, brought together modernity with a racial category historically seen as separate and distinct.[44] The Black artists seen on stage or in images were handsome, beautiful, wealthy, and, moreover, imitated by white artists (such as Elvis Presley, the Rolling Stones, and Johnny Hallyday) This racial discourse had a special significance in France given the nation's relationship to Black American racialness. It helped fill the gap of positive representations of Black postcolonial populations, caught between an invisibility evident in portraits of the nation (with the exception of sports where performance remains the principal selection criterion) and a discourse of Blackness emphasizing poverty and inferiority.[45] The politics of images used by the mass media or even more so by humanitarian campaigns illustrate this by placing otherness at the center of its discourse.[46] A coding of race according to the ideological line of Black Power meets, confronts, and in particular balances another coding of race, one that is based on Black (especially African) miserabilism. Together they produce "controlling images," normative categories in which the meaning of Blackness in France is contained.[47] These codings dispose of a performative force giving Blacks references that serve to define their identity. As Stuart Hall notes, "There is no escape from the politics of representation."[48] In this context, the ideological representation contributed principally by American neoliberalism and especially its Black capitalism branch is one of the rare sources for the Black population of France (and elsewhere) of a positive image of their racialization. These representations integrate themselves into a much larger economy of racial discourse that defines Black existence in France.

The *Black* Model of Republican Integration

The massive export of African American popular culture by the entertainment industry has contributed to the emergence of a phenomenon of "hegemonic racialness" throughout the Black Atlantic. The use of the term Black in France became popular in the 1980s following the success of the 1983 "March for Equality and against Racism" and of the institutionalization of the question of racism by SOS Racisme, which created the republican slogan *"Black-Blanc-Beur"* and used the anglicism during its publicity campaigns.[49]

The use of the term Black came first from its appropriation by racially stigmatized French youths from suburban neighborhoods of large urban areas that could see in the Black American experience a model for its struggles against racism and for emancipation. The formation of "gangs" like the Black Dragons or the Black Fist in the Paris region that took part in the hunt for the racist "skins" illustrated the influence of urban and masculine Black American representations (mediated by hip hop culture) on the Black French of lower-class neighborhoods.[50]

The term Black held a central role in the construction of these youths' identity. For example, in 2000 the rapper Busta Flex hammered home the theme "We are Black, Black, Black" ("On est Black, Black, Black") to express pride in belonging to a transnational identity group centered around African American cultural codes (principally hip hop).[51] Nonetheless for some artists this identification went farther, taking on an explicitly neoliberal ideological tone. The rapper Booba (whose albums have all gone gold in France) claims in a song that "My president is Black, my Visa card [*carte bleue*] is Black" ("Mon président est Black, ma carte bleue est Black").[52] If the term Black clearly refers to the United States, it equally emphasizes the successful economic and political integration of Blacks in a country that the artist portrays as a model, because it was capable of electing a Black president and permitting Blacks to succeed, according to the rules of meritocracy.

Black French artists reflected a social discourse popular since at least 2005 (when the lower-class suburban revolts erupted) about the necessity of ending the social exclusion of oppressed and racialized (because of the colonial heritage) young people by mounting a primarily economic response inspired by the American model of Black capitalism. For example, the CRAN (Conseil Représentatif des Associations Noires, Representative Council of Black Associations) organized on May 12, 2008, a "Summit of Economic Diversity Initiatives" featuring the "strong presence of African American entrepreneurs" with the goal of creating an Economic Association of the African Diaspora in France.[53]

This phenomenon of the mimicry of Black American identity goes back to what Nacira Guénif-Souilamas has termed "subjectivized ethnicization." This concept describes a "conversion operation" by which racialized individuals "endow different personalities of their being with a personal content."[54] From slavery to the election of the first Black president, the official history of Black Americans reads like a continual forward march. Black American racialization is therefore viewed through a fantasy of success and accomplishment in which French Blacks can find positive models of recognition that contrast with the stereotypes of postcolonial discourse.[55] One can see an ideological slippage in these identity models: if during the 1983 march they emphasized leaders in the political struggle for emancipation (like Angela Davis or Martin Luther King), in contrast they took a neoliberal turn with the promotion of individual and meritocratic success (by rappers, athletes, and some associations).[56]

Moreover, the institutionalization of the term Black shows that the "subjectivized ethnicization" experienced through that term can coexist with the "lived ethnicization" linked to republican discourse, which is concerned with promoting the integration of marginalized populations.[57] The appearance in 1983 and then the resurgence in 1998 of the term Black in the republican rhetoric used by political leaders and media heads was systematically placed next to the term "Beur" (slang for Arab), the two terms surrounding the word White (the only one that remained unchanging) to form the "multicultural version" of the Republic.[58] The bringing together of these three "ethno-racial" components constituted the republican response to the emergence and the exacerbation of tensions that endangered national unity. The 1970s and 1980s were marked by a series of traumatic police killings of young Arabs and Blacks in working-class neighborhoods. The decades that proceeded France's 1998 victory in the World Cup were marked by the rise of the National Front and the increasing acceptance of its ideas in republican debates.[59] The recurrence of urban revolts heralded, moreover, the birth of the suburbs as a symbol of the problematic integration of postcolonial populations.

However, as Nacira Guénif-Souilamas has observed, for Blacks and Arabs, inclusion into this republican communion came with conditions that highlighted their semantic "conversion." Guénif explains that the figure of the Beur/Beurette became politically significant starting in the 1980s (when the "March for Equality" of 1983 was rebaptized the "March of the Beurs"): the designation Beur was supposed to demonstrate to French youth whose parents had come from the former North African colonies that "integration [was] not only possible but [that it also represented] the only foreseeable future."[60] The result of the inversion of syllables, the expression Beur appeared as a euphemism that dispensed with the ethnic and colonial burden of these young people, suggesting that the only possible solution to the presence of Arabs in France was an assimilationist integration, that is to say the erasure of all physical, patronymic, cultural, and/or religious characteristics "which rendered them undesirable in the former metropole." The Beur and the Beurette thus appear not just as alternative figures but also those whose existence equally contributes to a hostile and intolerable vision of the "veiled girl" and the "Arab boy."

Continuing with this analysis that illustrates the normative and political character of a designation intended to sanitize a social group seen as a problem, the identity label Black also seems like a tool of domination. It constitutes an alternative to the use of the term Noir. But avoiding the use of the French term masks the degrading connotations that it continues to have in a national imagination still marked by colonial discourse. Highly publicized expressions like "the noise and the smell" (by French president Jacques Chirac in 1991), "savages" (from minister of interior J. P. Chevènement in 1999), "N—" (by the perfumer J. P. Guerlain in 2010), "ape" (a National Front candidate's description of Minister of Justice Christiane Taubira in 2013) are all brutal examples of the linguistic racism that continues to surround the term Noir in France. However, like the term Beur, does Black aim to conceal the colonial charge associated with the representations of the Noir in France?

The use of and recourse to the English language term Black in republican rhetoric of "France Black-Blanc-Beur" shows, in my opinion, that Blacks in France (like the Arab-Berber population) cannot be integrated as they are and that their right to national recognition comes above all from an individual will to "melt themselves" into national unity. The discourses that followed the 1998 victory of the French team in the World Cup and those that commented on the defeat of this same team in 2010 are very revealing in this sense. From a national fervor about Blacks and Beurs to the opposite sentiment of national distrust of these "immature caïds" from the suburbs, these different perspectives underline the state of insecurity in which these postcolonial populations find themselves, and the necessity constantly to call into question their allegiance to the nation by medias and politics. The expressions Black and Beur can be understood as a republican attempt to reconcile minority racial affiliations with membership in the imagined national community. This double membership is made possible for Black populations on the condition that they reject any supposed "lack of civic responsibility" (to which the stigma of noir is linked) and to rehabilitate their image by borrowing Black American representations, which the national imaginary has historically recognized as modern and beautiful.

The use of the word Black recalls the Black American impact on the French postcolonial imaginary. Although principally taking the form of entertainment, Black American culture has never stopped posing important ideological stakes in situations in France where the question of race arises. The definition of race as a floating signifier, exemplified in the new meaning infused into the designation Black and particularly through Black popular culture, shows that its ideological content is never definitive. A vector of a dominant social order, it is equally a process that allows the double consciousness of Noir and French to be (re)thought.

NOTES

1. The title is inspired by the novel by Eddy Harris, *Paris en noir et black* (Paris: Liana Levi, 2008).

2. Reconstruction (1865–77) designates the Federal government's creation of measures to deal with the freeing of four million Black slaves. In this context President Abraham Lincoln authorized the creation of services charged with aiding Blacks during the first years of the war, services that eventually came under the aegis of the Freedmen's Bureau.

3. Valérie Bonnet, "Don't call me Nigger, Whitey," *Communication* 28, no. 2 (2011), http://communication.revuews.org/1803.

4. Colette Guillaumin, *L'idéologie raciste—Genèse et langage actuel* (Paris: Gallimard, 2002), 229–30.

5. See Pastoureau, Michel, *Noir: histoire d'une couleur* (Paris, Editions du Seuil, 2008); Pascal Blanchard, Eric Deroo, Gilles Manceron, *Le Paris noir* (Paris: Éditions Hazan, 2001), 8.

6. See Law # 94–665 of August 4, 1994, relative to the use of the French language (the Toubon Law), particularly intended to reinforce the primacy of French over English (or anglicisms).

7. Marc Angenot, *L'histoire des idées: problématiques, objets, concepts, méthodes, enjeux, débats* 2 (Quebec: Discours social, 2011), 18.

8. Nicolas Bancel, Pascal Blanchard, and Sandrine Lemaire, "Ces zoos humains de la République colonial," *Le Monde Diplomatique*, http://www.monde-diplomatique.fr/2000/08/BANCEL/1944.

9. Tyler Stovall, *Paris Noir: African Americans in the City of Light* (Boston: Houghton-Mifflin, 1996), 71.

10. See Tyler Stovall, "The Color Line behind the Lines: Racial Violence in France during the Great War," *The American Historical Review* 103, no. 3 (1998): 737–69.

11. I borrow the expression from Michel de Certeau. See De Certeau, *L'invention du quotidien, l'arts de faire* (Paris: Gallimard, 1990). Macherey synthesizes the definition in this way: "'The art of doing' which 'plays' upon the weakness of the system and which, without going outside the system, invents margins of maneuver which, for lack of being able to liberate oneself from the system, enables one to liberate oneself within the limits imposed by the system, despite the constraints that it imposes, and even in some ways because of these constraints, by cleverly exploiting them." Macherey Pierre, *Michel De Certeau et la Mystique du quotidien*, http://stl.recherche.univ-lille3.fr/seminaires/philosophie/macherey/macherey20042005/macherey06042005.html.

12. Houston A. Baker, "To Move without Moving: An Analysis of Creativity and Commerce in Ralph Ellison's Trueblood Episode," *PMLA* 98, no. 5 (October 1983), 831. See also Matthew Brown, "Boxing Darwin's Shadow: Jack Johnson and Joe Louis's Historical Challenges to American Racism," (undergraduate thesis, Wesleyan University, April 2007), http://wesscholar.wesleyan.edu/cgi/viewcontent.cgi?article=1008&contest=etd_hon_theses. Both of these works underline the ways that Black Americans produced a Black identity in order to make it attractive to whites.

13. Theresa Runstedtler, "Visible Men: African American Boxers, the New Negro, and the Global Color Line," *Radical History Review* 103 (Winter 2009): 65.

14. Stovall, *Paris Noir*, 53.

15. Stovall, *Paris Noir*, 31.

16. Rachel Gillett, "Jazz and the Evolution of Black American Cosmopolitanism in Interwar Paris," *Journal of World History* 21, no. 3 (September 2010): 491.

17. Runstedtler, "Visible Men," 1.

18. When he came to Paris, Richard Wright wrote "I tell you frankly that there Is more freedom in one square block of Paris than there is in the entire United States of America!."

19. Runstedtler, "Visible Men," 6.

20. Studs Terkel, *P.S.: Further Thoughts from a Lifetime of Listening* (New York: New Press, 2008); "Être Noir dans un monde de Blancs—Entretien avec James Baldwin," Studs Terkel, translated in French by Charlotte Nordman, *Revue Internationale des Livres et des Idées (RILI)* 13 (September-October 2009): 27.

21. Claude McKay, *Banjo* (New York: Harper, 1929); Didier Gondola, "'But I Ain't African, I'm American!': Black American Exiles and the Constitution of Racial Identities in Twentieth-Century France," in *Blackening Europe: The African American Presence*, ed. Heike Raphael-Hernandez (New York: Routledge, 2004); Stovall, *Paris Noir*.

22. See Nicolas Bancel, Pascal Blanchard, and Françoise Vergès, *La République coloniale: Essai sur une utopie* (Paris: Albin Michel, 2003).

23. Pap Ndiaye, *La condition noire: essai sur une minorité française* (Paris: Calmann-Lévy, 2008), 147.

24. Gondola "'But I Ain't African, I'm American!,'" 202–3.

25. Stuart Hall, "Race, The Floating Signifier" (transcript), *Media Education Foundation* (1997), https://www.mediaed.org/transcripts/Stuart-Hall-Race-the-Floating-Signifier-Transcript.pdf, accessed October 8, 2020.

26. Hall, "Race, The Floating Signifier."

27. The Harlem Renaissance was a literary and intellectual movement that emerged in New York during the 1920s and 1930s. Some of its leading representatives were Alain Locke, Langston Hughes, Zora Neale Hurston, and Claude McKay. The movement proposed to create a revolutionary new Black aesthetic.

28. Paulla Ebron, "Strike a Pose: Capitalism's Black Identity," in *Recharting the Black Atlantic*, ed. Annalisa Oboe and Anna Scacchi (London: Routledge, 2008), 320.

29. Ebron, "Strike a Pose," 324.

30. See Franck F. Ekué, "'Blackness à la demande': Production narrative de l'authenticité raciale' dans l'industrie du rap américain," *Volume!* 8–2 (2012).

31. Rickey Vincent, *Party Music: The Inside Story of the Black Panther's Band and How Black Power Transformed Soul Music* (Chicago: Lawrence Hill, 2013), 92.

32. Stokely Carmichael and Charles V. Hamilton, *Black Power: The Politics of Liberation in America* (New York: Penguin, 1967), 51.

33. Vincent, *Party Music*, 52.

34. Vincent, *Party Music*, 88.

35. Bonnet, "Don't Call Me Nigger, Whitey," 30.

36. Vincent, *Party Music*, 106.

37. Al Sharpton, "The Godfather and Dr. King," *Rolling Stone*, January 25, 2007, cited in Vincent, *Party Music*, 107.

38. Al Sharpton, in "James Brown—Say It Proud," *CNN: Special Investigations Unit*, aired May 5, 2007, cited in Vincent, *Party Music*, 105.

39. Bonnet, "Don't Call Me Nigger, Whitey," 106.

40. Roland Barthes, *Mythologies* (Paris: Éditions du Seuil, 1957), 219.

41. Ebron, "Strike a Pose," 329.

42. Ebron, "Strike a Pose," 329.

43. Naomi Klein, *No Logo: No Space, No Choice, No Jobs* (London: Flamingo, 2002), 265.

44. For Gilles Deleuze "reterritorialization" meant the insertion of a phenomenon or experience into a different context from the one it had left (the stage of "deterritorialization"), giving it a different meaning. See also Rémy Bazenguissa-Ganga, "Paint it 'Black': How Africans and Afro-Caribbeans Became 'Black' in France," in Trica Danielle Keaton, T. Denean Sharpley-Whiting, and Tyler Stovall, *Black France/France noire: The History and Politics of Blackness* (Durham NC: Duke University Press, 2012), 157.

45. "I will also meet with leaders of the audiovisual sector. The media must better reflect the reality of France today. I also invite the leaders of the political parties to assume their share of responsibility for this; elected politicians and national political representation in general must also reflect the diversity of France." "Déclaration aux Français de Monsieur Jacques Chirac, Président de la République," Palais de l'Élysée, November 14, 2005, http://tempsreel.nouvelobs.com/societe/20061026.OBS7064/le-discours-de-chirac-le-14-novembre-2005.html.

46. Michela Fusaschi, "Victimes à tout jamais. Les enfants et les femmes d'Afrique," *Cahiers d'études africaines* 198-199-200 (2010): 1034.

47. Patricia Hill Collins associates this concept of "controlling images" with that of "representations" and "stereotypes." But representations do not need to be stereotypical" and stereotypes do not necessarily function as controlling images. Collins explains, "The use of the expression 'controlling images' allows one to underline the power relations of race, class, gender, and sexuality." "Glossary," in Patricia Hill Collins, *Black Sexual Politics: African Americans, Gender, and the New Racism* (New York: Routledge, 2005), 350.

48. Stuart Hall, "What Is This 'Black' in Black Popular Culture," *Social History* 20, no. 1–2 (Spring-Summer 1993): 111.

49. For example, see the 1998 SOS Racisme ad, "This evening all French people were scandalized by the expulsion of a *Black*" (emphasis added).

50. Arnaud Ducome, "Dans le Paris des années 80, skinheads contre 'chasseurs,'" *Rue89*, https://www.nouvelobs.com/rue89/rue89-nos-vies-connectees/20091116.RUE3504/dans-le-paris-des-annees-80-skinheads-contre-chasseurs.html. See also Bazenguissa-Ganga, "Paint It 'Black,'" 166.

51. Busta Flex, "Black," *Sexe, Violence, Rap & Flooze*, Warner Music, 2010.

52. Booba, "Saddam Haut d'Seine," *Lunatic*, Tallac Records, Because Music, 2000.

53. Communiqué de presse du CRAN, Paris, April 28, 2008, http://newsletterappa.over-blog.com/article-19116304.html.

54. Nacira Guénif-Souilamas, *Des beurettes* (Paris: Hachette Pluriel, 2004), 183.

55. In the same sense, for example, Busta Flex opposes his "Black" identity to the stereotype of Blacks as cannibals.

56. Stéphane Beaud and Olivier Masclet, "Des 'marcheurs' de 1983 aux 'emeutiers' de 2005. Deux générations sociales d'enfants d'immigrés," *Annales: Histoire, Sciences Sociales* 4 (2006): 814.

57. Nacira Guénif-Souilamas describes lived ethnicization as the "product of the assignment to a culture given to them directly or in veiled form by their family or 'the French.' It takes the form of the affirmation of an essentialized identity (Arab, Muslim, woman) based not in their personal experience but inherited from a mythic traditional past." Guénif-Souilamas, *Des beurettes*, 183.

58. Eric Collier, "Zidane, Doucouré et les succès de la generation 'multi,'" *Le Monde*, August 20, 2005.

59. For example, in 1991 Prime Minister Jacques Chirac implied (without naming them directly) that African families had "unrefined" customs characterized by "the noise and the smell." Jacques Chirac, *Le Discours d'Orléans*, June 19, 1991.

60. Nacira Guénif, "Le Beur, la Beurette, pseudo-français," *Ravages* 5 (2011): 62.

11

Solidarity or Difference?

African Americans and the Making of Black France

TYLER STOVALL

In the introduction to his seminal study *La condition noire*, Pap Ndiaye notes that when he wrote his book there were more studies of African Americans published in France than those of French Black people. While that may remain literally true, it is also noteworthy that the balance has at least shifted, and that today there are many more studies of Black life in France than a decade ago. Since the beginning of the twenty-first century a number of books and articles about Blacks in France have appeared, challenging the erstwhile color-blindness of French universalism.[1] They have been merely one manifestation of a broader series of public debates about race and difference in contemporary French society, in particular the extent to which a common racial background can serve as the grounds for a unified social identity in a universalist French republic.[2]

This essay considers the role played by African Americans and particularly African American expatriates in these new debates about Blackness in France. It is perhaps no accident that Ndiaye begins his book with a comparative reference to Black Americans and Black French people. African Americans have often served as the model and the referent, both positive and negative, for not only Black communities but racialized minorities in France and elsewhere during the modern era.[3] As this chapter will argue, the history and contemporary condition of Blacks in the United States continues to play an important role in debates about the experience of French peoples of African descent.

At the same time I wish to pose several questions: to what extent has this new Black consciousness in France regarded the African American presence in France as part of its own history and contemporary reality?

Are the storied African American expatriate communities of Paris part of what we consider Black France? An exploration of this issue provides an alternate way of considering the relationship between Blacks in the United States and France and between those nations in general. Such a question also suggests a diasporic and transnational approach to the history of what Ndiaye has called a "French minority." Can citizens of another country be considered part of a French minority, and to what extent does a study of Black France in general challenge the traditional boundaries of the nation-state?

Diaspora and the Nation-State

The rise of the diasporic approach to Black history has tended to emphasize the heterogeneity of peoples of African descent both historically and today. In particular, Black European studies have generally focused on the many ways in which the Black experience in Britain, France, Germany, and other European countries diverges from the African American model.[4] Rather than attempt to construct an alternate hegemonic model of Blackness, it has underscored a postmodern focus on hybridity as opposed to nationalist cohesion. In addition, diasporic studies has tended to ignore, overlook, or challenge the importance of the nation-state, focusing instead on intellectuals who transgressed national boundaries and aspired to global citizenship.[5]

Studies of the relationship between Black France and Black America have tended to adopt one of two perspectives. The first, grounded in the history of Nègritude and the anti-imperialist struggles of the postwar years, sees this relationship as one of racial solidarity transcending national boundaries. From this perspective, Black intellectuals in France and America came together at times to create new insights into Black modernity.[6] The second, on the contrary, tends to focus on the interactions between African Americans and Black French people as grounded in a certain tendency toward dominance of the former over the latter, even a kind of cultural imperialism that replicated that exercised by the United States over France in general since World War II. In particular, it argues that many African Americans have tended to impose a view of race grounded in the American experience in ways not always sensitive or relevant to France.[7] This contrast at times replicates the divergence between theories of Black nationalism and unity on the one hand and diasporic approaches to Blackness on the other.[8]

Both approaches tend to ignore the question posed earlier in this chapter: are African Americans in France part of the French Black experience, and if so, how? In tackling this issue today I will take two approaches. First, I will give an overview of the history of African Americans in France with a focus on their interactions with Blacks from both the metropole and the colonies. Second, I will analyze several recent French texts, both academic studies and popular manifestos, on Black life in France to consider how they treat the presence of African Americans in French Black life and France in general.[9]

Taken together, these approaches reveal that African Americans have certainly played a role in Black life in France, but that this role has changed significantly over time. Moreover, if one looks at contemporary French texts on Black life, one encounters a contrast between a tendency to view African Americans in France as distinct (if they are in fact viewed at all), and an intense focus on Black society and culture in the United States more generally. In particular, changes in Black life in both the United States and France, and the insistence in recent French writings about Blackness that Black people are an integral part of the French nation, have tended to render the African American presence in France both invisible and omnipresent at the same time.

African Americans and French of African Descent in France

Blacks have traveled from the United States to France almost as long as there has been a United States. During the nineteenth century Creoles of African descent from Louisiana at times settled in France, often sending their sons to be educated there.[10] A number of African Americans also visited France as performers, dignitaries, or tourists. In 1886, for example, the statesman Frederick Douglass vacationed in France, in particular enjoying standing in Marseille and trying to catch his first glimpse of Africa across the sea.[11]

It wasn't until the beginning of the twentieth century, however, that African Americans established a substantial and sustained presence in

France. The birth of a Black expatriate community in Paris in particular corresponded to two broader changes that would reshape life in France: the advent of America as a global military and cultural power and the new prominence of empire that would see the beginnings of postcolonial society in France. The Paris Exposition of 1900 featured a major exhibition on the life of Black Americans organized by sociologist and civil rights leader W. E. B. Du Bois.[12] More significantly, some two hundred thousand African American soldiers would journey to France during World War I, by far the largest migration of Blacks out of the United States until that point.[13] At the same time the new popularity of jazz in France and elsewhere in Europe created opportunities for those Black Americans who chose not to return home after the armistice and for those hoping to find new opportunities outside the United States.[14] By the mid–1920s several hundred African Americans, primarily but not exclusively jazz performers, had settled in Paris, giving the neighborhood of Montmartre in particular some of the flavor of an overseas Harlem.[15]

While this small expatriate colony came to France primarily because of economic opportunities, many were also attracted by the idea that French people were not only color-blind but indeed pro-Black, in contrast to the racism that dominated Black life in the United States. This idea of African American expatriates as refugees from racism became a key leitmotif of Black expatriate life in France, resurfacing with a vengeance after the Second World War. The literary circle that formed around Richard Wright and James Baldwin during the 1950s used overseas exile as a means of attacking American racism at the dawn of the civil rights movement.[16] However, both the increasing challenges to Black subordination brought by that struggle and a new awareness of racism in France caused by the Algerian war undermined the traditional opposition between a racist America and a tolerant France.[17] Since the 1960s France has retained a small African American community spurred by the growth of the Black middle class and by increasing globalization. Paris in particular has a collection of Black music clubs, restaurants, and social organizations, including city tours oriented toward African Americans. The idea of an expatriate community, first born in the 1920s, continues to shape Black American life in France.

A key theme of that community's life has been interaction with Blacks from France and the French empire. As many studies have recently noted, the Black presence in France is an ancient one that dates back to Roman Gaul. The modern history of Black France began with the establishment of a French colonial presence in both Africa and the Caribbean. In the 1620s and 1630s French traders began establishing settlements and trading posts, or *comptoirs*, along the coast of West Africa. In 1635 the French government annexed Martinique and Guadeloupe in the Caribbean, and in 1660 it created the colony of Saint-Domingue on the island of Hispaniola. In the late seventeenth century and throughout the eighteenth century, France used its position in both Africa and the Caribbean to play a leading role in the transatlantic slave trade, bringing millions of Black Africans to the New World.[18]

The history of Blacks in metropolitan France during the modern era is closely linked to both the colonization of Africa and the slave trade. By the early eighteenth century several thousand Blacks lived in the metropole, concentrated primarily in Paris and the great slaving ports of Nantes and Bordeaux. Many had come to France as slaves accompanying their masters from the Caribbean, and some successfully sued for their freedom based on the ancient principle that France was a land of free men and women. By the era of the French Revolution some Blacks had achieved prominence in French life, including the Chevalier de Saint-Georges of Guadeloupe, a leading classical musician and soldier, and Alexandre Dumas of Saint-Domingue, son of a French count and the father of the great novelist Alexandre Dumas.[19]

During the nineteenth and early twentieth centuries small numbers of French Blacks continued to settle in the metropole. Blacks from Martinique, Guadeloupe, and French Guiana who became French citizens after the final end of slavery in 1848 came as students, politicians, musicians, and journalists. Smaller numbers of Africans also visited or took residence in metropolitan France, sometimes as part of traveling exhibits on display during the great Parisian world's fairs of the late-nineteenth century.[20] Like African Americans, Blacks from the French colonies first came to the metropole *en masse* during World War I. Over one hundred thousand *tirailleurs sénégalais* fought in the battlefields of France during the great conflict.[21] Even though virtually all returned home after the armistice, the Great War established the fact that Blacks were an integral part of life in France.

The confluence of both French Blacks and African Americans in the metropole during the war and the interwar years led to a number of interactions between their communities. In 1919 Du Bois and Blaise Diagne, the first African member of the French National Assembly, worked together to organize the Pan-African congress in Paris.[22] The 1920s and 1930s brought numerous interactions between the American writers of the Harlem Renaissance and the poets of Nègritude: both groups frequented the Clamart salon of Pauline Nardal, and the resulting *Revue du monde noir* was published in a bilingual edition.[23] The manifesto of the first issue of the *Revue* stated that its aim was to: "Créer entre les Noirs du monde entier, sans distinction de nationalité, un lien intellectuel et moral qui leur permette de se mieux connaître, de s'aimer fraternellement."[24] Similarly, during the 1950s Richard Wright and his American colleagues worked closely with the French intellectuals of *Présence Africaine*, together organizing the 1956 Congress of Black Writers and Artists in Paris.[25]

At the same time, however, as Brent Hayes Edwards has argued, the two groups had many differences, not the least those of language. Even during the interwar years, for example, African American musicians concentrated in Montmartre, whereas Antillais performers lived primarily in Montparnasse. In a 1928 review of the Bal Nègre, a Caribbean dance hall, African American columnist J. A. Rogers noted both its the similarities with and differences from Black American nightclubs, writing "The visitor who speaks only English had better take his interpreter with him."[26] Frequent interactions between the two communities did not erase their essentially separate character.

Black France vs. Black America

In some ways these differences have increased since the golden age of African American expatriates in Paris from World War II to the 1960s. Most African American expatriates are solidly middle class and many do not live there permanently but alternate between stays in France and in the United States.[27] Most live in Paris itself, not in the *banlieue* home to so much of the French Black population; the 2005 suburban uprisings in France had relatively little impact on Black Americans because so few of them lived there. At the same time the African and Afro-Caribbean population of France has changed notably since the First World War. Whereas during the interwar years it was, like the Black American expatriate community, very small and dominated to a significant degree by students, intellectuals, and musicians, since 1945 it has grown much larger and more diverse. During the Second World War Black French soldiers fought for France both in the Free French armies and in the Resistance, and the nation's African and Caribbean colonies generally rallied to De Gaulle in the struggle against Vichy.[28] By the end of the twentieth century various estimates placed the population of French people of African descent at well over a million, possible as many as five million.[29] African Americans in France, by contrast, probably did not number more than a few thousand. Expatriates from the United States thus constitute a much smaller percentage of France's Black population than they did in the 1920s or even 1950s.[30]

In the contemporary era, therefore, Black French life resembles less the Black American community in Paris and more the broader African American society back in the United States.[31] Few members of the overwhelmingly middle class Black American expatriate population live in the banlieue, but many Blacks in the United States live in ghettos every bit as grim.

In general, then, African Americans in France have had experiences very different from those of their African and Afro-Caribbean neighbors. To a certain extent, as any African American who has ever escaped police harassment by producing an American passport can testify, it has been one of relative privilege. Nonetheless, it is also true that many other differences divide Blacks in France, so much so that one usually speaks of Black populations, not a Black community. The question therefore remains: to what extent are African Americans considered to be part of Black life in France? In what remains of this chapter I will address this question by considering how some important texts written by Blacks in France have viewed African Americans, both those living in France and the broader population as a whole.

One theme that emerges clearly is the tendency to view African Americans as part of the history of Black France more than of its present-day reality. This is especially true of the two primarily historical texts I analyzed: Pap Ndiaye's *La condition noire* and *Paris Noir* by Pascal Blanchard, Eric Deroo, and Gilles Manceron. Both note the important presence Black Americans established in France. In analyzing the deployment of thousands of African colonial soldiers in the metropole during World War I, for example, Ndiaye also notes the arrival of African American troops, seeing both migrations as part of the creation of Black France in the early twentieth century. As he writes, "La Première Guerre mondiale eut pour conséquence l'arrivée massive de Noirs d'Afrique et des Amériques en France metropolitaine. Au total, environ 300.000 soldats noirs (citoyens des vielles colonies, sujets des colonies africaines, Afro-Américains d'Amérique du Nord) stationnèrent en France."[32] Similarly, Pascal Blanchard and his colleagues devote a lot of attention to the popularity of African American jazz and performance in interwar France, entitling one chapter "Harlem à Paris."[33]

To a certain extent this is also true of recent nonhistorical texts about Blacks in France. In *Nous les noirs de France* Patrick Lozès rhapsodizes about the impact of African Americans on Parisian culture: "Le Paris Noir, c'est enfin 'l'art nègre' et son influence sur le cubisme, c'est la Revue nègre avec Josephine Baker, la première star noire de l'histoire, c'est le jazz (Louis Armstrong, Miles Davis), le gospel, les sportifs, du boxeur au footballeur, les écrivains (Richard Wright, James Baldwin, William Gardner Smith, Chester Himes, Richard Gibson)."[34] In his study *Les Nègres de la République* Claude Ribbe also notes the importance of Josephine Baker, along with the writers of the Nègritude school, during the 1930s.

United and Divided by the Same Color

In general, however, current studies of Blacks in France pay little attention to the presence of Black American expatriates, and rarely see them as part of Black France. The fact that the few indications of their presence are generally historical serves to relegate African Americans to a somewhat romanticized past, a legacy perhaps for the French Blacks of today, but not much more than that. One of the first major studies of Black life in contemporary France appeared in 1983 in a special issue of the journal *Autrement* titled simply "Black: Africains, Antillais . . . Culture noires en France." The title alone is highly significant: in it African Americans are both present and absent at the same time. The journal issue consisted of a number of articles by specialists on the condition of Africans and Afro-Caribbeans in France, most notably Maryse Condé, as well as a discussion of the Black presence in Paris by *arrondissement*. It remains an excellent source for Caribbean and African cultures in France but it says nothing about Black Americans even in its discussion of areas like Montmartre, Pigalle, and the Latin Quarter that retained at the time a certain African American presence. For example, its extensive discussion of the Theatre Noir founded by Martinican playwright Benjamin Jules-Rosette in 1975 barely mentions the significant participation of Black American performers.[35]

The same is true of other major studies of Black life in France. In spite of the fact that the African American community in contemporary Paris is probably larger and more diverse than it was in the early twentieth century, it has received less attention from commentators on French Black communities. The only time Rama Yada-Zimet mentions African Americans in France in her *Noirs de France* is to discuss the June 2005 incident where Oprah Winfrey, probably the wealthiest Black woman in the world, was denied entry to Hermès in Paris.[36] Overall, the portrait of Black France in these texts is almost exclusively a postcolonial one, focusing on individuals and communities from Francophone Africa and the French Caribbean.

In contrast, all these texts have lots to say about African Americans in general. Contemporary French discourses about race have tended to look to the Black American experience as a template for that of racialized minorities in the modern era, and studies of Blacks in France have generally followed that pattern. François Durpaire devotes much of the beginning of his book *France blanche, colère noire* to a discussion of the Black condition in the United States and to comparisons between French and American thinking about race. At times this takes the form of attacking French condemnations of American racism as hypocritical. For example Durpaire notes that many commentators characterized America's reaction to Hurricane Katrina in 2005 as discriminatory against Blacks while ignoring the plight of the many French Blacks who died in apartment fires at the same time.[37]

In particular, books about Black France often look to African American culture and politics as a model, if at times an imperfect one. In a chapter entitled "Français, made in USA," Rama Yade-Zimet portrays Black America as an inspiration for Black France: "Leur inspiration? L'Amérique, ses clips, ses stars de basket et de rap, ses héros de cinéma. Pourquoi pas la France? Parce que notre pays ne leur montre pas de modèles auxquels ils pourraient si'identifier. Alors, ils vont chercher outre-Atlantique des héros noirs. Au moins, là-bas, *Black is beautiful*."[38] Yade-Zimet also discusses in her book the tremendous impact that African American television shows, notably *Roots* and *The Cosby Show*, have had on her personally, at one point stating, "I am a child of the Cosby Show."[39] Francois Durpaire similarly underscores the influence of Black American culture in France, noting that "La culture afro-américaine est un puissant creuset commun entre jeunes Antillais et jeunes Africains. Du jazz au hip-hop, la communauté noire américaine n'a cessé d'exporter tout au long du XXe siècle une culture qui a fédéré les diasporas noires."[40]

As Yade-Zimet makes clear, these texts tend to present the Black French interest in African American culture as a negative referent on the condition of Africans and Afro-Caribbeans in France itself, rather than as a desire to imitate another people or society. In general they use the vitality of African American culture to call upon France to make room for a similar Black presence at home. Just as Black expatriates from the United States traditionally embraced France in part because of its prestige in American eyes, so have Black French writers promoted African American culture not just because of its merits but also because of the tremendous role played by America in contemporary French life. The experience of Black America appears in these texts not so much as something to be imitated but rather as one potential lesson for how to build a unified Black culture in France itself.

This tendency to see African American expatriates as distinct from the Black presence in France also exists among Black Americans themselves. The literature on African American expatriates in France does often mention French Blacks, but generally in passing and not as an integral part of their history.[41] In part the fact that the two communities in France have diverged significantly since the Second World War may explain this, as well as the fact that after 1945 Black Americans became more integrated into the American expatriate community in Paris in general. As a result African Americans in France have remained largely peripheral to the rise of a new Black conscious in France that paradoxically has often looked to the United States as a role model.

Perhaps most important is the focus of many African Americans in Paris on integrating the expatriate experience into Black history: the view of Josephine Baker as the first Black American diva, for example, rather than an integral part of the history of Black France. There is a tendency among not just French Blacks but many African Americans themselves to regard the expatriate presence in the capital as an historical artifact, something that effectively died with Richard Wright. In recent years France has seen the rise of several companies run by African American women that stage tours of Black Paris. The tours not only focus almost exclusively on the African American experience but to a large extent on the past. Catering largely to Black American tourists, they stage walking tours of Montmartre and the Latin Quarter, evoking the lives of African American expatriates during the 1920s and 1950s. In her guidebook *Paris Reflections: Walks through African-American Paris*, Monique Y. Wells describes her fascination with African American history in the French capital:

> I began to see the streets of Paris in a new light. I read and read and walked the streets again. And I began to see traces of the presence of Black people in Paris-a painting of a Black man serving a hot beverage to a white woman on the façade of a building, a plaque dedicated to Richard Wright on an apartment building, a statue honoring Alexandre Dumas. . . . It became evident that I had only scratched the surface of what promised to be a treasure trove of history. I continue to investigate the events of our past in Paris, and also to chronicle current events involving African Americans here.[42]

Interestingly, in this passage even images and testimonials from the history of French Blacks are assimilated into the African American past.

Another example of this tendency among African Americans in Paris to see themselves as distinct from Black France is the *salon* of Patricia Laplante-Collins. Originally from Atlanta, Laplante-Collins lived in Paris for several decades before her death there in 2019, and for over twenty years staged a regular gathering where American expatriates and others would enjoy food and drink and listen to a speaker, discuss a book, or listen to a musical performance. Many of these *soirées* involved African American expatriates, but relatively few touched upon the lives of French Blacks and the politics of Blackness in France. During the 2005 suburban uprisings, for example, the Laplante-Collins salon featured talks by an African American fitness instructor living in Paris and an American specialist in walking tours of the city, as well as a celebration of Thanksgiving.[43]

Conclusion

It seems clear that contemporary writers about the Black condition in France see African Americans as ultimately foreign to that experience even if they live there. Several reasons explain this. Black expatriates constitute a very small percentage of French peoples of African descent, much smaller than in the interwar years. Moreover, Blacks now constitute a large and diverse French population, much more like the African American general population than its representatives in Paris. In addition, an emphasis on African Americans as an historical presence, tied to the myth of color-blind France that not only no longer carries much weight but is also directly contradicted by the experience of French Blacks, certainly plays an important role. If the current vogue of Black consciousness has drawn attention to racism in contemporary France, it is perhaps difficult to square that emphasis with a narrative of African Americans finding refuge from racism in France.

Finally, it is worth considering another factor. Books like Patrick Lozès' *Nous les noirs de France* and Claude Ribbe's *Les Nègres de la République* emphasize the Frenchness of Blacks in France, the importance of considering them as equal citizens of the French nation. For example Patrick Lozès concludes his book with the following ringing declaration: "Le CRAN regroupe en son sein des Noirs originaires d'Afrique et des Noirs originaires des Antilles. La solidarité est la condition même de notre réussite.

Car il faut le dire, le répéter . . . Nous sommes tous des Noirs de France!"[44] It is difficult, perhaps, at the same time to embrace so heartily the idea of national inclusion and extend that vision to a population that is proud to be foreign and guards its American passports jealously.

Ultimately the exclusion of African American expatriates represents a distinct approach to diasporic and transnational perspectives on Blackness. Black French writers embrace Black American culture as part of their own experience, yet at the same time see its representatives in France as foreigners who don't really belong to the idea of Black French community. Similarly, African American expatriates hold themselves at arm's length from Francophone Blacks. This interplay between diasporic and nationalist perspectives underscores the importance of both in modern Black life, and not just in France. At a time when many Black French writers see their task as both building a sense of common identity and fighting for inclusion in French mainstream life, such an approach plays an important role in the creation of a community both Black and French at the same time.

NOTES

1. See, for example, Jean-Baptiste Onana, *Sois nègre et tais-toi!* (Nantes, France: Éditions du Temps, 2007); Serg Mokanda, *Un Noir en colère: lettre ouverte d'un Noir de France à Marianne* (Paris: Afromundi, 2011); Erick Noël, *Être noir en France au XVIIIè siècle* (Paris: Tallandier, 2006); Pierre H. Boulle and Sue Peabody, *Le Droit des Noirs en France au temps de l'esclavage* (Paris: Harmattan, 2014).

2. Pap Ndiaye, *La condition noire: essai sur une minorité française* (Paris: Calmann-Lévy, 2008).

3. See, for example, Dominic Thomas, *Africa and France: Postcolonial Cultures, Migration, and Racism* (Bloomington: Indiana University Press, 2013); Susan D. Pennypacker, *From Scottsboro to Munich: Race and Political Culture in 1930s Britain* (Princeton NJ: Princeton University Press, 2009).

4. On Blacks in Europe see Darlene Clark Hine, et. al., *Black Europe and the African Diaspora* (Urbana: University of Illinois Press, 2009); Eve Rosenhaft and Robbie Aitken, eds., *Africa in Europe: Studies in Transnational Practice in the Long Twentieth Century* (Liverpool, UK: Liverpool University Press, 2013); T. F. Earle and K. J. P. Lowe, eds., *Black Africans in Renaissance Europe* (New York: Cambridge University Press, 2010); Lynn T. Ramey, *Black Legacies: Race and the European*

Middle Ages (Gainesville: University of Florida Press, 2014). For a useful summary see Allison Blakely, "Coda: Black Identity in France in European Perspective," in *Black France/France Noire: The History and Politics of Blackness*, ed. Trica Keaton, et. al. (Durham NC: Duke University Press, 2012).

5. The classic example of this is Paul Gilroy, *The Black Atlantic: Modernity and Double Consciousness* (Cambridge MA: Harvard University Press, 1995). For a more recent, and French, perspective, see Jeremy Braddock and Jonathan P. Eburne, *Paris, Capital of the Black Atlantic: Literature, Modernity, and Diaspora* (Baltimore: Johns Hopkins University Press, 2013).

6. Lilyan Kesteloot, *Black Writers in French: A Literary History of Negritude* (Washington DC: Howard University Press, 1991); Chidi Ikonné, *Links and Bridges: A Comparative Study of the Writings of the New Negro and Negritude Movements* (Ibadan, Nigeria: University Press PLC, 2003).

7. See Ch. Didier Gondola, "'But I Ain't African, I'm American!' Black American Exiles and the Construction of Racial Identities in Twentieth Century France," in *Blackening Europe: The African American Presence*, ed. Heike Raphael-Hernandez (New York: Routledge, 2003).

8. For a particularly nuanced view of these questions, see Brent Hayes Edwards, *The Practice of Diaspora: Literature, Translation, and the Rise of Black Internationalism* (Cambridge MA: Harvard University Press, 2003).

9. In this essay I will consider the following texts: Ndiaye, *La condition noire*; Pascal Blanchard, Eric Deroo, Gilles Manceron, *Le Paris Noir* (Paris: Éditions Hazan, 2001); "Black: Africains, Antillais . . . Cultures noires en France," *Autrement* 49 (April 1983); Patrick Lozès, *Nous les noirs de France* (Paris: Éditions Danger Public, 2007); Claude Ribbe, *Les Nègres de la République* (Paris: Éditions Alphée, 2007); Rama Yade-Zimet, *Noirs de France* (Paris: Calmann-Lévy, 2007); François Durpaire, *France blanche, colère noire* (Paris: Odile Jacob, 2006).

10. Mary Gehman, *The Free People of Color of New Orleans* (New Orleans: Margaret Media, 1994); Sybil Kein, *Creole: The History and Legacy of Louisiana's Free People of Color* (Baton Rouge: Louisiana State University Press, 2000).

11. Frederick Douglass, *The Life and Times of Frederick Douglass* (New York: Collier, 1962), 568.

12. Marcus Bruce, "The New Negro in Paris: Booker T. Washington, the New Negro, and the Paris Exposition of 1900," in *Black France/France Noir*, ed. Keaton; Rebecka Rutledge Fisher, "Cultural Artifact and the Narrative of History: W. E. B. Du Bois and the Exhibiting of Culture at the 1900 Paris Exposition Universelle," in *Paris, Capital of the Black Atlantic*, ed. Braddock and Eburne, 17–51.

13. On African American soldiers in World War I, see Chad Louis Williams, *Torchbearers of Democracy: African American Soldiers in the World War I Era* (Chapel Hill: University of North Carolina Press, 2010); Adriane Danette Lenz-Smith, *Freedom Struggles: African Americans and World War I* (Cambridge MA: Harvard University Press, 2009); Arthur E. Barbeau and Florette Henri, *The Unknown*

Soldiers: Black American Troops in World War I (Philadelphia: Temple University Press, 1974).

14. On the history of jazz in France see Ludovic Tournès, *New Orleans-sur-Seine: Histoire du jazz en France* (Paris: Fayard, 1999); Jeffrey H. Jackson, *Making Jazz French: Music and Modern Life in Interwar Paris* (Durham NC: Duke University Press, 2003); Jeremy F. Lane, *Jazz and Machine-Age Imperialism: Music, "Race," and Intellectuals in France, 1918–1945* (Ann Arbor: University of Michigan Press, 2013); Andy Fry, *Paris Blues: African American Music and French Popular Culture, 1920–1960* (Chicago: University of Chicago Press, 2014).

15. Tyler Stovall, *Paris Noir: African Americans in the City of Light* (Boston: Houghton Mifflin, 1996); William Shack, *Harlem in Montmartre: A Paris Jazz Story between the Great Wars* (Berkeley: University of California Press, 2001); Michel Fabre, *La rive noire: de Harlem à la Seine* (Paris: lieu commun, 1985); Jody Blake, *Le Tumulte noir: Modernist Art and Popular Entertainment in Jazz Age Paris* (University Park: Pennsylvania State University Press, 1999); Brett A. Berliner, *Ambivalent Desire: The Exotic Black Other in Jazz-Age France* (Amherst: University of Massachusetts Press, 2002); Petrine Archer-Shaw, *Negrophilia: Avant-Garde Paris and Black Culture in the 1920s* (New York: Thames & Hudson, 2000).

16. Michel Fabre, *The Unfinished Quest of Richard Wright* (New York: Morrow, 1973); Hazel Rowley, *Richard Wright: The Life and Times* (New York: Henry Holt, 2001).

17. William Gardner Smith, *The Stone Face* (New York: Farrar Strauss, 1963); Tyler Stovall, "The Fire this Time: Black American Expatriates and the Algerian War," *Yale French Studies* 98 (2000): 182–200.

18. See William A. Cohen, *The French Encounter with Africans: White Response to Blacks, 1530–1880* (Bloomington: Indiana University Press, 1980); Shelby T. McCloy, *The Negro in France* (Lexington: University of Kentucky Press, 1961); Sue Peabody and Tyler Stovall, eds., *The Color of Liberty: Histories of Race in France* (Durham NC: Duke University Press, 2003).

19. Alain Guédé, *Monsieur de Saint-Georges: le nègre des Lumières* (Arles, France: Actes sud, 1999); Tom Reiss, *The Black Count: Glory, Revolution, Betrayal, and the Real Count of Monte Cristo* (New York: Crown Trade, 2012); Noël, *Être noir en France au XVIIIè siècle*; Jean-Daniel Piquet, *L'Emancipation des Noirs dans la révolution française* (Paris: Karthala, 2002); Pierre H. Boulle, *Race et esclavage dans la France de l'Ancien Régime* (Paris: Perin, 2007); Sue Peabody, *"There Are No Slaves in France:" The Political Culture of Race and Slavery in the Ancien Régime* (Oxford, UK: Oxford University Press, 1996); Boulle and Peabody, eds., *Le Droit des Noirs*.

20. Pascal Blanchard, et. al., *Zoos humains et exhibitions coloniales: 150 ans de l'invention de l'autre* (Paris: La Découverte, 2011); Lynn E. Palermo, "Identity under Construction: Representing the Colonies at the Paris Exposition Universelle of 1889," in *The Color of Liberty*, ed. Peabody and Stovall, 185–201; Jean-Michel

Bergougniou, *"Village noirs" et autres visiteurs africains et malgaches en France et en Europe: 1870–1940* (Paris: Karthala, 2001).

21. On the history of African soldiers in France during the Great War, see Marc Michel, *Les Africains et la grande guerre: l'appel à l'Afrique* (Paris: Karthala, 2003); Joe Harris Lunn, *Memoirs of the Maelstrom: A Senegalese Oral History of the First World War* (Portsmouth NH: Heinemann, 1999); Richard Fogarty, *Race and War in France: Colonial Subjects in the French Army, 1914–1918* (Baltimore: Johns Hopkins University Press, 2008).

22. W. E. B. Du Bois, "The Pan-African Congress," *Crisis* 17, no. 6 (April 1919): 271–74.

23. T. Denean Sharpley-Whiting, *Negritude Women* (Minneapolis: University of Minnesota Press, 2002).

24. "Ce Que Nous Voulons Faire . . . ," *Le Revue du Monde Noir* 1 (1931): 3.

25. V. Y. Mudimbe, *The Surreptitious Speech: Présence Africaine and the Politics of Otherness, 1947–1987* (Chicago: University of Chicago Press, 1992); Bennetta Jules-Rosette, *Black Paris: The African Writers' Landscape* (Urbana: University of Illinois Press, 1998).

26. J. A. Rogers, "The French Harlem," *New York Amsterdam News*, April 4, 1928.

27. Christiann Anderson and Monique Y. Wells, *Paris Reflections: Walks through African American Paris* (Lincoln: University of Nebraska Press, 2002); Florence Ladd, *The Spirit of Josephine: A Family Reunion in Paris* (n.p.: Cote d'Or, 2014).

28. Tierno Monénembo, *Le terroriste noir: roman* (Paris: Editions du Seuil, 2012); Martin Thomas, *The French Empire at War, 1940–1945* (Manchester, UK: Manchester University Press, 2007).

29. Thanks to the ban on collecting racial and ethnic statistics by government authorities in France, the exact number remains unknown, and controversial. See Louis-Georges Tin, "Who is Afraid of Blacks in France? The Black Question: The Name Taboo, the Number Taboo," *French Politics, Culture, and Society* 26, no. 1 (Spring 2008): 32–44.

30. Tyler Stovall, "No Green Pastures: the African-Americanization of France," in *Empire Lost: France and its Other Worlds*, ed. Elisabeth Mudimbe-Boyi (Lanham MD: Lexington, 2009).

31. Mar Fall, *Les Africains noirs en France: des tirailleurs sénégalais aux . . . Blacks* (Paris: Harmattan, 1986); Jean-Pierre Ndiaye, *Nègriers modernes: les travailleurs noirs en France* (Paris: Présence Africaine, 1970); Dominic Thomas: *Black France: Colonialism, Immigration, and Transnationalism* (Bloomington: Indiana University Press, 2007); David Beriss, *Black Skins, French Voices: Caribbean Ethnicity and Activism in Urban France* (Boulder CO: Westview, 2004).

32. Ndiaye, *La condition noire*, 137.

33. See also Pascal Blanchard, dir., *La France noire: présences et migrations des Afriques, des Amériques et de l'océan indien en france* (Paris: La Découverte, 2011).

34. Lozès, *Nous les noirs de France*, 116.

35. "Black," *Autrement*; Benjamin Jules Rosette, *Itinéraire du Théatre Noir: mémoires mëlées* (Paris: Harmattan, 1999).
36. Yade-Zimet, *Noirs de France*, 53.
37. Durpaire, *France blanche, colère noire*, 48–50.
38. Yade-Zimet, *Noirs de France*, 74.
39. Yade-Zimet, *Noirs de France*, 200.
40. Durpaire, *France blanche, colère noire*, 143.
41. This is true of my own work on the subject. Interestingly, however, when I have given talks on the history of African Americans in France invariably people ask about their interactions with French Blacks. Clearly, many African Americans see such transnational experiences as an integral part of Black expatriate history.
42. Anderson and Wells, *Paris Reflections*, x.
43. On Patricia Laplante-Collins see "Black Paris Profiles: Patricia Laplante-Collins," in *Entreé to Black Paris*, entreetoBlackparis.blogspot.com.
44. Lozès, *Nous les noirs de France*, 158.

Conclusion

Toward a History of Black France, and a Black History of France

SYLVAIN PATTIEU, EMMANUELLE SIBEUD,
AND TYLER STOVALL

Bastille Day is not only France's great national holiday, but also an occasion for people throughout the world to consider conditions there and mark the achievements and challenges of the French nation. On July 14, 2020, the *New York Times* published an article, titled "A Racial Awakening in France, Where Race is a Taboo Topic," addressing the question of race and Blackness in France after the uproar over the police execution of George Floyd in Minneapolis.

Growing up in France, Maboula Soumahoro, who the *Times* described as "an expert on race who lived in the United States for a decade," never thought of herself as Black. At home her immigrant parents stressed the culture of the Dioula, a Muslim ethnic group from Ivory Coast in West Africa. She identified as Ivorian to the other children of African immigrants in her neighborhood.

It was only as a teenager—years after her discovery of Whitney Houston, Michael Jackson, "The Cosby Show," and hip hop made her "dream of being cool like African-Americans"—that Soumahoro began feeling a racial affinity with her friends. As she recalled, "We were all children of immigrants from Guadeloupe, Martinique, Africa, and we are all a little bit unlike our parents . . . . We were French in our new way and we weren't white French. It was different in our homes, but we found one another regardless, and that's when you become Black."[1] For the *New York Times* and for many commentators on questions of race in France, this new assertiveness of French Blacks was at least in part stamped "made in the USA."[2]

Soumahoro's quotation contrasts in interesting ways with the anecdote that opened the introduction to this study. Whereas that earlier example illustrated the complexities and difficulties surrounding Black identity in France, this story shows how one woman decided nonetheless to embrace that identity. The contrast between public event and private reflection highlights the different ways in which people, both as individuals and as part of a group, select or reject ideas of racial consciousness. Both stories have an important transnational Anglophone dimension: rejected in one case, embraced in the other. At the same time, however, both anecdotes underscore the complex and at times contested nature of French Blackness. The story of Maboula Soumahoro addresses two important themes in this history of Blacks in France: heterogeneity and diasporic transnationalism. These themes have proved central in guiding the research in this volume.

As noted in the introduction, this book arose out of the seminar on the Black populations of France that began at the University of Paris 8 in 2011 and has continued to the present day. Like this volume, the seminar is now drawing to a conclusion after many years of fruitful inquiry and discussion. In bringing this book to an end, it is therefore worthwhile to reflect not only on its findings but also to consider the prospects for the study of Blackness in France more generally and create a field that would bring together and carry forward into the future the work of both the seminar and the book.

Contemporary conditions continue to underscore the importance of this field for the history of France. The murder of George Floyd in Minneapolis struck a deep nerve among French Blacks, bringing thousands out into the streets in protest marches across the country. For many it revived memories of the case of Adama Traoré, a young Black Frenchman who died in police custody in the Paris suburbs in July 2016. Led by Assa Traoré, Adama's sister, activists renewed their demands for an investigation and for justice. In June 2020 the French artist JR painted a large mural of George Floyd and Adama Traoré on the side of a Parisian building, and similar murals sprang up elsewhere in the country.[3] Commenting on the movement for racial justice in France, Lova Rinel, vice president of the CRAN, declared, "In the 1960s, it was politicians and intellectuals who made their voices heard. In the 1980s and 1990s there were big anti-racism movements . . . Now it's the families of the victims who are talking."[4]

This contemporary movement represents a new manifestation of racial consciousness in France, protesting against racist police violence and calling for the removal of names of slaveholders and colonialists from French streets and public spaces. It both addresses specifically French concerns and has arisen in the context of a global movement for racial justice. Whether or not it symbolizes the embrace of racial identity by large numbers of Blacks in France, however, remains to be seen. It certainly indicates one path forward in the development of Blackness in France, but not by any means the only one. Differences of ethnicity, class, region, and gender all constitute salient challenges to the idea of a common Black identity. At the same time, the powerful lure of French universalism and the emphasis on France as a color-blind nation retains its considerable attraction for many of African descent in the country.

In the context of this process that is still unfolding, the world of Black America constitutes a reference that is not only historical and cultural but also political and economic. Whereas many African Americans shared a common heritage and citizenship, citizen migrants from the Caribbean and Réunion and immigrant workers from Africa may belong to working class communities but have nonetheless had different postcolonial experiences. The memory of "Negro" associations and unions of the 1920s, victims both of government repression and Communist hegemonic politics at the time, did not survive. The same was true for the few organizations that arose during the 1970s. The absence of a slave or segregationist past, however, in no way prevented the existence of elements of systemic racism, impacting the social positions and representations of Blacks in France.

Certain French elites present the United States as a negative referent when it comes to issues of race. As Minister of Education Jean-Michel Blanquer argued in the *Journal du Dimanche*: "One must fight against an intellectual matrix originating in American universities of intersectionalism, which essentializes communities and identities, in sharp opposition to our republican model which argues for the equality of human beings, independent of their characteristics of origin, of sex, of religion. [Such a perspective] is the breeding ground of the fragmentation of our society which converges with the interests of the Islamists. This perspective has already corrupted a considerable part of French social science."[5] In contrast to such fantastical representations, a detour through the United States offers Blacks in France resources to forge the tools for their struggle for respect and pride, just as many African Americans took inspiration from France's universalist discourse.

Such contrasting interpretations only underscore the importance of studying Blackness and Black identity in France both as a way of understanding the meanings of the concept for peoples of African descent there and its broader implications for the nation as a whole. Many of the peoples studied in the pages of this book would not necessarily have identified as Black; in particular, most of those Africans whose histories we encounter in Section One would probably have found little in the term that spoke to their own lives. Yet any social identity is shaped both by insiders and outsiders: we are not only who we perceive ourselves to be, but also who we are perceived to be by others both in the past and the present. The essays in this book give important insights into how Blacks in France and the French empire conceived of their own lives while also exploring their place in the French nation. They were Sainte-Marian, Somali, Martiniquan, American; they were also Blacks of France, and their histories belong to that of Black France.

Based on the lessons derived from this book, how then shall we conceive of the history of Blacks in France? One should state first of all that this study only constitutes one small aspect of this much broader history; there are many other stories of Black life in France, and our work can most usefully serve as a beginning that suggests further approaches. For example, following the lead of Pierre Boulle we need to know much more about the lives of Blacks in the premodern era, not just the eighteenth century but even earlier, going all the way back to Roman times. Another fruitful avenue of inquiry is the relationship between different Black communities in France and the empire, as suggested by the work of Jennifer Boittin. The essays of Franck F. Ekué and Tyler Stovall serve as a model for studies of the relationship between Blackness in France and elsewhere, not just the United States. It would be very interesting, for example, to place the theoretical work of Frantz Fanon in a Black context, exploring its influence on and intersections with Black consciousness movements in America, Britain, and beyond.

That said, one can nonetheless note a few central themes in this book that will help to outline the shape of Black French studies going forward. Most obviously is the theme of race itself, particularly the extent to which one can consider a population defined on racial grounds a group with a common identity, historically and in the present. Scholars have long debated the question whether race is a biological or social and political construct; most today see it as the latter, yet the debate remains open.[6] More specifically, many in France refuse to see race as a social reality that characterizes and perhaps divides French citizens. The French state's refusal to gather statistical information about race in official government documents is only the most well-known example of this.[7]

The authors of this study take the overall position that race does constitute a social reality, that it has played a significant role in the history of France, and that it probably will continue to do so in the future. We do so by analyzing the specific case of Blackness in France as not only interesting in and of itself but also as one that sheds light on this broader debate. In doing so, we reject any kind of racial essentialism, exploring rather the diversity of Black cultures and of conceptions of Blackness in this population. We also recognize that racial identity can be approached in many different ways, that it can be accepted, rejected, and transformed, and that it is created both by the gaze of outsiders, especially the dominant white society as well as one's own individual and community identities. Above all it is a lived and living process, one that like history itself changes over time.

Gender constitutes another vitally important aspect of the history of Blackness in France, one that connects it to broader questions of difference in human societies. Did Black men and women experience Blackness differently, and if so how? How did French authorities and French society in general view and treat Black women and men differently? Many of the essays in this book address the question of gender, often focusing on the history of Black women. They analyze the communities formed by Black women in both the colonies and the metropole, both together with and at times separate from Black men. Gender was an issue for Black men as well, especially soldiers who spent extended periods of time in all-male regiments. Moreover, one should note that gender often played a central role in interracial contacts as well. Love and sex across the color line brought Blacks and whites together at times, both in France and in the empire, and anxieties about such contacts often shaped thoughts about racial difference in general. Gender constituted a key aspect of the diversity of the Black French experience, one that showed how the experience of Blackness manifested itself in different ways throughout French history.[8]

Another key theme is geographic diversity and transnationalism. France is a country with many different and often distinct regions both within the metropole and throughout the Francophone world, and Blacks can be found in almost all of them. One of the key questions for this book, and this field in general, concerns the relationship between regional identities and Blackness as a whole. What do Blacks from sub-Saharan Africa and the Caribbean have in common, for example? To what extent are African American expatriates in Paris part of Black France? Do individuals of mixed race form part of French Black communities? These questions speak directly to the work that scholars of the African diaspora have done on the nature of Black identity in the modern world, which is often extremely diverse while at the same time frequently embraces unifying themes of cultural pride and resistance to discrimination.

Blacks in France also represent an important example of transnational history, especially if one sees transnationalism not as the rejection of the nation state but rather interwoven with national cultures. The contribution of African Americans to Black French life is perhaps the most important example of this, but certainly not the only one. France is not the only country in Europe with a significant Black population, and the exploration of relations between French Blacks and peoples of African descent elsewhere on the continent and in Britain will make an important contribution to a transnational understanding of Blackness in France, especially in an era of growing European integration. The story of Blacks in France is part of both French history and world history, and a transnational approach enables and requires us to explore the intersections between the two.[9]

A key part of this theme is the issue raised by the quotation from Maboula Soumahoro at the outset of this conclusion: the relationship between

French Blacks and Blacks in America and more generally that between the United States and France in the modern and contemporary eras. Is Blackness in effect an American import, an attempt to apply cultural norms taken from the United States to a vastly different culture, and if so can it legitimately claim to be French? Some Blacks in France would agree with this position, others would reject it. In part, such an argument reflects the difference between frequent and open discussions of race in America as opposed to the resistance of many in France to consider race a meaningful social or political category.

Yet as members of the CRAN have argued, such resistance tends to silence Blacks in France, to render them invisible; in response it has pushed the French state to collect racial statistics on the national population as a way of concretely measuring the realities of Black life and anti-Black discrimination in the country. Portraying discussions of race as an American corruption of French culture thus tends to hide disagreements among French people about this issue. Moreover, it is a mistake to conceive of the relationship between Blackness in France and in America as a one-way street, to see the former as derivative of the latter. To take one example, the great Black French author Frantz Fanon had a profound ideological influence on American Black militants, notably the Black Panthers.[10] The relationship of Black America to Blackness in France should be seen as an illustration of the transnational character of the French nation.

These are some of the themes that have emerged from our study of the history of Blacks in France, and hopefully these essays will continue to inspire scholars and students of the topic. As the field grows other questions will emerge to add new dimensions to this history and historiography. We wish to end with some reflections on how this field will address not just the history of Blacks in France but the history of Black France more generally. To put it differently, to what extent can we consider France a Black nation, not just a nation that counts Black populations among its inhabitants? Even to pose the question is to insist on the importance of race in the making of the French nation, an insistence that ultimately suggests that Blackness is not the only form of racial identity in France. Just as whiteness theory rose out of ethnic studies in the United States, such an approach could easily prompt the study of France as a white nation as well. To conceive of France as a Black nation is to see Blacks not as recent arrivals but rather as communities whose presence in the country has helped define what it means to be French in general. Such an idea is implied by Soumahoro's assertion that she and her friends were "French in a new way." It suggests that France is a country with a unique blend of cultures from the African diaspora and that this unique blend is one of the things that makes France a unique country. In other words, Black history and Black people are one of the things that gives the French nation its distinct and rich character, that make France . . . France.

Permit us to conclude this study with a fantastic vision of reality. Imagine a video advertisement promoting tourism to France. This particular video would include a variety of images of the nation, ranging from Parisian exhibitions of African art, to beaches in the French Caribbean, to summertime jazz festivals. It would be full of smiling French women and men, all of whom were Black. At no point would it mention the fact that it overwhelmingly featured Black themes and people; instead of portraying Blacks in France, it would offer a Black vision of the country. Over and over again, it would simply welcome visitors to France. Such a video would embrace the French tradition of color-blindness while at the same time making Blackness visible and central to the national heritage. It would portray France as a Black nation. This study of the history of Blacks in France, and the broader field of Black French studies to which it hopes to contribute, represents an attempt to render such a vision at least conceivable and perhaps one day realistic. If it succeeds in doing so it will have accomplished its task.

NOTES

1. *New York Times*, July 14, 2020.
2. Didier and Eric Fassin, eds., *De la question sociale à la question raciale: représenter la société française* (Paris: Découverte, 2006); Alexis Buisson, "Why French and Americans Can't Understand Each Others' Perspectives on Race," *Frenchly*, July 13, 2018.
3. "Paris Protestors Mark Fourth Anniversary of Adama Traoré's Death," *Guardian*, July 18, 2020; Zineb Dryef, "Comment Assa Traoré est devenue une figure de l'antiracisme en France," *Le Monde*, July 3, 2020.

4. *Financial Times*, June 11, 2020; Patrick Lozès, *Nous les noirs de France* (Paris: Danger Public, 2007).

5. *Le Journal du Dimance*, October 25, 2020.

6. For example, some geneticists and other scientists argue today that race does have an objective biological reality. See Nicholas Wade, *A Troublesome Inheritance: Genes, Race and Human History* (New York: Penguin, 2015); David Reich, *Who We Are and How We Got Here: Ancient DNA and the New Science of the Human Past* (New York: Pantheon, 2018).

7. Michèle Tribalat, *Statistiques ethniques, une querelle bien française* (Paris: L'Artilleur, 2016); Alexander Stille, "Can the French Talk About Race?" *New Yorker*, July 11, 2014; Katrina Piser, "Breaking France's Race Taboo: A new generation of activists is trying to change the way France conceives of race," *Nation*, August 10, 2018.

8. Robin Mitchell, *Venus noire: Black Women and Colonial Fantasies in Nineteenth-Century France* (Athens: University of Georgia Press, 2020); Annette K. Joseph-Gabriel, *Reimagining Liberation: How Black Women Transformed Citizenship in the French Empire* (Urbana: University of Illinois Press, 2020); Felix Germain and Silyane Larcher, eds., *Black French Women and the Struggle for Equality, 1848–2016* (Lincoln: University of Nebraska Press, 2018).

9. Tyler Stovall, *Transnational France: The Modern History of a Universal Nation* (Boulder CO: Westview, 2015); Dominic Thomas, *Black France: Colonialism, Immigration, and Transnationalism* (Bloomington: Indiana University Press, 2007); Nancy L. Green, *The Limits of Transnationalism* (Chicago: University of Chicago Press, 2019).

10. Sean L. Malloy, *Out of Oakland: Black Panther Party Internationalism during the Cold War* (Ithaca NY: Cornell University Press, 2017).

Contributors

JENNIFER ANNE BOITTIN is an associate professor of French, Francophone studies, and history at the Pennsylvania State University. She is the author of *Colonial Metropolis: The Urban Grounds of Anti-Imperialism and Feminism in Interwar France*. Her research focuses upon colonialism and how race, gender, class, and sexuality have shaped peoples' experiences in France, Africa, Southeast Asia, and the French Caribbean.

PIERRE H. BOULLE taught at McGill University in Montreal until his retirement in 2005 and is the author of *Race et esclavage dans la France de l'Ancien régime* (2007). He has specialized on the issues of race and slavery and is preparing to publish his online database on Blacks in France in the eighteenth and nineteenth centuries, focused on the censuses taken of them in 1777, 1801, and 1824.

AUDREY CÉLESTINE is a social scientist and associate professor in American studies at the University of Lille. Her work focuses on migration, memory, race, and identity in France, the French Caribbean (Martinique and Guadeloupe), and the United States. Her first book, *La Fabrique des identités* (2018), deals with the collective trajectories of Puerto Ricans in New York and French Caribbeans in Paris since the mid–twentieth century.

SARAH FILA-BAKABADIO is an associate professor in American and African American studies at the CY Cergy Paris University (France) and member of the research center AGORA. Her work explores the African diasporas from the Black Atlantic, African American nationalisms, Black studies in Europe, Black beauty, and cosmopolitanism.

FRANCK FREITAS-EKUÉ is a PhD candidate and is teaching in the Culture Department of the University of Lille (France). His research examines the way capitalism contributes to the shaping of subjectivities within the Black Atlantic. He has co-edited the book *Penser avec Stuart Hall* (2021).

RUTH GINIO is an associate professor of history at Ben Gurion University of the Negev. She works on murder investigations in French West Africa. She is the author of two books: *The French Army and Its African Soldiers: The Years of Decolonization* (2017) and *French Colonialism Unmasked: The Vichy Years in French West Africa* (2006).

MINAYO NASIALI is an associate professor of history at the University of California, Los Angeles. Her first book, *Native to the Republic: Empire, Social Citizenship, and Everyday Life in Marseille since 1945*, was published in 2016 by Cornell University Press. She is currently working on her second monograph, *Sea Traffic: A Clandestine History of Shipping, Exploitation, and Rebel Sailors Across Empires*.

SYLVAIN PATTIEU is an associate professor in history at the University of Paris 8. He has published widely on the social history of tourism, including his 2009 book *Tourisme et Travail*. His current research focuses on Black people in France. He is also a literary writer, with five novels and three nonfiction works to his credit.

EMMANUELLE SIBEUD is a professor in the Department of History at the University of Paris 8. Her publications include *Une science impériale pour l'Afrique (1878–1930)* and several essays on imperial cultures and the intellectual history empires in the twentieth century.

TYLER STOVALL is a professor of history and dean of the Graduate School of Arts and Sciences at Fordham University. He has written widely on questions of race, class, and transnationalism in modern France. His most recent book, *White Freedom: The Racial History of an Idea*, was published by Princeton University Press in 2021.

SARAH J. ZIMMERMAN is an associate professor of history at Western Washington University. She studies the experiences of women and the operation of gender in West Africa, the French Empire, and the Atlantic World. Her monograph, *Militarizing Marriage: West African Soldiers' Conjugal Traditions in Modern French Empire*, appeared in 2020. Her new research attends to the gendered production of history and memory on Gorée Island—a UNESCO World Heritage site in Senegal.

Index

colonial soldiers, 50, 51, 110, 176, 197

colonial subjects, 5, 14, 19, 24, 25n3

colonization, 37, 38, 107, 113, 159, 194

color-blind nation, 49, 160–61, 166, 177, 201, 209

color prejudice, 69–71, 73, 83, 89n76

Congress of Black Writers and Artists, 161, 195

"controlling images," 181, 188n47

day-laborers, 77, 78, 81

de Breteuil, Michel, 163

decree 2007–1062, 147, 156n29

demobilization, 49, 50, 51, 52, 54–59

Diagne, Blaise, 15, 21, 22, 28n40, 195

discrimination: against African soldiers, 53, 55, 60, 61; in France, 53; against migrants, 141–42, 144, 146–47, 149–54; racial, 14, 52, 53

Djibouti Inscription Maritime, 93, 94

Du Bois, W. E. B., 24, 25n6, 121n36, 193, 195

Dumas, Alexandre, 83, 194, 200

Dumersan, 78, 79, 80, 88n56

Dyer, William Holmes, 49

equality: aim of, 62; demand for, 14; racial, 19, 26; semblance of, 58; struggle for, 50, 51, 59, 62, 63

expatriate communities, 191, 193, 196, 200

family reunification, 126, 127, *129*

Fanon, Frantz, 158, 159, 210, 213

Ferrier, Louis, 73

Firinga, Joachim, 5, 13–18, 20, 22, 26n19, 27n33

floating signifier, 7, 178–81, 185

Floyd, George, 1, 4, 207, 208

France: Bastille Day in, 207; Black feminine press in, 158, 162, 166, 169, 170; Black French life in, 196; as a color-blind nation, 49; community's life in,

193–94; discrimination in, 53; expatriate communities in, 191; French of African descent in, 192–95; marriage ban of 1778 and, 69–72; nonwhite population in, 69–70, 83, 84, 84n4; power play by, 36; racial discourse in, 181; racism in, 53, 63, 193; "woke culture" in, 4, 5

freedom of assembly, 26n17

French Blacks, 7, 194–97, 199–201, 206n41, 207–8

French Caribbean, 1, 2, 6, 198, 214

French civilians, 50, 51, 52, 53, 57, 63

The French Encounter with Africans (Cohen), 30

French identification papers, 90, 92, 93, 94

French identity, 6, 108

French imperialism, 3, 91, 92, 95, 99

French military, 30, 31, 35–36, 38–44, 61

French of Overseas Origin, 142, 143, 147, 150, 151, 152

French population, 20, 70

French Revolution, 2, 194

French West Africa (FWA), 34; Black villages and, 40; importance of, 64n4; mobility and sex in, 112–17; slavery outlawed in, 35, 36; social relationships in, 42. *See also* African soldiers; mesdames tirailleurs; North Africa

French women, 51–53, 56–57, 214

gangs, 26n24, 182

Gasparin, Lucien, 21, 23, 24

Geisser, Vincent, 144–45

gender: race issue and, 8, 106, 112, 113, 114, 211–12; sex and sexuality and, 106–8

godparents, 76, 79

Grand Orient of France, 22, 28n40

Great Fear of 1789, 74

Great War, 98, 176, 195

ing woman from, 29–30, 44; Black villages and, 38–44; colonization of, 38; conclusion about, 44–45; conquest of, 29, 30, 38, 39, 41; "pacification" of, 31–38; sub-Saharan African soldiers and, 31, 33, 37, 43

Municipal Center for the Reception and Information for the French of overseas origin, the CMAI-Dom-Tom, 143, 153

Nama Diara, 37
nappy hair fashion, 168, 169, 173n38
Nardal, Jane, 110, 111
Nardal, Paulette, 110, 111
National Front, 183, 184
nation-state, 191–92
naturalization, 14, 16, 21, 23, 24
Négritude movement, 103, 110, 170
nonwhite population, 69–70, 83, 84, 84n4
North Africa: colonization of, 37; slave trade in, 30; tirailleurs sénégalais and, 31–32, 36

overseas departments (DOM), 123, 125
overseas populations, 142–45, 147, 149, 153–54
Overseas Secretary of State, 147, 148, 149

Paris Exposition of 1900, 193, 203n12
Parisian families, 71, 83, 84
police harassment, 196, 209
popular culture, 104, 108, 111, 175, 178, 181
populations: colonized, 19, 177; French, 20, 70; marginalized, 183; overseas, 142, 143, 145, 147, 149, 153–54; postcolonial, 181, 183, 185. *See also* Blackness and Blacks
POW camps, 51–52
pregnancies, 52, 114, 115, 116, 117

prostitutes, 112, 117

race consciousness, 103–4, 106, 108–9, 111–12, 116–18, 209
race issue, 3–5; as a biological and social reality, 211, 215n6; as a floating signifier, 178–81, 185; gender and, 8, 106, 112, 113, 114, 211–12; in Madagascar, 22; policy of, 18; sex and, 104, 106, 108, 117, 119n14; statistical information about, 211, 213
racial boundaries, 31, 51, 52, 54–59
racial discourse, 51, 174, 177, 178, 180, 181
racial discrimination, 14, 52, 53
racial identities, 8, 141, 176, 209, 211, 213
racialized minorities, 190, 198
racialized systems of labor, 91, 100n5
racial prejudice, 135, 166
racial segregation, 176, 177, 178
racism, 2, 22, 23; against African workers, 53; American, 2, 193, 198; colonial, 24, 50, 53; in France, 53, 63, 193
Reconstruction, 174, 185n2
Red Sea region, 90–92, 96, 99
Representative Council of Black Institutions (CRAN), 1, 2, 157, 182, 208, 213
Representative Council of the French from Overseas (CREFOM), 151, 155n21
representative institutions, 150, 154
repression, 15, 51, 56, 209
Ressemblement Démocratique Africaine (RDA), 59, 65n25

sailor unions, 91, 95, 99
Saint-Geniès-de-Malgoirès village, 72–75
Saint-Marians, 14–20, 23–24, 26n19, 26n24, 27n33
Sarkozy, Nicolas, 141, 145–47, 149, 151, 153
Second Empire, 81, 177
semiskilled workers, 126, 132, 133

CPSIA information can be obtained
at www.ICGtesting.com
Printed in the USA
LVHW012236090122
708050LV00012B/1096

9 781496 228994